UNDERSTANDING FAITH

Understanding Buddhism

UNDERSTANDING FAITH

SERIES EDITOR: PROFESSOR FRANK WHALING

Also Available

Understanding the Baha'i Faith, *Wendi Momen with Moojan Momen*
Understanding Christianity, *Gilleasbuig Macmillan*
Understanding Islam, *Cafer Yaran*
Understanding Judaism, *Jeremy Rosen*
Understanding Sikhism, *Owen Cole*

Forthcoming

Understanding the Brahma Kumaris, *Frank Whaling*
Understanding Chinese Religions, *Xinzhong Yao*
Understanding Hinduism, *Frank Whaling*

UNDERSTANDING FAITH

SERIES EDITOR: PROFESSOR FRANK WHALING

Understanding Buddhism

Perry Schmidt-Leukel

Professor of

Systematic Theology and Religious Studies

University of Glasgow

DUNEDIN ACADEMIC PRESS

Edinburgh

For Edda Brouwers
and Kim Lan Thai Thi
who first introduced me to the riches of Buddhism

Published by
Dunedin Academic Press Ltd
Hudson House
8 Albany Street
Edinburgh EH1 3QB
Scotland

ISBN 1 903765 18 8
ISBN 13: 978-1-903765-18-0
ISSN 1744-5833

First published 2006, reprinted 2008.

British Library Cataloguing in Publication Data
A catalogue record for this book is available from the British Library

Typeset by Makar Publishing Production
Printed in Great Britain by Cpod, Trowbridge, Wiltshire

Contents

List of Figures

Sources: Fig. 1: Microsoft ® Encarta ® Premium Suite 2005 © 1993–2004 Microsoft Corporation. Fig. 3: Gandhara (Pakistan), 3rd–5th cent. CE, in: Jeannine Auboyer, Jean-Louis Nou: *Buddha. Der Weg der Erleuchtung*, Freiburg-Basel-Wien: Herder 1982, no. 49. Fig. 4: Gandhara (Pakistan), 3rd–4th cent. CE, in: ibid. no. 78. Fig. 6 and 7: the Wheel of Samsaric Existence and enlarged inner circle detail therefrom from *Buddhistische Bilderwelt* von Hans Wolfgang Schumann erschienen bei Diederichs 1986 in Heinreich Hugendubel Verlag Kreuzlingen/ Munchen. Fig. 10: Painting (detail) from Pemayangste monastery (Sikkim); photo with kind permission from J. Chwaszcza (www.editionsummit.de).

List of Abbreviations

AN	Aṅguttara Nikāya
AP	Aṣṭasāhasrikā Prajñāpāramitā Sūtra
BCA	Bodhicaryāvatāra
Cv	Cullavagga des Vinayapiṭaka
CT	Caṇḍamahāroṣaṇa Tantra
Dhp	Dhammapada
DN	Dīgha Nikāya
HT	Hevajra Tantra
Itv	Itivuttaka
Jat	Jātaka
Kv	Kathāvatthu
Lv	Lalitavistara
Mhv	Mahāvaṃsa
MMK	Mūlamadhyamakakārikā
MN	Majjhima Nikāya
Mph	Milindapañha
Ms	Mahāyānasaṃgraha
Mv	Mahāvagga des Vinayapiṭaka
Ndk	Nidānakathā
NP	Netti Pakaraṇa
SN	Saṃyutta Nikāya
Sn	Sutta Nipāta
SpS	Saddharmapuṇḍarīka Sūtra (= Lotus-Sūtra)
SS	Śikṣāsamuccaya
SVV	Sukhāvatīvūha Sūtra
Thag	Theragāthā
Thig	Therīgāthā
Ud	Udāna
Vism	Visuddhimagga
Vn	Vimalakīrtinirdeśa Sūtra

(Next to abbreviations, numbers with 'p.' or 'pp.' indicate pages; otherwise numbers refer to the respective Sūtras and their sections/subsections.)

Preface

This book would not have been written without Frank Whaling's gentle but irresistible talent to persuade me. What made me hesitant is that there are already so many introductions to Buddhism. But perhaps there is some justification in adding one which highlights the religious aspects of Buddhism and tries to make these intelligible as a genuine and essential dimension.

Apart from Frank, my gratitude goes to a number of people who in various ways contributed to the genesis of this book. In the first place I would like to mention my students. Their questions sometimes teach us teachers more than our explanations – or at least, it is through their questions that we make some progress too (hopefully). My great colleagues Ernst Steinkellner and Lambert Schmithausen were always generous in sharing their outstanding competence when I needed philological advice. I hope that, from their point of view, this little book does not contain too many errors for which, of course, I alone am to blame. I am absolutely indebted to Carolina Weening who took great pains in transforming my teutonic draft into readable English. If there is style in the book, it's her merit – any awkward formulations still left are so only because I insisted on them. Last, but not least my gratitude goes to Anthony Kinahan from Dunedin Press for showing so much patience, an important Bodhisattva-virtue, in waiting for the final manuscript.

In the transcription of Buddhist and other technical terms I mostly followed the 'Oxford Dictionary of World Religions', and when I had to choose between Pāli- and Sanskrit-forms, I usually preferred the latter.

Two outstanding women, one Buddhist – one Christian, introduced me to Buddhism about thirty years ago. To them this book is dedicated.

Perry Schmidt-Leukel, Glasgow, May 2006

Introduction

'Understanding Faith', 'Understanding Buddhism' – is this really possible? And if so, how? What would it mean to understand Buddhism? Would I have to be (or become) a Buddhist? And which kind of 'Buddhism' are we talking about? Are there not far too many different forms of Buddhism? Is it not an extremely diversified religion, quite different in Thailand or Sri Lanka from what we see in Japan or Korea or Tibet – not to mention Europe or America? Is not this diversity simply too extensive to be 'understood'? Is not Buddhism very different today from its beginnings circa 2500 years ago? How much would we need to know about the history of this multifarious religion so as to be able to say that we have gained some understanding of it?

Such questions are quite justified and it is important to face them right at the start to drive home the point that neither we (nor even the most learned experts perhaps) can ever reach anything like an all-encompassing understanding of Buddhism. Moreover, we should be aware that Buddhism (and analogously any religion) is made up of two fundamental components. Firstly, there are the Buddhists: the real concrete people who lived and live under the influence and with the inspiration of the second component: the Buddhist tradition. It was Wilfred Cantwell Smith (1916–2000) who emphasized that what we usually call 'a religion' consists essentially of these two basic elements, the *cumulative tradition* and the *personal faith* of those who live within this particular tradition (see Smith, 1978). The tradition encompasses scriptures, doctrines, beliefs, philosophies, rules, precepts, institutions, buildings, rituals, songs and prayers, customs, artwork, etc. – everything that can be observed and investigated as a historical object. Faith, however, is what the tradition means to individual persons, or better: what life means to them as seen in the light of that tradition. It is through personal, existential faith that people relate themselves to what they perceive as reality and to what they accept as ultimate, transcendent reality. Faith and tradition are interdependent. Faith expresses itself within a given religious tradition, and therefore the tradition is in constant change and transformation with each new generation which takes it up and every new environment which it enters. Without faith the tradition would die. Conversely, tradition also shapes and nourishes faith. Without the inspiration of a living tradition faith would be cut off from its major resources: the media in which the experiences of generations have been preserved and condensed, and which thus can serve as channels for bringing others in contact with that same ultimate reality in relation to which those previous generations lived.

Whatever makes up a religious tradition can be observed and studied directly. Faith can not be investigated in this way, and yet it is essential that we try to understand the faith if we want to understand the tradition, for otherwise we miss the very heart of the tradition. We need to understand what the tradition meant and means to the real people who embrace it. Hence we need to understand the people. But in order to understand people we need to understand them as they understand themselves – if not, we have not understood *them*. Does this mean that if we want to understand their faith we need to share it? Some scholars of religion, Raimon Panikkar for example (1978, p.9f), have indeed insisted that only if we ourselves are convinced of a given faith's truth can we understand the faith of others *as they do*. I believe this to be an exaggeration, for it would imply that we could never understand someone's view and at the same time reject it as false. For Panikkar, what we don't share we simply misunderstand. Surely this is an absurd conclusion, one that leaves no room for informed and justified rejection. Nevertheless, Panikkar rightly stresses the need to look at things with the insiders' perspective – through their eyes. To quote Wilfred Cantwell Smith (1997, p. 132f):

> … to understand the faith of Buddhists, one must not look at something called 'Buddhism'. Rather, one must look at the world – so far as possible, through Buddhist eyes. In order to do that, one must know the data of what I have called the Buddhist tradition …

This statement rests upon two very important premises. For one thing, we need to look *at* the Buddhist tradition in order to look *through* it. We need to understand how this tradition served as the lenses through which Buddhists perceived their lives and their world. Secondly – as Smith says elsewhere (1979, p. 137) – if there are any truths to be found these are, strictly speaking, not Buddhist truths but cosmic truths, not truths in Buddhism but truths in the universe as detected by Buddhists.

These premises will guide me in the subsequent chapters. That is, I will focus on basic Buddhist insights into life, into its existential challenges, its hopes and its promises because I am interested in the truths that Buddhists possibly discovered. And I will deal with the historical settings and developments of Buddhist views. I will point out what I see as the interconnectedness among Buddhist ideas, and what I understand as the inner logic behind the development of these ideas in the course of history. But I will also be rather selective. This is inevitable given the immense age of this tradition and the vast variety of forms it has assumed within the various cultures to which it spread. I will concentrate more on the formative period than on later developments, for what comes later can best be understood from what came first. And I will concentrate more on ideas than on practice or sociological aspects. This is a rather conservative approach, often snubbed nowadays as old-fashioned or even obsolete. But I have chosen this approach because I am convinced that our practice is significantly guided by our ideas and that in any case it is easier to understand practice through the ideas behind it than the other way around. I do not accept the Marxist dogma, shared by so many sociologists today, that religions are simply the product and epiphenomenon of their social environment and economical conditions. Undoubtedly they are considerably conditioned by their socio-economic context, but the opposite is no less true: Religions have shaped and changed societies, and in any case sociological explanations do not render an exhaustive explanation of our religious life.

In another respect I am far less conservative: I do not share the standard view in religious studies that the scholar has to deliver an entirely neutral and objective presentation of the phenomena under consideration. I believe that total objectivity and neutrality (at least in matters of religion) are impossible. It goes without saying that we must not deliberately distort any of the views and data with which we dealing. But when we try to understand a particular religion it is always *we* who do so. And we are not blank. When we try sincerely to look at the world through Buddhist eyes and take seriously what we thereby see, when we expose ourselves to Buddhist viewpoints and attempt to grasp what Buddhists have understood, we will not emerge from the encounter untouched or unchallenged. Our own personality is always a constitutive component of this process of understanding, and always lingering in the air will be the question of what all this could imply for our own life. This state of affairs is not something that we should deny, ignore, or exclude, but something we should openly and consciously reckon with. While objectivity and neutrality seem to me illusionary goals, we can and should strive for honesty and reflective subjectivity.

My own perception of Buddhism and my ongoing efforts to understand Buddhists are undoubtedly influenced by my own personal background which is primarily formed by Christianity. For more than twenty years, however, my particular way of being Christian is also permeated by what I have learned through my exposure to Buddhism and by a deep fascination with this spiritually and intellectually rich tradition. Some may think that this Christian background cuts me off from an adequate understanding of Buddhism. For my part I have serious doubts that the atheist, naturalist, materialist, secularist background of so many contemporary Western interpreters of Buddhism (and even of some Asian Buddhists who are under strong Western influence) provides them with a more appropriate disposition. Of course the Buddha was not a theist in the sense of someone who believed in a personal Creator-God. But neither was the Buddha one of the Cārvākas, those early Indian materialists and atheists who were his contemporaries. Quite the contrary: The Buddha considered the teachings of the Cārvākas as unwholesome because they denied universal moral laws, life after death, karmic retribution and final release in and through an ultimate transcendent reality. The Buddha presented and still presents a challenge for theists and atheists alike.

Any attempt to understand Buddhism will have to confront what are seen as misunderstandings. Measured in historical terms, Western knowledge of Buddhism is still quite young. Only in the second half of the nineteenth century did scientific and philosophic exploration of Buddhism in the West get under way. The ideological conflicts of that time have significantly influenced the occidental perception of Buddhism, leading to a number of misunderstandings which still greatly affect the image of Buddhism in the West. Buddhism was seen as materialism, nihilism, pessimism, escapism, and so on. At times Western interpreters were very reluctant to amend their views even when an increased knowledge of the Buddhist tradition required this. Max Weber, in his (in-)famous assessment of Buddhism as the 'asocial' religion par excellence, had deliberately neglected the role of the Saṅgha (the Buddhist community) and 'right livelihood' for the Buddhist path of salvation (see Weber, 1958, pp. 213–221). Albert Schweitzer understood Buddhist ethics as being entirely passive and incapable of motivating practical charitable deeds, and thus when he came across the canonical record of the Buddha's caring with his own hands for a severely ill monk and instructing the disciples to follow this example, he concluded that here the Buddha acted against his own teaching (see Schweitzer, 1936, p. 114). Many such clichés still persist, as for example in Pope John Paul II's characterisation of Buddhism as 'an almost exclusively negative soteriology' in his book *Crossing the Threshold of Hope*. New clichés have developed as well, presenting Buddhism as the easy pop-religion, a spirituality without dogmas or beliefs, without precepts or commandments, always peaceful, tolerant of almost everything. Or as no religion at all but rather a form of wisdom-psychology, a lifestyle or trendy worldview most appropriate for the slightly weary but well-heeled post-modern intellectual. I hope that the following attempt to understand Buddhism may also contribute to rectifying at least some of these misunderstandings.

For further reading: Cahill (1982); Panikkar (1978); Smith (1981); Smith (1997); Streng (1985).

1

Buddhism: A Brief Overview

Buddhism arose in north-eastern India some 2500 years ago. It developed into one of the major religious forces of Asia, and in the twentieth century made its presence felt in almost every country of the world. To get an initial idea of how Buddhism developed it is helpful to look at its long history in terms of five periods of roughly five hundred years each (see Conze, 1980).

The Formative Period (500–0 BCE)

Buddhism originated as one of the Śrāmaṇa movements revolting against the traditional religious life of Brahmanical India (see Chapter 2). The Śrāmaṇas introduced a new religious goal: ultimate salvation or liberation, and a new way of life for pursuing this goal: the life of religious drop-outs as homeless wanderers and ascetics. While early Buddhism shared many of the Śrāmaṇa motives and ideas – particularly their anti-Brahmanical attitude – it managed to combine the 'otherworldliness' of the Śrāmaṇas with a 'this-worldly' orientation: Active missionary efforts consciously promoted and propagated the Buddha's teachings 'within the world', and the establishment of the *Saṅgha*, i.e. the 'four-fold community' (*catuṣ pariṣad*), brought together the monks and nuns of the monastic orders *with* their secular supporters, the male and female laity. Buddhist teachings were directed to monastics and to lay-people, and practical rules and guidelines were developed for both. Thereby Buddhism rapidly became a major religious factor in India. When Emperor Aśoka (272–232 BCE) united most of the Indian peninsula under his rule, he adopted Buddhism and became its strongest patron. Under Aśoka Buddhism spread throughout the country and was – with imperial support – exported to non-Indian countries, entering Sri Lanka to the southeast where it is still present today, and reaching the Hellenistic kingdoms of Bactria and Sogdia to the north and northwest. Towards the end of its first five hundred years Buddhism became firmly established in Central Asia; the mission of the Dharmaguptakas, one of the early Buddhist schools, extended even as far as eastern Iran.

During this formative period the foundation for a progressively growing and expanding teaching was laid. It is difficult to say which of the early

Buddhist doctrines can be directly attributed to the Buddha himself, but certainly not all of them. For several hundred years the Buddhist *sūtras* (the texts claiming to preserve the Buddha's words) were not written down but memorized and transmitted orally. Whatever was truly important in life had to be learned by heart so that it could always be available. As the Buddhist doctrines became more elaborate, Buddhists did begin to write out their earlier, hitherto only memorized texts and scholastic-systematic treatises, apologetical and commentarial texts appeared on the scene. The Pāli Canon, an early scriptural collection accepted by the Theravāda School as its canonical work, was written down in the first century BCE in Sri Lanka in order to preserve the true teaching during a time of increasing doctrinal disputes (see Mhv 33:100f). Yet the ancient tradition of memorizing and commonly reciting the sūtras was never completely abolished.

Evidently at no stage of its history was Buddhism a homogenous movement. The Pāli Canon reports that sometimes whole groups of other masters with their disciples joined the early Buddhists and accepted the Buddha as their enlightened teacher. Surely however these groups brought their own pre-Buddhist heritage with them. Differences over important issues of doctrine and practice can be detected even in the oldest strata of Buddhist texts. Such differences became increasingly visible after Aśoka, and we hear about eighteen or perhaps more than twenty schools which clashed over doctrinal as well as practical issues. A major institutional schism occurred roughly a hundred years after the Buddha's death based on a dispute between the more liberal Mahāsaṅghikas and the more conservative Sthaviravādins as to the exact status of the Arhat, the enlightened saint, as well as over matters of monastic discipline. While the Sthaviravādins are forerunners of the Theravādins (now the most important Buddhist school in South and South-East Asia) the Mahāsaṅghikas are often seen as preparing the ground for Mahāyāna Buddhism, which dominates eastern Asia today.

The Rise of Mahāyāna (0–500 CE)

The literal meaning of 'Mahāyāna' is 'Great Vehicle' – 'Great' in the sense of 'noble' or 'eminent' as in Mahārāja, the 'Great King', and 'Vehicle' with reference to the doctrine and discipline leading to salvation. Correspondingly the Mahāyānins called the non-Mahāyānins and their teachings 'Hīnayāna', i.e., 'Small' or 'Inferior Vehicle', a derogatory term which should not be used in any scholarly treatment of Buddhism.

The roots of Mahāyāna certainly extend far back into the earliest period of Buddhist history though their distinguishing features are still a matter of much scholarly debate. The possibly major influence of the Mahāsaṅghikas notwithstanding, it seems that the basic ideas of Mahāyāna emerged among several pre-Mahāyāna schools and cannot be traced back to merely one of them. Mahāyānins themselves understood their teachings as a revelation of the true and deeper meaning of traditional Buddhist doctrines, surfacing later only because the time had not yet been ripe for them. These Mahāyāna ideas took shape in a number of new sūtras which, it was claimed, were revealed by the Buddha to an elect circle of disciples and afterwards hidden for several centuries. Some of the earliest layers of these texts – sections of the 'Perfection of Wisdom-Sūtras' (Prajñāpāramitā Sūtras) for instance, or of the Lotus-Sūtra (Saddharmapuṇḍarīka-Sūtra) – may have been composed already in the first century BCE. But it was during the second period of Buddhist history that ever more Mahāyāna texts, often quite voluminous ones, were written and became public.

This increase of doctrinal diversity fostered the development of Buddhist philosophy. The crucial and most influential figure of the nascent Mahāyāna philosophy was Nāgārjuna, who probably lived between 150 and 250 CE. His thought laid the foundation for the Madhyamaka School ('Middle Way' School), though his influence stretched far beyond that, even inspiring indirectly the philosophical renaissance of Hinduism set in motion by Śankara (8–9th cent. CE). The fourth century witnessed the development of the second major school of Mahāyāna philosophy, the so-called Yogācāra ('Yoga-Practice') or Vijñānavāda School ('Consciousness-School'), based on the writings of Asaṅga and Vasubandhu. By this point, non-Mahāyāna schools were also producing systematic treatises offering philosophically sophisticated presentations of their doctrines: Vasubandhu's important Abhidharmakośabhāṣya ('Commentary on the Treasure House of the Higher Doctrine'), for example. According to a Mahāyāna tradition this Vasubandhu is identical with Vasubandhu the Yogācārin, alleged to have converted to Mahāyāna after the completion of this work (though modern scholarship has raised considerable doubts about the identity of the two Vasubandhus). We can also cite Buddhaghosa's Visuddhimagga ('The Path of Purity') composed in fifth-century Sri Lanka. Thanks to this work and to his extensive commentaries on the Pāli Canon he became the major representative – indeed a kind of 'Church-Father' – of Theravāda orthodoxy.

This second period of Buddhist history is also a period of tremendous geographical expansion. Beginning in the first century CE, Buddhism progressed from Central Asia into China, and by the end of the fifth century it had spread throughout the country. More than 1300 Buddhist works were translated into Chinese during this time, the most eminent of the translators being Kumārajīva (344–413). From China Buddhism was introduced to Vietnam in the third century and to Korea in the fourth/fifth century. Between the second and fifth centuries Indian Buddhist missionaries took Buddhism to Cambodia and Burma, whence it gradually gained entry into Thailand.

The Rise of Tantric Buddhism (500–1,000 CE)

During its third 500 years Buddhist expansion in Asia proceeded yet further, and in some of the countries added to the Buddhist world during this period Buddhism continues to thrive even today.

In the sixth century Buddhism was officially recognized in Korea; between the seventh and tenth centuries it enjoyed royal patronage in the newly unified kingdom of Silla. In the middle of the sixth century Buddhism spread from Korea to Japan where Prince Shōtoku (574–622) became a dedicated supporter. In the seventh century Buddhism entered Tibet in two movements: Buddhist missionaries arrived from the flourishing Buddhist cultures of North India and Central Asia, and there was Buddhist influence coming from China as well. The Indian strand proved stronger. During the ninth century Buddhism in Tibet suffered a brief but vigorous persecution, yet it survived and subsequently became even more robust. China, though maintaining unbroken contact with India so as to have access to as many Indian Buddhist scriptures as possible, also furthered the evolution of new doctrinal schools (T'ien-t'ai, centred around the Lotus-Sūtra; Hua-yen, centred around the Avataṁsaka-Sūtra) and of new or modified forms of practice (Ch'an = Zen, with meditative practice as the focal point; Ching-t'u = Pure Land, with the veneration of Amida Buddha as the focal point). While these new schools and practices were clearly rooted in Indian sources, they also developed their own typical Chinese flavour, spiced by Taoist and Confucian ingredients. In mid-ninth-century China, Buddhism was subjected to severe persecution instigated by Taoist and Confucian circles, and never regained its former power. Both Ch'an and Pure Land Buddhism did survive however and now sought even more actively to link up with Confucianism and Taoism. Chinese forms of Buddhism also entered Vietnam where they gradually superseded non-Mahāyāna forms of Buddhism, while further to the south Buddhism flourished in Indonesia, where the remains of the famous Borobudur temple compound have left us with an unmistakeable sign of its strength during that period. Westward expansion, however, had come to a halt: the Muslim countries constituted an impenetrable barrier.

This period witnessed the heyday of Buddhist philosophy in India. Large monastic universities as, for example, Nālandā, Vikramaśīla or Odantapurī, became vibrant centres of a highly sophisticated intellectual culture. Both strands of Mahāyāna philosophy, Madhyamaka as well as Yogācāra, produced an array of splendid thinkers: Bhāvaviveka (6th cent.), Candrakīrti (7th cent.), Dignāga (6th cent.) and Dharmakīrti (7th cent.) – to mention but a few.

Apart from its continued expansion and its burgeoning religious and intellectual life, the most startling feature of the third period of Buddhist history is the rise of Tantric Buddhism (Tantra = 'loom' or 'warp', but also 'underlying principle' or 'main point'), also called Vajrayāna (Vajra = 'diamond' or 'thunderbolt', though the term is properly applied only to a later form of Tantric Buddhism). Tantrism is not an exclusively Buddhist phenomenon but developed synchronically in Hinduism and Buddhism. Within Buddhism it usually presupposes Mahāyāna teachings, which were expanded into psychological and/or cosmological systems. It emphasizes particular forms of ritual and meditational practice promising a more rapid path to enlightenment. Some Tantric texts make frequent use of erotic symbolism, and Tantric techniques at times entail provocatively antinomian elements. Tantra's religious ideal is the Siddha ('perfected', 'accomplished'), someone who is not only perfect in wisdom and compassion but also possesses extraordinary supernatural powers.

Tantrism not only spread swiftly over India, but in fact made its presence felt throughout the Buddhist world within a fairly short time. At the end of this period we find forms of Tantric Buddhism in Central Asia, China, Korea, Japan (where Kūkai, 774–835, established the small but influential Tantric Shingon School), Vietnam, Indonesia, and Sri Lanka. Nowhere however did it become so powerful and successful as in Tibet. The eighth-century Buddhist mission to Tibet was carried out by an interesting mix of philosophically minded monks, such as the famous Śāntarakṣita and his disciple Kamalaśīla, along with Tantric masters like the mysterious Padmasambhava whom the oldest of the Tibetan orders, Nyingma, designates as its founder. The symbiosis of scholarly Buddhism and Buddhist Tantrism, so typical for the North Indian and Central Asian Buddhism of that time, found its perfect continuation – and preservation – in Tibetan Lamaism.

Decline and Consolidation (1000–1500 CE)

The next period can be distinguished by the formation and denominational consolidation of the Buddhist world as it more or less persists in Asia up to the present day (see Figs. 1 and 2). That is, Buddhism ceased to exist in some of the formerly Buddhist countries while in other countries certain schools or forms of Buddhism became dominant or even monopolist.

First of all, Buddhism gradually disappeared from its land of origin, India. The reasons for this are manifold and have been the subject of considerable speculation. For one thing, there was a mighty resurgence of Hinduism, particularly in its theistic variants though also in the form of Hindu Tantrism. Moreover, Buddhism suffered some heavy blows from the advances of Islam onto Indian territory. Several of the Buddhist universities were raided and sacked by Muslim troops (Nālandā in 1197, Vīkramaśīla in 1203) and never recovered. Such explanations however simply beg the question: Why could Buddhism, which had survived heavy persecutions in other countries, not recoup its losses on its own home turf, India? One possible answer is that over the centuries it had become too similar to Hinduism such that it no longer presented a vivid alternative. This, however, should be understood

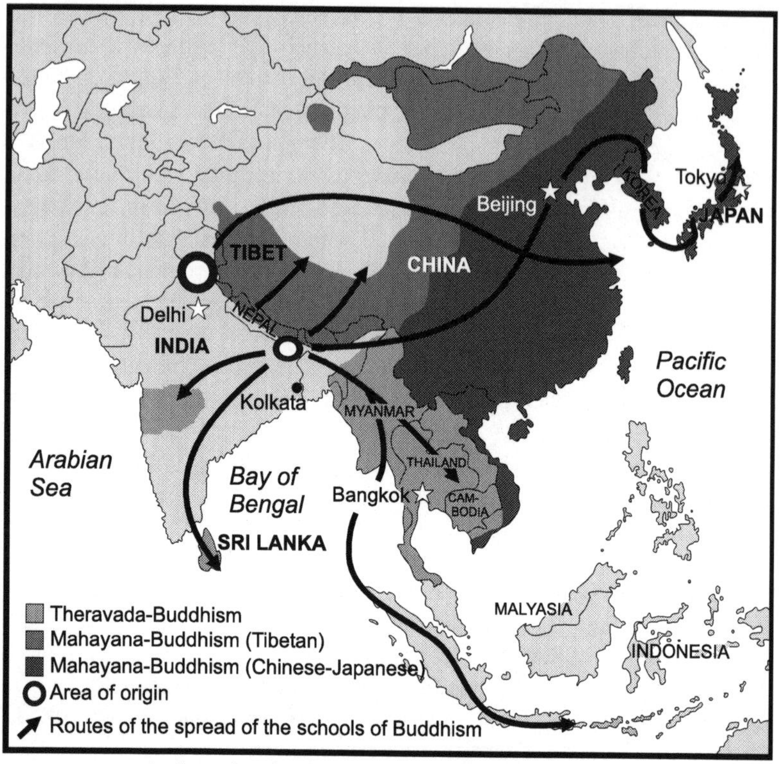

1. Spread and current location of Buddhism in Asia.

not only in the sense of Buddhism's excessive accommodation to Hinduism (as is often said of Buddhist Tantrism and late Indian Mahāyāna). Equally, if not even more so, the similarity suggests that Hinduism had gained so much and learned so profoundly from Buddhist spirituality and philosophy, that much of what once made Buddhism formidably unique was now to be found in Hinduism as well. If this is the case, then Buddhism never did disappear from India, or at least not entirely. Only its institutional form died out; much of its religious flavour remained. In addition to India, Buddhism also declined and gradually died out in Central Asia and Indonesia where it was superseded by Islam. But here again one may rightly ask whether Buddhism did not indeed leave its particular imprint on the Islam of the formerly Buddhist countries, inasmuch as Islam now developed a vibrant tradition of contemplative mystical Sufism.

In China Buddhism continued in the form of Ch'an (Zen) and Pure Land Buddhism. Learned Chinese Buddhists frequently maintained that Confucianism, Taoism and Buddhism differ only in function and not in substance, or that they are different manifestations of the same principle. While this claim ensured centuries of a fairly stable cohabitation, it worked less well in

Non-Mahāyāna	**Mahāyāna**	**Tantric Buddhism**
Theravāda, dominant in: • Sri Lanka • Thailand • Laos • Cambodia • Myanmar (Burma)	Fusions of various Mahāyāna traditions, particularly *Pure Land* and *Ch'an*, are dominant in: • China/Taiwan • Korea • Vietnam	Vajrayāna orders (*Nyingma*, *Kagyü*, *Sakya*, *Geluk*) • Tibet • Mongolia • Ladakh, Sikkim, Butan
Neo-Buddhism / *Ambedkar-Buddhism* • India (Maharashtra)	Lotus Schools (*Tendai* and *Nichiren Schools*) • Japan	Fusions of Hindu and Buddhist Tantrism • Nepal
	Pure Land (*Jōdo shū* and *Jōdo Shin shū*) • Japan	Shingon • Japan
	Zen (*Rinzai*, *Sōtō*, *Ōbaku*) • Japan	

2. Major currently existent schools and their main areas.

Korea. Though at first greatly promoted during Korea's Koryo period (10th–14th cent.) Buddhism subsequently became the target of a hostile Confucian reaction which deprived it of most of its former privileges.

In the Japan of the Kamakura period (1185–1333) Buddhism enjoyed its religiously most fruitful phase. All three of the great popular forms of Japanese Buddhism: Pure Land, Lotus and Zen, received their major impulses during this period, primarily through such outstanding religious personalities as the Pure Land Buddhists Hōnen (1133–1212) and Shinran (1173–1263), the Zen Buddhists Eisai (1141–1215) and Dōgen (1200–53), and the energetic propagator of the Lotus Sūtra, Nichiren (1222–83).

Something similar can be said for Tibet. A range of extraordinary personalities laid the foundation for Buddhism in its present form: Atīśa (11th cent.) played a crucial role in re-establishing Buddhism after the heavy persecution of the ninth century, spearheading in fact a missionary campaign which is remembered in Tibet as the "second diffusion" of the Dharma. The teachings of Marpa (1012–97), his disciple Milarepa (Mi-la-ras-pa, 1040–1123), and Milarepa's disciple Gampopa (sGam-po-pa, 1079–1153) led to the establishment of the Kagyü Order. The Sakya Order was founded by Konchok Gyalpo (11th cent.) and his son Gunga Nyingpo (12th cent.). In the fourteenth century, the great reformer of Tibetan Buddhism, Tsong Khapa (1357–1419), established the Geluk Order, the leaders of which became also the political rulers of Tibet in the fifteenth century with the title 'Dalai Lama' ('Ocean [of wisdom] Teacher').

Buddhism enjoyed one further geographical expansion: In its Tibetan form it was introduced into Mongolia in the thirteenth century, becoming firmly established there during the sixteenth and seventeenth centuries.

In a number of South and South-East Asian countries the Theravāda form of Buddhism prevailed and gradually displaced all other schools. This is true of Sri Lanka, Myanmar (Burma), Laos, Cambodia and Thailand as well as of some smaller regions in bordering countries (as for example Chittagong in Bangladesh). In Vietnam, on the other hand, despite strong and ongoing Theravāda influence, the dominant form of Buddhist doctrine remained Mahāyāna as inspired by China.

Buddhism Encounters the West (1,500–2,000 CE)

The arrival of the Portuguese in Sri Lanka in 1505 opened a new and exciting, though all too often painful, chapter of Buddhist history: Buddhism's encounter with the West. Until that time only a handful of adventurers had managed to traverse the barrier presented by the Islamic cultures. Now, however, the Western nations were able to proceed to the East by sea, and arrived as religious and political conquerors. Sri Lanka experienced three successive phases of Western colonial rule of roughly 150 years each: first the Portuguese (1505–1658), followed by the Dutch (1658–1795) and then the British (1795–1948), until it finally regained its independence.

In 1549 Christian missionaries entered Japan. In 1557 the Portuguese colony of Macao was established, whence the missionaries entered China in 1583. Apart from a few notable exceptions the encounter between Buddhists and Christians was hostile. In Sri Lanka the Portuguese began a sanguinary persecution of Buddhists. In Japan Christians encouraged newly converted regional rulers to suppress Buddhism, and as a result the Japanese authorities finally forbade Christianity: During the seventeenth century Japanese Christians (approx. 300,000) suffered one of the worst persecutions Christianity had ever seen, leading to the almost total extinction of Christianity. Subsequently the country isolated itself from virtually all foreign influence until the United States forced it to reopen in the middle of the nineteenth century. Though in China anti-Christian reactions were comparatively milder, Christianity was nevertheless officially forbidden in 1724.

During the nineteenth century Western colonialism in Asia reached its climax. Britain controlled Sri Lanka and Burma, France ruled over Vietnam, Laos and Cambodia and both nations, together with Portugal, Germany and Russia, controlled parts of China. Japan followed the Western example and established colonial rule in Korea and parts of China.

On the plus side, the missionary and imperialist activities of Western countries in Asia increased the knowledge of Buddhism in the West considerably, at first through the extensive reports of missionaries and travellers, and in the course of the nineteenth century through the study of Buddhist scriptures as well. The spread of these texts together with the appearance of the first Western books on Buddhism led a number of Europeans to identify themselves as Buddhists, most notably among them the German philosopher Arthur Schopenhauer (1788–1860). German Buddhists founded the first 'Buddhist Missionary Association' for Germany in 1903, and the influential 'Buddhist Society of Great Britain and Ireland' was established in 1907. Buddhism had reached Europe without a single Asian missionary setting foot on European soil. In the United States the situation was quite different: Buddhism entered the country with Buddhist immigrants from China and Japan, first through California and later primarily through Hawaii.

The massive presence of Westerners and Western ideas in the East and the far humbler and 'cleaner' but nevertheless influential presence of Buddhists and Buddhist ideas in the West proved to be a productive challenge for both sides. Is Buddhism more suitable to the modern world than Christianity, such that it should replace the latter? Or could Christianity receive vital impulses from the less dogmatic spirituality of Buddhism and its wealth of meditative experience? While these are major questions in the West, the East started to ask its own questions: How much could and should Buddhism learn from Western culture in order to renew itself and successfully resist the pressure from Christianity?

While the encounter with Christianity was and still is a crucial feature of Buddhism's encounter with the West, many Buddhist countries in Asia had to face another Western phenomenon which brought tremendous suffering: the post-Christian ideology of atheist and materialist Communism. Particularly in the second half of the twentieth century the vast majority of Asian Buddhist countries: China, Tibet, Mongolia, North-Korea, Vietnam, Laos, Cambodia, came under Communist rule. As a consequence Buddhism was subjected to many forms of restriction and suppression, and in some places, particularly in Cambodia, was even threatened with total extinction. Yet Buddhism survived in all these lands, and in Mongolia it was even declared the 'main' or state-religion after the country regained its independence and freedom from Communist rule.

In any event we have no certain knowledge as to the exact numbers of Buddhists in some Communist countries. We cannot assess the reliability of the official statistics in these countries, for it may well be the case that for various reasons the inhabitants do not readily identify themselves as Buddhists. Given China's large population this uncertainty makes it eminently difficult to produce a good estimate of the total number of Buddhists throughout the world. However it may be somewhere in the neighbourhood of 500 million (see Harvey, 1998, p. 5f).

Last but not least, one side-effect of the modern encounter between Buddhism and the West needs to be mentioned: the rebirth of Buddhism in India. Bhimrao Ambedkar (1891–1956), the first minister of justice in modern India, put together a highly political synthesis of traditional Buddhist ideas and Western Enlightenment ideals – particularly as regards the dignity and liberty of each individual being. For Ambedkar, this synthesis offered the most effective 'faith' for combating the Indian caste system with all its inhuman consequences. Indeed, Ambedkar's Neo-Buddhism gained much ground among the so-called Untouchables, the 'caste' of the casteless or outcasts. It is particularly robust today in the Indian state of Maharashtra.

Buddhism has shaped the face of Asia as no other religion, inspiring and guiding the lives of innumerable people in cultures as diverse as India and Japan, for example, or Mongolia and Thailand. Moreover it has begun to filter into the spirituality of growing numbers of people in the West. 'Why did Buddhism spread so successfully?' asks Oxford scholar Richard Gombrich (1988, p. 151). Several answers have been proposed. Many experts point to general sociological factors, to specific situations of social transition and change and, particularly, to political patronage – and clearly there is an element of truth in all of this. But to my mind the most simple and convincing answer is the one given by Gombrich himself: 'The major factor has no doubt been the power and beauty of its thought' (ibid.). To this we will now turn. But first we must look at the religious climate during the time of the Buddha under the influence of and in response to which he proclaimed his insight.

For further reading: Bechert and Gombrich (1984); Conze (1980); Conze (2001); Habito (2005); Harvey (1998); Skilton (1997).

2

The Religious Context of Early Buddhism

Brahmanism and the Ideal of a Good Life

At the time of the Buddha the dominant religion in India was Brahmanism. It was based on early sections of the Vedas believed to contain eternal truth as perceived by the Vedic seers. The world was understood to be filled with innumerable deities (*devas*). Every force in nature, every power in society and culture was associated with one or more divine personalities. There were gods of wind and water, of fire and earth, of the sun, moon and stars. Trees and plants were inhabited by spirits and there were gods watching over communal duties, the social order and customs.

Nevertheless, the impression of a strong polytheism here is deceptive. Polytheism was in fact moderated – and at times fully defeated – by two contrary tendencies: First, by the tendency to rank the gods into a hierarchy with one single deity at the top *(henotheism)* – and as soon as an idea of qualitative difference is introduced into the relationship between the highest god and all subordinate deities, one is already on the road leading to *monotheism*. Various gods were at times venerated as superior to the others, as the 'king of the gods' – particularly Varuṇa and Indra and, somewhat later, Brahmā and Prajāpati, whom Ṛg-Veda 10:121 praises as the 'God above Gods', the one who generates and encompasses everything else.

The second tendency working to offset polytheism was not monotheistic but *monistic*, reflecting the idea that ultimately everything is a manifestation of one single divine reality. Monism's beginnings can be detected in the frequent process of identifying various gods with each another, or even seeing them all as referring to one single ultimate reality, as famously stated in Ṛg-Veda 1:164:46: 'They call him Indra, Mitra, Varuṇa, Agni, and he is heavenly nobly-winged Garutmān. To what is one, sages give many a title…' (Radhakrishnan and Moore, 1989, p. 21). Keeping in mind that the vast pantheon of Vedic gods represented the sum of cosmic, natural and even social forces, the idea of seeing them as expressing one single divine reality could easily lead to a monistic understanding of reality itself. But that creates new questions: Who or what is the ultimate reality within and beyond everything? Is it itself a kind of existent being or is it more appropriately conceived as meta-reality similar to nothingness? And why has it now manifested in such a diverse range of phenomena? These questions are raised in a Vedic hymn (Ṛg-Veda 10:129), justly described as perhaps *the* key text underlying all later philosophical thought in India, whether Hindu or Buddhist (see Lindtner, 1999, pp. 40f; 48ff):

> Non-being then existed not nor being:
> There was no air, nor sky that is beyond it.
> What was concealed? Wherein? In whose protection?
> And was there deep unfathomable water?
>
> Death then existed not nor life immortal;
> Of neither night nor day was any token.
> By its inherent force the One breathed windless:
> No other thing than that beyond existed.
>
> … Creative force was there, and fertile power:
> Below was energy, above was impulse.
>
> Who knows for certain? Who shall here declare it?
> Whence was it born, and whence came this creation?
> The gods were born after this world's creation:
> Then who can know from whence it has arisen?
> (Radhakrishnan and Moore, 1989, p. 23)

Another celebrated hymn in the Ṛg-Veda (10:90) explains the world as the result of a primordial sacrifice. The whole universe is one single 'man' (*puruṣa*) or organism; as the hymn expresses it, or more precisely: the whole universe is but a quarter of what this primordial 'man' truly encompasses. The *puruṣa* is sacrificed by the gods, and from the various parts of his body the elements of the natural and social world are created – including the gods! That is, the sun-god, the fire-god, the wind, the earth, and Indra, are all made from various parts of the *puruṣa's* body. On the one hand then, the gods perform the sacrifice of the *puruṣa* and on the other they are themselves the result of the sacrifice. This suggests that the world with its vast diversity of beings, forces and elements comes into existence as a kind of divine self-sacrifice, whereby the primordial unity submits to an ordered diversity without ceasing to remain the one single divine organism in and behind everything.

The *puruṣa* myth also explains the origin of the caste system. The caste of the priests (*brāhmaṇas*) is born from the *puruṣa's* mouth. The caste of the rulers and warriors (*kṣatriyas*) is made of his arms. His thighs became the caste of traders and farmers (*vaiśyas*) and from his feet the caste of the servants (*śūdras*) was made (Ṛg-Veda 10:90:12). This relation between the castes and different parts of the *puruṣa's* body is not only indicative of their different functions within society but at the same time expressive of a social hierarchy – with the Brahmans at the top.

The Brahmans saw themselves as guardians of the social order which itself was seen as part of the eternal and divine cosmic order (*ṛta*). They knew and taught the *dharma*, i.e. the eternal 'law', encompassing not only general ethical rules but also the more specific 'duties' derived from the cosmic order for each and everyone according to his or her caste-status. To fulfil one's *dharma*, to live in accordance with *dharma*, was the overall ideal of the Brahmanic religion.

Apart from teaching the Dharma, the particular duty of the Brahmans was to perform the Vedic ritual-sacrifices, which might be private or domestic, or at times very large public affairs. Through the Vedas the Brahmans possessed the knowledge of how to perform the sacrifice properly and effectively. The purpose of the sacrifice was to offer the oblation (usually various kinds of food: milk, rice and barley, plants and domestic animals, but also valuable things like a good horse) to the gods by burning the oblation in the sacred fire. Fire, divinized as the god 'Agni', transported the oblation to the invisible realm of the deities. In return, the deities granted material benefits, success, social and personal well-being, a joyful life, and – quite importantly – male offspring. But communication with the gods was mediated not only through the fire-god Agni, but also through Soma, a god associated with a plant whose juice had hallucinogenic or stimulating properties. The altered states of consciousness induced by Soma were understood as glimpses of the beyond. Soma widened the 'doors of perception' and elevated the priest to the heavenly world (see Ṛg-Veda 8:48; 9:113).

Early Vedic religion testifies to a very *this-worldly* orientation: One needs to live in harmony with the gods, the powers of nature and culture in order to avoid mischief and enjoy life as much as possible. There are three general 'goals of men' (*puruṣārtha*), affirmed by the Vedas for all regardless of caste: living in accordance with *dharma*, gaining 'wealth' and 'power' (*artha*), enjoying the 'sensual pleasures' of life (*kāma*). In a Vedic hymn to the god Soma (Ṛg-Veda 9:112:1.3f), we read:

> Our thoughts bring us to diverse callings, setting people apart: the carpenter seeks what is broken, the physician a fracture, and the Brahmin priest seeks one who presses Soma. O drop Soma, flow for Indra. …
>
> I am a poet; my Dad's a physician and Mum a miller with grinding-stones. With diverse thoughts we all strive for wealth, going after it like cattle. O drop of Soma, flow for Indra.
>
> The harnessed horse longs for a light cart; seducers long for a woman's smile; the penis for the two hairy lips, and the frog for water. O drop of Soma, flow for Indra.
>
> (O'Flaherty, 1981, p. 235)

Artha (wealth/power) and *kāma* (sensual, particularly erotic pleasure) – this, according to the Vedas, is what we all long for and what, with the help of the gods, we can and should expect from life if we live in accordance with the *dharma*.

But what about life after death? The constituent parts of a human being return to the corresponding elements of nature: the light of the eyes to the sun, the breath to the wind, the limbs to the earth. The person itself goes to the realm of the 'fathers'. The cremation of the dead is again linked to the function of Agni, the fire god. As Agni bears the sacrifice to the gods by consuming the oblation, he is also called upon to bear the dead to a heavenly world, a world of reward for those who did what is good (see Ṛg-Veda 10:16:1–5). But this 'reward' was apparently not understood as essentially different from what one could enjoy here. Afterlife was conceived as a better (hopefully) continuation of life, but not as something totally other. This may explain why at some stage in the development of Vedic Brahmanism the idea arose that life after death could eventually come to an end as well: Given the ominous prospect of 're-death' (*punarmṛtyu*), a true liberation from death and redeath comes to be seen as a goal really worth pursuing.

The Challenge of the Śramaṇas

Belief in rebirth or redeath is simply not to be found in the early parts of the Vedas, and the origins of this belief – which subsequently became one of the most widely accepted ideas in the Indian religions – are still quite obscure. But the further development and spread of reincarnation-belief was closely linked to the Śramaṇa movement. Belief in reincarnation functioned as a major motivation behind the new religious ideal and lifestyle propagated by the Śramaṇas (Pāli: *samaṇas* = 'strivers'). In their eyes, the idea of a possibly endless repetition of one life after the other, of a 'cycle of rebirth' (*saṃsāra*), made the traditional life-goals of Vedic religion pointless: What would be the sense of repeatedly looking forward to the same sorts of little enjoyments and transient worldly successes, that is, for *kāma* and *artha*? Nothing was permanent except this unending transitoriness itself. Within this cycle of rebirth and redeath nothing could count as finally satisfying and worthy of ultimate pursuit:

> In this sort of cycle of existence (*saṃsāra*) what is the good of enjoyment of desires, when after a man has fed on them there is seen repeatedly his return here to earth?
> … In this cycle of existence I am like a frog in a waterless well.
> (Radhakrishnan and Moore, 1989, p. 93f)

This passage from one of the later Upaniṣads (Maitri Upaniṣad 1:4) captures quite aptly the motivation of the Śramaṇas. It uses the same metaphor we encountered earlier in a sampling of the Vedic endorsements of worldly pleasures: the frog longing for water as symbolic of all creatures' natural pursuit of satisfaction and happiness. But while early Brahmanism was convinced that human striving can be satisfied by *artha* and *kāma*, that wealth and sensual pleasures are to human beings what water is to a frog, the Śramaṇas rejected this. Life in *saṃsāra* is like being a 'frog in a waterless well'. The real satisfaction of human longing must be found somewhere else, outside the saṃsāric world, there where real immortality reigns, where we arrive at the ultimate ground of reality. Consequently, the sacrificial practices, with their focus on this-worldly benefits, were useless to the Śramaṇas – as was a life in conformance with the duties and purposes of society. They decided to renounce the world and live as homeless ascetics in the forests, ignoring all caste obligations and focussing on those practices which they believed would lead them to liberation from saṃsāra, to the discovery of ultimate reality and to the lasting satisfaction resulting from this:

> Thinking sacrifice and merit is the chiefest thing,
> Naught better do they know – deluded!
> Having had enjoyment on the top of the heaven won by good works,
> They re-enter this world, or a lower.
>
> They who practice austerity and faith in the forest,
> The peaceful knowers who live on alms,
> Depart passionless through the door of the sun,
> To where is that immortal Person (*puruṣa*) …
> (Muṇḍaka Upaniṣad 1:2:10f; Radhakrishnan and Moore, 1989, p. 52)

So the new religious goal introduced by the Śramaṇas was ultimate salvation or liberation. While a wide range of different opinions prevailed among the Śramaṇas, there was general agreement that this goal could be achieved through liberating knowledge – insight into the nature of what reality really is. Yet this sort of knowledge or insight is not something that can be learnt and understood intellectually. To be genuine and efficacious it must be perceptible, it must strike one's understanding with the irresistible force and certainty of a clear experience. Therefore the Śramaṇas pursued a lifestyle and spiritual practices which seemed conducive to that special experience of liberating insight. This meant cutting the bonds to the usual worldly life of a householder, practicing diverse forms of meditation and disciplining one's body and mind through living a celibate life and, at times, through enduring rather severe austerities such as various forms of fasting and self-inflicted pain.

Arising in India between the sixth and fourth centuries BCE, the Śramaṇa movements posed a tremendous challenge to religion and society. If the Śramaṇas were right, the life of ordinary people with their social obligations and goals was meaningless, the Vedic rituals pointless, and the 'knowledge' of the Vedas deceiving. Many of the subsequent developments in religion in India can be understood as different attempts to come to grips with this challenge: 'to reconcile the life of the householder … with the ideal of the ascetic renouncer …' (Krishna, 1996, p. 51).

Some of the religious groups which grew out of the Śramaṇas remained outside the boundaries of Vedic orthodoxy, rejecting the Vedas together with the socio-religious system the Vedas promoted, and developing instead their own religious institutions. This is true of the Jains and of the Buddhists. Even today some of the most severe forms of ascetic discipline are occasionally practiced among the Jains: When a spiritually highly-developed Jain follower approaches saintliness, he will refrain from eating and starve to death.

Established Brahmanism, however, made a successful attempt to integrate as much as possible of the Śramaṇa spirituality into their own religious system. Indeed, part of the Śramaṇa movement may have arisen within Brahmanic circles, as can be seen in the Upaniṣads, a group of scriptures primarily composed between 600 and 300 BCE. The Upaniṣads are replete with Śramaṇic ideas, including the criticism of the Vedic texts and rituals. Yet they present themselves as revealing the true and higher knowledge hidden behind the surface of traditional Vedic views. This approach permitted the Brahmans to incorporate the Upaniṣads into the Vedas as their final part (Vedānta = 'end of the Veda') and in fact as their ultimate meaning. Liberating insight is here understood as perceiving the inner unity between one's true self, *ātman*, and the ultimate divine reality, now frequently called *brahman* (perhaps as a consequence of the identification of *brahman* as the interior life-principle of the *puruṣa* – an identification found already in some Vedic texts [see Atharva-Veda 1:2]). The unity between *ātman* and *brahman* is sometimes conceived along monotheistic lines as a mystical union, but more often it is seen as a monistic unity, such that the self, *ātman*, is in truth identical with the all-pervasive divine *brahman*.

The new religious goal of the Śramaṇas, salvation *(mukti)*, or liberation *(mokṣa)*, was added to the three traditional goals of *dharma*, *artha*, *kāma*, as the final goal in life. In order to reconcile the new goals with the old, the defenders of Vedic orthodoxy insisted that one should first learn and respect the *dharma*, and thereafter start a family and pursue the goals of wealth, power and pleasure. Only when he sees his children's children is man free to abandon his social duties so as to lead the life of a hermit or homeless ascetic in pursuit of final liberation. Should he not feel spiritually ripe for this, the idea of reincarnation offers both a solution to his own situation and a new approach to consolidating the Vedic society: Fulfilling one's *dharma*, it was now declared, is as effective in the course of reincarnation as the performance (*karma*) of sacrifice. Through good *karma*, i.e. through living in accordance with *dharma*, one will attain a good rebirth, perhaps in an even higher caste, and gradually prepare oneself for the ultimate goal of salvation.

Another reaction to the religious disruptions and transitions set in motion by the Śramaṇas can be seen in the emergence of the Cārvākas. These retained the traditional Vedic goals and made no attempt to harmonize them with the new Śramaṇic ideals. However, while rejecting Śramaṇic asceticism they also abolished the whole religious context of Brahmanism and openly endorsed a form of atheism and materialism (*lokāyata*) that sounds astonishingly modern:

> There exists here no cause excepting nature.
>
> The soul is just the body …
>
> There is no world other than this; there is no heaven and no hell; the realm of Śiva and like regions are invented by stupid impostors of other schools of thought.
>
> The enjoyment of heaven lies in eating delicious food, keeping company of young women, using fine clothes, perfumes, garlands, sandal paste, etc.
>
> The pain of hell lies in the troubles that arise from enemies, weapons, diseases; while liberation (*mokṣa*) is death which is the cessation of life-breath.
>
> The wise therefore ought not to take pains on account of that (i.e. liberation); it is only the fool who wears himself out by penances, fasts, etc.
>
> Chastity and other such ordinances are laid down by clever weaklings …
>
> The wise should enjoy the pleasures of this world through the proper visible means of agriculture, keeping cattle, trade, political administration, etc.
>
> (as quoted in: Śaṅkara's Sarvasiddhāntasaṅgraha; Radhakrishnan and Moore, 1989, p. 235)

Such views were never adopted by the masses in traditional India, though they did have their supporters. At the time of the Buddha they were forcefully proclaimed by a teacher called Ajita Keśakambali (see DN 2:23).

What was the early Buddhist reaction to all of this? All groups, whether the traditional Vedic Brahmanists, or the various Śramaṇa circles or even the Cārvākas, agreed on the principle that 'all beings recoil from pain and desire happiness', as a Buddhist text expresses it (see MN 94). Buddhists affirmed this as well. The big question concerned the nature of genuine satisfaction or ultimate happiness and, accordingly, the right way to attain it. Together with the Śramaṇas, Buddhists proclaimed that ultimate happiness is linked to salvation. Buddhism too rejected the authority of the Vedas as well as that of the Brahmans. But faced with the more radical world-renouncers on the one hand, and the materialistic Cārvākas on the other, the Buddha proclaimed his discovery of a 'middle way', a path that leads to the 'deathless' and to

3

Siddhārtha Gautama, the Buddha

History and Legend

'Buddha' is not a proper name but a religious title meaning 'the Enlightened' or, literally, 'the Awakened One' – someone who has overcome the darkness of existential ignorance and awakened from illusion or delusion. The title usually refers to Siddhārtha Gautama (Pāli: Siddhattha Gotama). Unfortunately from a historical point of view, we do not have much which could count as fairly safe or highly probable knowledge about Siddhārtha. We may assume that he was in fact a real historical person and not entirely the fabrication of religious legend, as some indologists held in the past. Regarding the exact dates of Siddhārtha's life however there is a great deal of uncertainty. Traditional Theravāda Buddhism claims that he lived between 623 or 624 and 543 or 544 BCE, though most scholars see 563 or 566 to 483 or 486 BCE as more likely. More recently a number of historians have opted for an even younger dating, usually something like 450–370 BCE.

The unanimous assumption that Siddhārtha reached the age of eighty is based on the traditional information found in the Pāli Canon. The Pāli Canon is our oldest source for biographical knowledge about the Buddha, though all too often the reliability of this information may be doubted. Some of the narratives seem quite credible while others obviously bear the mark of legend. In subsequent centuries comprehensive accounts of the life of the Buddha were written: the Mahāvastu (2nd cent. BCE) for example, or the famous Lalitavistara (1st cent. BCE) and the poetical Buddhacarita composed by Aśvaghoṣa (1st cent. CE), or the Theravādic Nidānakathā (4th cent. CE). These 'biographies' contain a mixture of patently legendary features together with some older, perhaps more reliable accounts. But all testify to the development of a rather stable Buddha-legend with a clear set of standardised elements. The obvious purpose of the Buddha-legend is to illustrate crucial points of Buddhist teachings through the life of the Buddha, whereby the Buddha functions as the 'visible *dharma*' – an idea having fairly old roots (see AN 3,54f; SN 22:87). This is also expressed by another religious title frequently given to the Buddha: 'Tathāgata', the 'Thus-Gone', meaning that the Buddha himself has 'gone' as he had taught. This function of the Buddha-legend is further underlined by the traditional view that the lives of all Buddhas always follow the same pattern of the major events of the Buddha-legend: Every Buddha – if he really is a 'Buddha', an 'Awakened One' – manifests or incarnates the same eternal truth of the Buddhist *dharma*. And this idea is already found in the Pāli Canon (DN 14). In this chapter I will focus primarily on those accounts which seem to be historically more on the reliable side. But I will also include some elements of the Buddha-legend in so far as these convey what the Buddha means to Buddhists.

Becoming a Buddha

Siddhārtha was born in Lumbinī near Kapilavastu, in North-East India, north of the present-day Benares near the Nepalese border. At this time Kapilavastu belonged to the small republic of the Śākyas which is why Siddhārtha is also called Śākyamuni: 'the wise from the Śākyas'. His father, Śuddhodana, was the ruler of the republic and thus Siddhārtha belonged to the caste of the *kṣatriyas*. His mother, Māyādeva, died shortly after giving birth, and Siddhārtha was raised by his aunt Mahāprajāpatī. We may assume that young Siddhārtha received an elite education befitting his status as a higher member of the warrior-caste. By the age of sixteen he was married to Yaśodharā who gave birth to his son Rāhula.

According to an autobiographical fragment in the Pāli Canon, Siddhārtha lived a privileged, well-protected, indeed luxurious life:

> I used only sandal unguent from Benares and my head dress, my jacket, my undergarment and my tunic were made of Benares muslin. By day and by night a white canopy was held over me, lest cold and heat, dust, chaff or dew should trouble me. I had three palaces: one for the summer, one for the winter and one for the rainy season. In the palace for the rainy season, during the four months of the rains, I was waited upon by female musicians only, and I did not come down from the palace during these months.
>
> (AN 3:38; Nyanaponika and Bhikkhu Bodhi, 1999, p. 53f)

But 'amidst such splendour and an entirely carefree life' Siddhārtha began to ponder the inevitability of old age, illness and death with the result that 'all my pride in youthfulness, … all my pride in health, … all my pride in life vanished' (ibid.).

The Buddha-legend has given dramatic narrative expression to the development of young Siddhārtha in the famous story of the 'Four Sights': According to legend Siddhārtha was conceived virginally. His mother saw in a dream how he left Tuṣita heaven and entered her womb in the shape of the royal symbol of a white elephant. He was born by miraculously exiting his mother's womb through her right side (which is regarded as noble). Immediately after birth he took seven steps and proclaimed himself to be the 'highest in the world' and this life to be his last life. Wise Brahmans predicted that Siddhārtha, having the thirty-two bodily marks of a great man, would either become an emperor (*cakravartin*) or a fully 'enlightened one' – a Buddha. Preferring the former for his son, his father surrounded him with every kind of luxury and took care that Siddhārtha was secluded from anything which might rouse some sort of religious longing. As a young man Siddhārtha nonetheless became curious about life outside the palace walls and undertook an excursion. On that occasion he saw, for the first time in his life, an old man 'bent like a roof-beam, broken, leaning on a stick, tottering, sick, his youth all vanished'. When he asked his charioteer what was wrong with this man, he learned that this is simply old age, and that all, including Siddhārtha himself, 'are liable to become old'. Siddhārtha was shocked and returned to his palace. On a second excursion, he met for the first time 'a sick man, suffering, very ill, fallen in his own urine and excrement'. Again Siddhārtha asked his charioteer, and learnt of the inevitability of sickness. Yet a third excursion confronted him with the sight of death. Siddhārtha asked his charioteer:

> "Why is he called a dead man?"
> "Prince, he is called a dead man because now his parents and other relatives will not see him again, nor he them."
> "But am I subject to dying, not exempt from dying?"
> "Both you and I, Prince, are subject to dying, not exempt from it."

By now Siddhārtha was deeply disturbed: 'Shame on this thing birth, since to him who is born old age, sickness, death must manifest.' Nothing could dispel his worries or divert him. At night, when he saw himself surrounded by the sleeping bodies of his female musicians and consorts, he was struck by the feeling of being 'in the middle of a cemetery'.

On a fourth and final excursion Siddhārtha met a Śramaṇa. His charioteer explained that this is one who truly follows the Dharma, 'who truly lives in serenity, does good actions, performs meritorious deeds, is harmless and truly has compassion for living beings.' Now Siddhārtha made up his mind to become a Śramaṇa himself. With tears in his eyes his father tried to dissuade him, but Siddhārtha replied he would only stay if Śuddhodana could endow him with freedom from old age, sickness and death. At night Siddhārtha took a final look at his sleeping son Rāhula, and left his father's palace to start his search for the 'deathless' (see Lv, Ndk and DN 14; quotations from Walshe, 1995, 207–221).

Undoubtedly the traditional accounts of Buddha's life locate the driving motive underlying Buddha's religious quest in the existential confrontation with life's transitoriness. There is, though, a little fragment in the Pāli Canon which suggests a further experience which may have influenced Siddhārtha's decision, the confrontation with human violence:

> Fear results from resorting to violence – just look at how people quarrel and fight! But let me tell you now of the kind of dismay and terror that I have felt.
>
> Seeing people struggling, like fish, writhing in shallow water with enmity against one another, I became afraid.
>
> At one time, I had to find some place where I could take shelter, but I never saw any such place. There is nothing in this world that is solid at base and not a part of it that is changeless.
>
> I had seen them all trapped in mutual conflict and that is why I had felt so repelled.
>
> (Sutta-Nipāta 935–38a; Saddhatissa, 1987, p. 109)

The experience of violence and war, as recalled in these verses, may well have contributed to the decision of the young Siddhārtha – who himself belonged to the warrior-caste – not to pursue a career as a worldly ruler but to find a religious response to this aspect of life.

The Buddha-legend tells us that Siddhārtha, having now chosen the life of a Śramaṇa, first learned certain forms of meditation which led him into deep contemplative states – but not to liberation from old age, sickness and death, and so he intensified his efforts and took on the most severe ascetic practices of his day:

> Such was my asceticism, ... that I went naked, ... I took food once a day, once every two days ... thus up to once every fortnight ... I was one who pulled out hair and beard. I was one who stood continuously, rejecting seats. I was one who squatted continuously ... I was one who used a mattress of spikes ... Thus in such a variety of ways I dwelt pursuing the practice of tormenting and mortifying the body.
>
> (MN 12; Ñāṇamoli, Bodhi, 2001, p. 173)

This radical asceticism brought him near death but no nearer the goal of his search. Had everything been in vain? Was there perhaps another way?

At that stage Siddhārtha recalled an experience from his youth when he had been sitting under a shady tree and felt a state of inner calm apart from any sensual pleasures or unpleasant feelings. Could this experience have indicated the proper direction? Pointing towards a path beyond the extremes of his once-luxurious life and the subsequent years of painful self-torment? He gave up his ascetic practices and resumed a normal diet. Regaining health and strength he dedicated himself to a form of meditation which induced a state of complete equanimity and inner stillness, beyond any feelings of pleasure or pain. In that state Siddhārtha finally experienced enlightenment (*bodhi*). First he attained the complete recollection of his own past lives, and then understood the mechanism that binds all beings to the cycle of reincarnation. Finally he saw the truth regarding the ultimate roots of the human predicament and the path to a lasting liberation. He not only understood all this, he experienced it himself:

> When I knew and saw thus, my mind was liberated from the taint of sensual desire, from the taint of being, and from the taint of ignorance. When it was liberated there came the knowledge: 'It is liberated.' I directly knew: 'Birth is destroyed, the holy life has been lived, what had to be done has been done, there is no more coming to any state of being.'
>
> (MN 33; Ñāṇamoli, Bodhi, 2001, p. 342)

This inner certainty of a lasting liberation from *saṃsāra*, the cycle of rebirth and redeath, was but the negative expression of the positive attainment of Nirvāṇa (Pāli: *nibbāna*), the ultimate reality beyond birth and death and all suffering:

> I attained the unborn supreme security from bondage, Nibbāna …
> I attained the unaging supreme security from bondage, Nibbāna …
> I attained the unailing supreme security from bondage, Nibbāna …
> I attained the deathless supreme security from bondage, Nibbāna …
> I attained the sorrowless supreme security from bondage, Nibbāna …
> I attained the undefiled supreme security from bondage, Nibbāna …
> The knowledge and vision arose in me: 'My deliverance is unshakeable …'
>
> (MN 26; Ñāṇamoli, Bodhi, 2001, p. 259f)

Through this experience Siddhārtha Gautama had now become the 'Buddha', the Enlightened or Awakened One. But just as crucial as this 'enlightenment' for the origins of Buddhism, so too was the Buddha's decision to communicate his insight to others, sharing the truth he had found. And the grounding motivation for this decision is the Buddha's compassion. The Buddha-legend expresses this with two narratives.

According to one, the Buddha was at first inclined not to preach or teach but to remain silent, since the truth he had discovered is 'hard to see and hard to understand, peaceful and sublime, unattainable by mere reasoning'; it 'goes against the worldly stream' (MN 26). But when the deity Bahmā Sahampati realised that Buddha might refrain from teaching, he appeared before him and pleaded for the world. 'The world will be lost, the world will perish', if the Buddha should decide to keep silent. 'Open the doors to the Deathless! Let them hear the Dhamma (Dharma) that the Stainless One has found.' So 'out of compassion for beings' the Buddha agreed (MN 26).

According to the second narrative, it was Māra (an evil deity, the tempter, associated with the bonds of sensual pleasures and death) who attempted to persuade the Buddha immediately after the enlightenment to abstain from teaching and leave the world at once, thus entering final Nirvāṇa. The

3. The Buddha sitting in meditation, symbolizing his perfection in wisdom.

Buddha, though, replied that he would not leave the world until he had established orders for monks and nuns and also a community of lay-followers, so that the Dharma and the path to salvation would be firmly rooted and 'well-proclaimed among mankind everywhere' (DN 16:3:35).

Both narratives lay great emphasis upon the absence of self-interest in the Buddha's activity after his enlightenment. Everything that he himself had been looking for had been attained through his enlightenment – 'what had

4. The Buddha walking into the world, symbolizing his perfection in compassion.

to be done has been done' is the traditional formula in the various records of his enlightenment. Afterwards, his missionary activity and the establishment of the Buddhist community were entirely for the sake of the others, motivated by altruistic 'compassion' (*karuṇā*). Buddhists may have felt the need to emphasise this because of a tradition according to which an enlightened person would remain silent. Even the term for a 'wise one', *muni*, literally means the 'silent one' – and there are two reasons for this: first, because the highest truth transcends what can be expressed in words; and second, because missionary activity smacks of self-interest, of bonds to the world which have not yet been severed. So we read in the Pāli-Canon that Buddha was rebuked by a demon with the words: 'Having abandoned all the knots as one fully released, it isn't good for you, an ascetic, to be instructing others' (SN 10:2; Bodhi, 2000, p. 306) to which the Buddha replied that the instruction of others does not forge a new fetter if one's mind is clear and one's motivation compassionate. There are indications that such criticism was levelled against the Buddha by non-Buddhists – hence the Buddhists' defence of their claim that the Buddha was really an Enlightened One, arguing that the Buddha was perfect in wisdom *and* in compassion. While his wisdom (*prajñā*) had indeed attained to a sphere beyond words and set him free from all bonds to the world, his selfless compassion (*karuṇā*) nevertheless impelled him to 'open the doors of the deathless' to all. Without the Buddha's enlightenment and without his compassion, his decision to preach, 'Buddhism' would have never come into existence. Buddhism is founded precisely on this inner unity of wisdom and compassion (see Figs. 3 and 4).

The Life as a Buddha

At the time of his enlightenment the Buddha was thirty-five years old. He spent the next forty-five years of his life as a wandering teacher, counselling people from all levels of society, gathering them into the community of his monastic and lay-followers and instructing them as to how to pursue the path he had found. He opened his very first sermon with the words:

> Bhikkhus ('monks'), these two extremes should not be followed by one who has gone into homelessness. What two? The pursuit of sensual happiness in sensual pleasures, which is low, vulgar, the way of worldlings, ignoble, unbeneficial; and the pursuit of self-mortification, which is painful, ignoble, unbeneficial. Without veering towards either of these extremes, the Tathāgata has awakened to the middle way, which gives rise to vision, which gives rise to knowledge, which leads to peace, to direct knowledge, to enlightenment, to Nibbāna.
>
> (SN 5:56:11, Bodhi, 2000, p. 1844)

Let us pause here for a moment. The two major periods of Siddhārtha's life before his enlightenment – the life of luxury in his father's palaces, and the years spent in painful austerities – symbolically represent the two rival orientations of his time: on the one hand, the traditional goals of *artha* and *kāma* (wealth, power, sensual enjoyment, equally affirmed by Brahmans and Cārvākas); and on the other, the radical asceticism and world-renouncement endorsed by so many within the Śramaṇa movement. In rejecting both traditional Brahmanism and the materialism of the Cārvākas, the Buddha is basically in agreement with the Śramanas and their new religious ideal of searching for ultimate liberation. Yet he rejects their harsh forms of asceticism and their total other-worldliness, and the Buddha does not withdraw from the world as Māra had tempted him to do. To characterise the path now found and proclaimed by the Buddha as a 'middle way' is to indicate the founding of a new religious approach above and beyond the existent options. In fact, it marks the beginning of the long Buddhist history of making Śramaṇa insights and spirituality fruitful and practicable within a life in this world.

This new approach also finds expression in the other traditional accounts of Buddha's life, in the many details about his activity after enlightenment. At the same time, the two basic features that make him a Buddha are illustrated: He is presented as a teacher whose *wisdom* is superior to the rival religious or ideological views of his time, and as someone whose personality is filled with *compassion*.

First of all, the Buddha is shown to be highly critical of established Brahmanism: The ancient Vedic hymns were written by people who had not achieved any success in meditation (DN 27:23), and those who follow the Vedas are compared with blind men following blind leaders (DN 13). While their faith is groundless, the *dharma* taught by the Buddha is profound (MN 95). The Buddha's *dharma* is, of course, not his invention. It is a cosmic truth which he rediscovered, as someone discovers and renovates an ancient city that had been overgrown by jungle (SN 12:65). The ritual baths and purification acts recommended by the Brahmans are useless (MN 7), and their practice of sacrificing animals is not only useless but also barbaric. A *useful* sacrifice, on the other hand, would consist in supporting needy and virtuous ascetics (DN 5; Sn 284–315). To call upon the help of the gods in order to attain a heavenly rebirth after death is as futile as praying that a rock would emerge from a deep pond into which it had sunk (SN 42:6). The idea that whatever a person experiences is caused by a creator-god is met with disapproval because it entails a denial of human freedom and responsibility and thus undermines any motivation to strive for salvation (AN 3:61). The caste system, or more precisely, the assumption that the value and moral or spiritual state of a particular individual can be derived from birth or caste is strictly rejected (Sn 116–42; Dhp 383–423; MN 84). The Brahmans' contention that their birth has bestowed them with a morally and religiously elevated status meets with particular censure (MN 93): A 'true Brahman' can only be someone who lives by the principles of the *dharma* as taught by the Buddha (Dhp 383–423). Accordingly, the followers of the Buddha are declared to be those 'born of his mouth', because the body of the Buddha is the 'body of the dharma' and as such the 'body of Brahmā' (DN 27:9). Obviously, this is an overt allusion to the Brahmanical claim to be born from the *puruṣa's* mouth (MN 93; see above p. 12).

The Buddha also called Upaniṣadic ideas (in so far as he knew them) into question – perhaps because of their integration into official Brahmanism. Views apparently alluding to Upaniṣadic conceptions, such as 'That which is the self is the world; after death I shall be permanent, everlasting, eternal, not subject to change; I shall endure as long as eternity', are dismissed as 'utterly and completely foolish teaching' (MN 22). It is not the Brahmans but the Buddha who reveals the way leading to union with Brahmā, through the development of a loving, compassionate, sympathetic and equanimous mind (DN 13).

Understanding themselves as the 'true Brahmans', the Buddhists assert that they, and not the members of the Brahmanic caste, should be regarded as the true religious authority safeguarding the principles of right and wrong. Hence, the Buddha explains, a king should listen to those ascetics and Brahmans who follow the *dharma* and accept their counsels as to what is wholesome and unwholesome and what would lead to sorrow and what to welfare (DN 26:5; see Collins, 1998, p. 604). Indeed, the Buddha is frequently presented as talking to and advising rulers and monarchs.

The canonical records present the Buddha as quite critical of the other religious or non-religious worldviews of his time. The materialist denial of rebirth, of the law of karma and of final liberation (DN 1:23) is denounced as 'untrue' and 'malicious' (MN 110) and as a source of unwholesome states (MN 114). Deterministic worldviews as well as the opposing view whereby everything occurs through pure chance are rejected as denying freedom and responsibility, thus undermining any motivation for serious religious efforts (AN 3:61). The Jains were castigated for their practice of ascetic self-torture as well as for their gross and mechanistic understanding of karma – the latter regarded by the Buddha as the main cause of their false practice (MN 14; 56; 101). Yet the Buddha is also depicted as having a certain sympathy for the Jains: On one occasion, he urged a former lay-supporter of the Jain Śramaṇas, who just had become a follower of the Buddha, not to terminate his donations to the Jains (MN 56).

The Buddha's life was not free from conflicts, the most serious of which came about through his cousin Devadatta. Devadatta was a member of the Buddha's order but wanted to see stronger forms of ascetic discipline. The Pāli Canon reports that he not only tried to split the order (with some success), but also made three failed attempts on the Buddha's life (Cv 7:2–4).

Above and beyond all controversies and conflicts, the Buddha's personality is portrayed as sympathetic and compassionate. On a number of occasions he manifested his disregard for caste-distinctions and other forms of social discrimination. He publicly honoured the leper Suppabuddha by offering him the seat at his right hand (Ud 5:3). He did not turn down an invitation to dinner in the house of the prostitute Ambapālī, even when some noblemen tried to hold him back (DN 16:2:14–19). He spoke highly of the drunkard Sarakāni as someone who had attained the first stage of holiness

(SN 55:24). When he met Panthaka, a man cast out from house and home, the Buddha put his arm tenderly around him, comforted him with kind words, gave him a linen cloth for washing his feet and admitted him to the community (Thag 557–66). With his own hands the Buddha washed and tended a monk who suffered from severe diarrhoea and had been neglected by his fellow monks. They were chastised by the Buddha with the words: 'Whoever, monks, would wait upon me ... should wait upon the sick' (Mhv 8:26:1–4). He instructed children not to harm animals (Ud 5:4). He taught a loving-kindness which excludes no one, a loving-kindness which is forbearing and forgiving and includes even the worst enemy (MN 21). When a war once threatened to break out over a shortage of water, the Buddha actively intervened and managed to reconcile the hostile tribes, thereby preventing imminent carnage (Jat 536). What real love means, the Buddha said, can be seen in a mother who protects her child with her life (Sn 149). The image of the Buddha in the Pāli Canon is summarily stated in the words of the lay-follower Jīvaka: 'I have heard that Brahmā lives with love. But I saw with my own eyes that the Venerable One (the Buddha) is always living with love' (MN 55).

By the time he was eighty the Buddha had become ill and weak. On the way back to his hometown Kapilavastu, his health rapidly deteriorated due to food poisoning. He died in Kuśinagara, surrounded by a great group of followers. In his final words he once more took up the crucial issue of transitoriness: 'All conditioned things are of a nature to decay – strive on untiringly' (DN 16:6, 7; Walshe, 1995, p. 270). For one last time he entered into that meditative state in which he had once experienced enlightenment, and in that state he passed away to the ultimate peace of the unconditioned Nirvāṇa.

For further reading: Carrithers (1983); Pye (1979); Seth (1992); Thomas (1992).

4

The 'One Taste': Liberation

Liberation from Suffering

In one of his many parables and allegories the Buddha presents his doctrine with the following comparison:

> Just as the great ocean has but one taste, the taste of salt; even so this Dhamma and Discipline has but one taste, the taste of liberation …
> (AN 8:19; Nyanaponika and Bodhi, 1999, p. 204)

But liberation from what? From 'suffering' (*duḥkha*, Pāli: *dukkha*) – and this in two basic respects: the *experience of suffering* and the *infliction of suffering* (see MN 13). Two highly popular Buddhist narratives illustrate this well: the story of Kisāgotamī and the story of Aṅgulimāla.

Kisāgotamī was a beautiful young woman happily married to the only son of a wealthy merchant. When she gave birth to her first child, a little boy, her luck was perfect. But when her little son had just started walking, he suddenly died. In her utter distress, Kisāgotamī grasped the dead body of her baby and ran frantically in search of help. A Buddhist monk advised her to ask the Buddha. When she begged him for a remedy, the Buddha responded that he would need some mustard seeds to prepare it, but the seeds must come from a house where no one had ever died. Kisāgotamī immediately set off to find these – in vain. Realising at last the omnipresence of death, she left her dead child behind and returned to the Buddha. He then taught her the link between death and suffering, and liberation by means of non-attachment. Kisāgotamī became a Buddhist nun and soon attained enlightenment (from the commentarial tradition associated with Thig 212–23).

Aṅgulimāla was the head of a gang of bandits who attacked villagers and travellers in the area of Kosala. The king of Kosala, Pasenadi, was unable to capture him, and so the Buddha decided to go and meet Aṅgulimāla. Aṅgulimāla was 'murderous, bloody-handed, given to blows and violence, merciless to living beings'. He wore the cut off fingers of his victims as a garland around his neck (which is the literal meaning of his name). When Aṅgulimāla spotted the Buddha, he immediately took his sword to kill him. The Buddha however countered with his supernatural powers, and

Aṅgulimāla, though running as fast as he could, was unable get any closer to the Buddha who continued to walk calmly on his way. Finally the bewildered Aṅgulimāla stopped and shouted to the Buddha: 'Stop, recluse! Stop, recluse!', to which the Buddha replied: 'I have stopped, Aṅgulimāla, you stop too.' Aṅgulimāla was nonplussed:

> While you are walking, recluse, you tell me you have stopped;
> But now, when I have stopped, you say I have not stopped.
> I ask you now, O recluse, about the meaning:
> How is it that you have stopped and I have not?

And the Buddha replied:

> Aṅgulimāla, I have stopped forever,
> I abstain from violence towards living beings;
> But you have no restraint towards things that live:
> That is why I have stopped and you have not.
> (MN 86; Ñaṇamoli and Bodhi, 2001, p. 710f)

Aṅgulimāla was struck by the dreamlike contrast: on the one side, his own incessant pursuit of something he never attained; on the other, the serene and peaceful equanimity of the Buddha. In a flash he saw the predicament of his life. He decided to become a Buddhist monk and after a short time found enlightenment. When king Pasenadi heard about Aṅgulimāla's conversion, he said: 'It is wonderful, ... marvellous how the Blessed One tames the untamed, brings peace to the unpeaceful ... we ourselves could not tame him with force and weapons, yet the Blessed One has tamed him without force or weapons' (ibid. p. 713).

The Four Noble Truths

The 'one taste' of the Buddha's teaching is the liberation from suffering. This is brought about by extirpating both the roots of the *experience* of suffering, as in the case of Kisāgotamī, and the roots of the infliction of suffering, as in the case of Aṅgulimāla. But what are these roots, and how are they rooted out? This is the subject of one of the most crucial doctrinal formulas of early Buddhism, the so-called 'Four Noble Truths'. According to the Buddhist tradition the Buddha realised them in his enlightenment and expounded them in his first sermon:

> Now this ... is the noble truth of suffering: birth is suffering, aging is suffering, illness is suffering, death is suffering; union with what is displeasing is suffering; separation from what is pleasing is suffering; not to get what one wants is suffering; in brief, the five aggregates subject to clinging are suffering.

> Now this … is the noble truth of the origin of suffering: It is this craving which leads to renewed existence, accompanied by delight and lust, seeking delight here and there; that is, craving for sensual pleasures, craving for existence, craving for extermination.
>
> Now this … is the noble truth of the cessation of suffering: It is the remainderless fading away and cessation of that same craving, the giving up and relinquishing of it, freedom from it, nonreliance on it.
>
> Now this … is the noble truth of the way leading to the cessation of suffering: It is this Noble Eightfold Path; that is, right view, right intention, right speech, right action, right livelihood, right effort, right mindfulness, right concentration.
>
> (SN 56:11; Bodhi, 2000, p. 1844)

The Buddha is often praised as a 'capable physician' and indeed, his central doctrine as expressed in the Four Noble Truths is set out in the manner of a medical analysis – as was already observed in one of the early Buddhist treatises, the Vimuttimagga (11:2:11): The First Noble Truth lists the *symptoms* of the disease. Then the cause of the problem is *diagnosed* – a cause identified in the Second Noble Truth as 'craving' or literally 'thirst' (*tṛṣṇā*; Pāli: *taṇhā*). The Third Noble Truth presents the *prognosis*. And because the prognosis is optimistic the Fourth Noble Truth prescribes the *therapy*, which is the Noble Eightfold Path. The 'disease' itself is called *duḥkha*, usually translated into English as 'suffering'. The meaning of *duḥkha* however is much broader and far more profound than 'suffering' in any narrow sense. It is a technical term for the Buddhist conception of unredeemed human existence. This can be seen by taking a closer look at the First Noble Truth.

In the first line *duḥkha* is exemplified by birth, aging, illness and death. The triad *aging, illness, death* represents the most conspicuous aspects of life's transitoriness. In the Buddha-legend (see above p. 21) Siddhārtha realises his own transience through seeing an old man, an ill man and a dead man on his first three excursions. And he exclaims: 'Shame on this thing birth, since to him who is born old age, sickness, death must manifest.' Thus 'birth' too is included, for birth marks the entry into a transient existence inexorably resulting in old age, illness and death. But still, in which sense is this *duḥkha*? The next line provides us with an answer. '*Duḥkha*' or suffering in a wider sense, entails a union with something that one dislikes or a separation from something that one likes. Basically then the meaning of *duḥkha* is 'frustration', 'dissatisfied striving', or as it is said here: 'not to get what one wants'. Against this background, *duḥkha*/frustration is to be seen as a feature of transitory existence itself. Our deepest longing or striving is for freedom from old age, illness and death, and this longing is permanently frustrated (see DN 22:17 and MN 141:19). The last line of the First Noble

Truth speaks of *duḥkha* as the 'five aggregates subject to clinging'. Let us defer the interpretation of this expression until we have looked at the Second and Third Noble Truth.

The 'Ignoble' and the 'Noble Search'

Many interpreters of Buddhism concluded that if the human predicament basically consists in unfulfilled human longing or desire, the Buddhist solution would be to annihilate desire itself. 'Craving' or 'thirst' (*tṛṣṇā* – which the Second Noble Truth identifies as the cause of suffering and which, according to the Third Noble Truth, must cease) was understood by these interpreters as referring to all human desire in any form whatsoever. I believe this to be a grave misunderstanding. Recalling the Buddha's own search for liberation, the Ariyapariesanā Sutta of the Pāli-Canon (MN 26) distinguishes between two radically different forms of 'striving' as an existential orientation: the 'ignoble' and the 'noble search':

> And what is the ignoble search? Here someone being himself subject to birth, ageing, sickness, death, sorrow and defilement, seeks what is also subject to birth, ageing, sickness, death, sorrow and defilement.
>
> And what may be said to be subject to birth, ageing, sickness, death, sorrow and defilement? Wife and children, men and women slaves, goats and sheep, fowl and pigs, elephants, cattle, horses, and mares, gold and silver ... These acquisitions are subject to birth, ageing, sickness, death, sorrow and defilement; and one who is tied to these things, infatuated with them, and utterly committed to them, being himself subject to birth, ageing, sickness, death, sorrow and defilement, seeks what is also subject to birth, ageing, sickness, death, sorrow and defilement.
>
> And what is the noble search? Here someone being subject to birth, ageing, sickness, death, sorrow and defilement, having understood the danger in what is subject to birth, ageing, sickness, death, sorrow and defilement, seeks the unborn, unageing, unailing, deathless, sorrowless and undefiled supreme security from bondage, Nibbāna. This is the noble search.
>
> (MN 26; translation following Ñāṇamoli and Bodhi, 2001, pp. 254ff)

To strive after Nirvāṇa – the 'noble search' – is never criticised in the early Buddhist texts. Quite the contrary: Its deliberate and indeed vigorous pursuit is strongly encouraged and seen as an indispensable mental attitude on the Buddhist path; moreover, the Noble Eightfold Path speaks explicitly of 'right *effort*'. What is criticised is the 'ignoble search', the bondage to and fixation upon the perishable things of this world. Here the seeker remains 'insatiate, the slave of craving' (MN 82) and as such is 'subject to sorrow', for this search will never attain its real end but is destined to be frustrated. The 'noble search' on the other hand arrives at lasting fulfilment with the attainment of Nirvāṇa. The 'striving' for Nirvāṇa vanishes when the goal is reached (see SN 5:51:15); all suffering, all dissatisfaction ends. Though hidden and obscured, the true longing of all sentient beings is Nirvāṇa, the 'deathless' (*amṛta*), the ultimate peace and happiness.

I am suggesting then that the 'craving' or 'thirst' discussed in the Four Noble Truths should be understood in the sense of the 'ignoble search'. 'Thirst', stirred up by the sensual pleasures, is the deluded directing of one's existential striving towards the transitory things of the world. The metaphor of 'thirst' is quite telling: Thirst can be temporarily quenched but never brought to a final stillness. It is in this sense that 'thirst' is the cause of 'suffering', *duḥkha*. And because of this 'thirst', the sentient beings remain bound to *saṃsāra*, the cycle of constant rebirth and redeath: 'It is this craving which leads to renewed existence', as the Second Noble Truth explains. Because this craving for saṃsāric existence is bound to frustration, it can also easily turn into a 'craving for extermination': 'Not to get what one wants' becomes the root of negative, destructive tendencies, of inflicting suffering upon others and oneself

The solution recommended by the Third Noble Truth then is not to give up all striving whatsoever but to give up this particular form of deluded, wrongly-directed striving which is here called 'thirst' or the 'ignoble search'.

Now what does this entail?

Attachment and Non-Attachment

On the 'ignoble search' one is 'tied' to the perishable things of the world and 'infatuated with them', as our text says. Buddhism calls this condition 'attachment' or 'clinging' (*upādāna*). To overcome 'thirst' is thus to overcome 'attachment'. But how can attachment be given up? 'Thirst' and 'attachment' are based on a false expectation, on the illusion that the things of the world could satisfy our deepest longing. Therefore, 'thirst' and 'attachment' can only be overcome by a liberation from this delusion. Two distinct insights lead to this liberation. One is the *negative* insight, based in experience, that 'nothing is fit to be clung to' (AN 7:58; Nyanaponika and Bodhi, 1999, p. 189): All clinging is in vain because everything is subject to decay (*anitya*) such that we cannot hold onto it; moreover, nothing is really worth clinging to, since its possession does not provide the ultimate satisfaction we truly seek. Frequently the Buddhist scriptures cite the example of kings to illustrate this point: Does all the power and wealth they possess really satisfy them? Are they not constantly striving for 'more'? Whatever is perishable (*anitya*), so the conclusion, is also unsatisfactory or *duḥkha*.

This negative insight alone however is not sufficient to bring about a genuine liberation from attachment. It must be complemented by the *positive* insight, equally based in experience, that there is indeed a different happiness: an ultimate bliss and satisfaction compared to which all else loses its attraction. The Buddha has illustrated the latter with the following parable (MN 75): A leper soothes the painful itching of his skin by cauterising his body over a burning charcoal pit. While the heat of the charcoal indeed provides 'a certain measure of satisfaction and enjoyment', it nevertheless leads to a deterioration of the skin and makes the symptoms even worse – only intensifying his longing for the charcoal pit. But suppose the leper is cured by a capable physician: The charcoal pit, previously so desirable, is now perceived for what it really is: hot and dangerous. The man is no longer attracted to it at all, nor does he envy other lepers who are still using it as remedy!

Such is the attachment stirred up by sensual pleasures. It leads not to a final satisfaction but to a vicious circle. The circle can be broken open however – by a radical cure, by the experience of a satisfaction which is superior to and qualitatively completely different from the limited measure of satisfaction and enjoyment deriving from sensual pleasures. And the Buddha explains:

> ... I abandoned craving for sensual pleasures ... and I abide without thirst, with a mind inwardly at peace. ... Why is that? Because there is ... a delight apart from sensual pleasures, apart from unwholesome states, which surpasses even divine bliss. Since I take delight in that, I do not envy what is inferior, nor do I delight therein.
>
> (MN 75; Ñāṇamoli and Bodhi, 2001, p. 611; similarly MN 14)

Only the experience of Nirvāṇa in enlightenment will bring about complete liberation from attachment. Nevertheless, the negative insight into the inevitable disappointment inherent in perishable things, together with the positive foretaste of Nirvāṇa gained through meditative experience, can weaken the bonds and reduce the craving, thereby creating a disposition towards the final liberating experience.

Attachment manifests itself in hunger for pleasant sensations and repugnance or hatred in the face of unpleasant sensations. Overcoming attachment does not mean that there are no longer any pleasant or unpleasant sensations. It means that one is no longer tied to these sensations by an attitude of avariciousness or aversion. When a pleasant feeling arises, 'the well-taught noble disciple ... does not lust after pleasure or continue to lust after pleasure'. And when with the cessation of a pleasant feeling a painful feeling arises, 'he does not sorrow, grieve, and lament ... and become distraught'. Neither the pleasant nor the unpleasant feeling is able to 'invade his mind' (MN 36; Ñāṇamoli and Bodhi, 2001, p. 334). The Buddha compares such a person with a forest deer which can lie down on a mound of snares without becoming trapped or caught by the hunter (see MN 26). And with the liberation from clinging comes the liberation from suffering: 'One does not sorrow in the midst of sorrow' (SN 1:31:1; Bodhi, 2000, p. 105).

The Not-Self Teaching

Attachment refers not only to things we possess or would like to possess, or people upon whom we are fixated in attraction or aversion. In an even stronger sense it refers to the constituent elements of our own individual existence. The Western tradition usually posits two (body and soul) or three (body, mind and soul) such constituents, whereas Buddhism distinguishes five – one material component, our body, and four mental components: feelings, perceptions, formations (that is, mental phenomena constructing and forming our mindset; these include our will and karmic inclinations), and consciousness. These five factors constituting an individual human being are referred to in the last line of the First Noble Truth: 'the five aggregates subject to clinging are suffering' (see above p. 31). They too are impermanent and incapable of providing lasting satisfaction; hence any attachment to them should be given up. Here attachment centres on the idea of an 'I' or 'self'. Clinging to the five constituents of individual existence manifests itself through the thought or attitude of: 'This is mine, this I am, this is my self (*ātman*)'. The Buddhist tradition relates that the Buddha, shortly after his first sermon in which he expounded the Four Noble Truths, instructed his first disciples to regard each of the five constituents as 'This is not mine, this I am not, this is not my self' (Mv 6:38–47).

The major point of this so-called 'Not-Self' (*anātman*, Pāli: *anattā*) teaching is to cultivate an attitude of non-attachment towards that which we usually see as constituting our very own self. The Buddha underlines this spiritual/practical aspect of the Not-Self teaching by emphasising that the cultivation of such a self-less attitude leads to 'disenchantment' and 'liberation'. Once more an illuminating parable is given: If one sees gardeners in a public park carrying off and burning the grass, sticks, branches or leaves, would one then think: 'They are carrying off and burning me?' Surely not, for one would not regard the garden-waste as one's self or as belonging to one's self. Likewise, the Buddha continues:

> Whatever is not yours, abandon it; when you have abandoned it, that will lead to your welfare and happiness for a long time. What is not yours? Material form is not yours … Feeling is not yours … Perception is not yours … Formations are not yours … Consciousness is not yours. Abandon it.
>
> (MN 22; Ñāṇamoli and Bodhi, 2001, p. 235)

Obviously the collecting and burning of the garden-waste is a metaphor for the impermanence of the five constituents – a metaphor, that is for our mortality. So altogether the *negative insight* conducive to non-attachment has three facets (*trilakṣana*): All things within saṃsāric existence should be regarded as impermanent (*anitya*), as incapable of providing lasting satisfaction (*duḥkha*), and as being 'not the self' (*anātman*).

In consequence of his Not-Self teaching the Buddha disapproved of any doctrine of 'self'. All such doctrines lead to clinging and suffering. In particular, it seemed absurd – from a Buddhist point of view – to identify any of the impermanent and unsatisfying constituents with a divine, unchangeable and blissful *ātman*. Therefore the Buddha rejected the Upaniṣadic Brahman-Ātman teaching (or what he knew of it) as complete foolishness (see MN 22). In fact, however, liberation from attachment was also the great goal of the Upaniṣads, and later Upaniṣadic texts, implicitly responding to the Buddhist criticism, made it clear that what they meant by the Self or *ātman* is not at all identical with the transitory constituents of which Buddhism speaks (e.g. Maitri Upaniṣad 3:1–2).

Though the Buddha rejected any self-doctrine whatsoever, he also abstained from a definitive assertion that there is no self at all. When he was once asked openly whether there is a self or not, he remained silent (see SN 44:10). Nonetheless the Buddhist tradition did not always stick to this restriction and tended to assert that there is no self. Here too there are exceptions however, most notably perhaps the great Mahāyāna philosopher Nāgārjuna who stated explicitly that the Buddha had taught neither that there is a self nor that there is no self (see MMK 18:6).

Now if, as I have argued, the early Buddhist Not-Self teaching pragmatically works to support the 'noble search' inasmuch as its principal aim is to trigger non-attachment, could it then not be concluded that we should identify ourselves, or our 'true self', with the 'noble search'? If we are called to detach ourselves from the transitory and unsatisfying world and to follow consciously our true inclination towards the 'deathless', towards Nirvāṇa, would we then not be entitled to see this inclination as our true nature or true self? Early Buddhist texts refrain from directly saying this, but at some places there are expressions coming close to it indeed: when for example it is stated that 'all things have release for their *essence*, plunge into the deathless, with *nirvāṇa* for their conclusion' (AN 10:58), or when it is expressed that our mind is essentially or originally pure and luminous whereas all its defilements come from without (see AN 1:10–11). Clearly this implies that attachment and all its negative effects go against our true nature whose 'luminosity' may be understood as signifying its inclination to Nirvāṇa (see Harvey, 2004, 166–79; Gowans, 2003, 154–6). This ancient tradition became the basis for the later Mahāyāna idea that all beings have the potential to become a Buddha for they all have a 'Buddha-Nature' – at times even called their *ātman* or the 'Ultimate Self' (*paramātman*) (see Hookham, 1991, pp. 100–4).

The Noble Eightfold Path and the Role of Insight

The Fourth Noble Truth speaks of the 'therapy' for the human predicament: What should we do in order to gain liberation from 'thirst', attachment and the resulting suffering? How can we reach the deathless and sorrowless Nirvāṇa? The answer is presented as a path with eight members. They are not eight successive steps but more like eight important areas of endeavour within which one should strive for personal development. They are mutually interlinked so that progress in any one area has an impact on progress in any other area. And 'just as the river Ganges slants, slopes, and inclines towards the east, so too a bhikkhu who develops and cultivates the Noble Eightfold Path slants, slopes, and inclines towards Nibbāna' (SN 5:45:91; Bodhi, 2000, p. 1548).

The eight members of the path are traditionally distributed among the three principles of insight or wisdom (*prajñā*), morality or ethics (*śīla*) and meditation or concentration (*samādhi*) as follows:

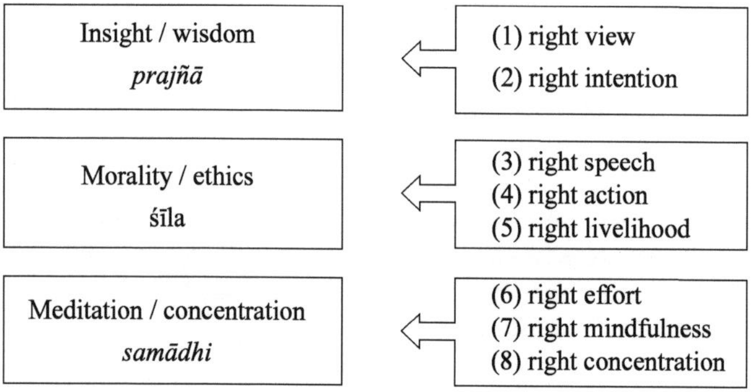

5. The Noble Eightfold Path.

The basic idea is that how we live depends upon how we perceive and understand life. Therefore *morality*, a morally good life, presupposes *insight*, an understanding as to what is really important in and about life. But in order to awaken, deepen and complete such insight and make moral virtue flow from one's heart, *meditation* is needed. In Chapters Six and Seven I will discuss in more detail the themes of Buddhist meditation and Buddhist ethics so as to provide a better understanding of the corresponding members of the Noble Eightfold Path. Let me conclude this chapter with some remarks on the first of the three principles and its role within the Noble Eightfold Path.

Liberating knowledge or *insight* in its fullest sense is enlightenment itself, and as such marks the goal and end of the path. On the other hand it also appears at the path's very beginning – as that to which the first two aspects of the path are allocated. In one place it is said that insight is the 'dawn' of all wholesome things, precisely because it is the harbinger of the full sunrise (see AN 10:121).

Insight is accorded such importance because, as we have seen, liberation from attachment can come about only through insight, and 'right intention', the second member of the path, springs from 'right view'. But it must be one's own, experience-based insight in order to be spiritually efficacious. One cannot become free of any attachment unless one understands for oneself that 'nothing is fit to be clung to' and that there is another 'delight which surpasses even divine bliss'. This insight however is fully realised only at the end of the path, i.e. in one's own enlightenment; while one is still on the way its status can be characterised as a fruitful tension between autonomous knowledge and confident trust (*śraddhā*) in the enlightened word of the Buddha.

So on the one hand, the Buddha encouraged people not to do something simply because it is accepted as a tradition, prescribed by the scriptures or based on reasoning or on the authority of a guru. Only if we realise by ourselves that something denounced by the wise is indeed unwholesome and leads to harm and suffering, should we refrain from it or, conversely, do it – not merely because it has been praised by the wise but because we ourselves see that it is wholesome and leads to welfare and happiness (see AN 3:65). At times the Buddha asks his own disciples whether they accept something merely because he teaches it or because they themselves have understood it (e.g. MN 38).

On the other hand, the teaching of the Buddha, flowing from his enlightenment, provides the pivotal impulse for triggering one's own understanding. In this light faith and trust are indispensable. A traditional standard account of the Buddhist path of salvation frequently repeated throughout the Pāli-Canon (e.g. DN 2; 3; etc.; MN 27; 38; etc.) underlines this point: When a fully-enlightened Buddha, a Tathāgata, arises in the world, he preaches the Dharma. And when a householder hears the Dharma, 'he gains faith in the Tathāgata'. Hence the initial insight of which the Noble Eightfold Path speaks – the 'right view' – is to a considerable extent a 'right *belief*'. The Buddha knows the goal and the path to it from his own experience; the disciple, however, needs to trust him. Like a wise cowherd who knows the place where his cattle can safely cross the river, the Buddha is able to lead his followers safely to the 'other shore'. As the cattle follow their cowherd so the disciple should 'place faith' in the Buddha (MN 34). In guiding his disciples towards their own insight the Buddha teaches them in a gradual and individually adapted way, depending on the kind and degree of their own understanding (see DN 9; 28).

But did the Buddha proclaim or reveal everything? Was he able to answer all questions? While later Buddhist traditions almost unanimously affirmed the omniscience of the Buddha, they nevertheless conceded that for pragmatic reasons he restricted his teaching entirely to those things necessary for salvation.

The Pāli-Canon relates the story of Mālunkyāputta, one of the Buddha's disciples who wanted to leave the order because the Buddha had not explained to him whether the world is eternal or not eternal, finite or infinite; whether the soul and the body are the same or different; whether after death a Tathāgata exists, does not exist, both exists and does not exist, or neither exists nor does not exist. When the Buddha heard of this he told Mālunkyāputta the following parable: Suppose a man were wounded by a poisoned arrow, but luckily his friends bring a physician who could save his life. Would the man then say that he will not allow the physician to pull out the arrow and treat him until he has first explained to him who had shot the arrow, to which caste that man belonged, whether he was tall or short, of dark or light complexion, in which village he lives, what sort of bow and which sort of bowstring he used, which kind of arrow and arrow feathers, and so on? The wounded man would surely die before all his questions were answered. But, the Buddha continued, whatever the answer to Mālunkyāputta's question might be, 'there is birth, there is ageing, there is death, there are sorrow, lamentation, pain, grief, and despair, the destruction of which I prescribe here and now' (MN 63; Ñāṇamoli and Bodhi, 2001, p. 535). He did not answer Mālunkyāputta's questions because their explanation 'is unbeneficial, it does not belong to the fundamental of the holy life, it does not lead to disenchantment, to dispassion, to cessation, to peace, to direct knowledge, to enlightenment, to Nibbāna' (ibid. p. 536). The only thing the Buddha ever explained is suffering (*duḥkha*), its cause, its cessation and the path leading to its cessation. Therefore, the text says, one should leave unexplained what has not been explained and stick to that which has been explained. A similar point is made in the famous parable of the raft. Just as a raft is only constructed in order to reach the other shore and not so as to be carried around on dry land, the only purpose of the Dharma proclaimed by the Buddha is 'crossing over'. It should not itself be made the object of grasping and attachment (see MN 22).

Does this mean that the Buddha rejected any form of metaphysics, that his teaching entails no metaphysical or cosmological claims at all? He is frequently thus understood by contemporary Western, and sometimes even Eastern, interpreters. I believe this to be a misunderstanding. The Buddha did not reject all metaphysical claims. He rejected only those kinds of metaphysical speculation which he regarded as not conducive to ultimate liberation. His explanation of suffering and of the path to overcome suffering however did indeed presuppose some crucial metaphysical beliefs which conclusively distinguished his teachings from the views of the materialist Cārvākas: belief in rebirth, belief in karma and belief in the ultimate bliss of unconditioned Nirvāṇa.

For further reading: Burton (2004); Collins (1982); Gowans (2003); Harvey (2004); Matthews (1994); Pérez-Remón (1980).

5

Many Lives and Ultimate Bliss

Saṃsāra: the Cycle of Reincarnation

> Bhikkhus, this saṃsāra is without discoverable beginning. A first point is not discerned of beings roaming and wandering on hindered by ignorance and fettered by craving …
>
> The stream of tears that you have shed as you roamed and wandered through this long course, weeping and wailing because of being united with the disagreeable and separated from the agreeable – this alone is more than the water in the four great oceans. For a long time, bhikkhus, you have experienced the death of a mother, … the death of a father, … the death of a brother, … the death of a sister, … the death of a son, … the death of a daughter, … the loss of relatives, … the loss of wealth, … loss through illness …
>
> It is enough to experience revulsion towards all formations, enough to become dispassionate towards them, enough to be liberated from them.
>
> (SN 15:3; Bodhi, 2000, p. 652f)

Early Buddhists shared the view of many of their contemporaries in the Śramaṇa movements that the idea of reincarnation fully exposes the unsatisfactory and indeed painful character of unredeemed existence. The cycle of reincarnation, *saṃsāra*, is by no means celebrated as a kind of everlasting life. On the contrary: it is seen as everlasting death, the potentially endless continuation of transitory existence, extending back indefinitely with no 'point zero' discernable.

The Buddhist understanding of *saṃsāra* is vividly depicted in a standardised graphical representation, usually called the *bhavacakra:* the 'Wheel of Becoming'. The earliest preserved example is one of the famous cave-paintings of Ajaṇta (6th cent. CE), but there is also a much older instruction in a Buddhist scripture (*Divyāvadāna*) as to how to paint the image. Let us now consider one of the more recent Tibetan versions of the *bhavacakra* (see Figure 6) and follow it in our attempt to understand the Buddhist doctrine of reincarnation.

6. The wheel of saṃsāric existence.

The 'wheel of becoming' is held in the claws of a monstrous being, originally explained as transitoriness itself, and later personified as mythological beings closely associated with death: either Yama or Māra, whom we know from the Buddha-legend as the evil tempter. In any case, the monster symbolically represents the transience of all forms of saṃsāric existence. The wheel itself is divided in four rings or levels: The first, external ring contains twelve pictures symbolizing the twelve members of the chain of 'Dependent Origination' (*pratītyasamutpāda*, see below pp. 46–8). The next and largest ring displays the six (according to other versions, five) realms of reincarnation. The ring next to the hub depicts the movements of descent and ascent: On the right, people are drawn downwards by Māra with a rope to which they are fettered, while on the left people move upwards by listening to the word of the Buddha. The centre, finally, shows a cockerel, a pig and a snake forming a circle by reciprocally biting into one another's tails. They stand for the three root evils: greed, delusion and hatred.

The six realms of reincarnation depicted in the second ring are divided into three lower and three upper fields. The lower fields show the unpleasant forms of reincarnation, while the upper ones display the more pleasant realms. In the lower part we see, clockwise, first the animal realm, then, at the very bottom, the cold and hot hells, and, to the left, the realm of the hungry ghosts. Moving further up we first find the human world, then, on top, the heaven of the peaceful deities, and, next to this, the realm of wrathful gods, the *asuras*. Those versions of the *bhavacakra* which have only five sections usually show the peaceful and wrathful gods as belonging to one single heavenly realm.

These five or six realms indicate the forms and worlds in which saṃsāric beings are reborn, for reincarnation occurs not only in human form. If their karma is bad, beings are reborn into one of the lower worlds: as an animal, as a denizen of one of the numerous hot or cold hells, or as a hungry ghost. And if their karma is good, they are reborn as human beings or as one of the peaceful or wrathful deities. Moreover only sentient beings are reborn, or, to put it differently, rebirth takes place only in the form of a being capable of consciously experiencing happiness or sorrow. According to traditional Buddhism, this excludes rebirth as a plant or as a material object like a mountain, though plants (particularly trees) and mountains or rivers can be inhabited by ghostly beings and these are part of the saṃsāra.

In none of its forms is saṃsāric existence eternal. Of course the duration of life varies considerably between life as an insect, for instance, and life as a deity (*deva*). The life of the *devas*, as the lives of those suffering in the hells, lasts inconceivably long and can even encompass many world-periods, but it is not everlasting. One day every 'god' will have to die and be reborn in some other form of existence. His former place – as the divine Indra or Brahma, for example – is then immediately taken by another being so that there is never any vacancy in heaven. But the particular individual existence of each deity is as perishable as everything else within *saṃsāra*. Thus existence in hell too comes to an end one day, after a similarly long period, and is followed by a new rebirth. The idea of irreversible, unredeemable, everlasting suffering in hell is unknown to Buddhism, though there were at times discussions as to whether there might be beings lacking any potential for enlightenment (the so-called *icchantikas*).

While existence in the lower realms is, to varying degrees, painful and undesirable, existence in the heavenly realms is full of divine enjoyments. It is simply too pleasant! Too pleasant and too long for fully realising the transitory and unsatisfactory character of saṃsāric life. It is human existence which provides the best conditions for true insight and for the achievement of ultimate salvation. This makes human life special and indeed precious. Frequently the Buddhist scriptures emphasise how difficult it is and how long it takes to regain human rebirth if one has fallen into the lower realms, and they encourage one to make the best use of the rare opportunity which human life offers for finding the way out of saṃsāric existence. This is depicted in the two inner sections of the wheel (see Figure 7).

7. Greed, delusion and hatred (detail from Fig. 6).

Karma

In the centre of the wheel we find greed, delusion, and hatred, symbolised through the cockerel, the pig and the snake. They belong inseparably together since greed is the deluded reaction to a pleasant sensation and hatred the deluded reaction to an unpleasant sensation (see AN 3:68). This triad of greed, hatred and delusion keeps the entire wheel going (see AN 10:174). In order to understand this, we need to analyse the Buddhist concept of karma.

The literal meaning of 'karma' is 'deed' or 'action'. Originally it referred to the religious acts of the Brahmans, particularly to the Vedic sacrifice as an efficacious action. Among the Śramaṇas 'karma' came to mean human actions in so far as they affect rebirth and determine the form of the rebirth: good actions leading to a good reincarnation and bad actions leading to a bad reincarnation. Buddhism developed a psychologically refined version of this view. Our 'actions' not only affect our future rebirth, they also impact upon our spiritual development. In its most fundamental sense 'karma' *is* our 'volition' or 'intention', for our actions in thought, word and deed follow from what we have willed (AN 6:63; MN 56). The generating of good or bad karma, or more precisely, of good or bad karmic tendencies, is therefore primarily a mental process.

The volition which produces bad karmic effects (in leading to morally bad actions in thought, word and deed, to a spiritually negative character disposition and finally to a bad rebirth) is a volition permeated by great greed, hatred and delusion. Conversely, the moderation and reduction of greed, hatred and delusion and their gradual replacement by the opposite qualities of equanimity, loving-kindness and insight, lead to morally good actions in thought, word and deed, to a spiritually positive character disposition and to a good rebirth (see AN 3:70). The life-sum of our volitions and their respective actions manifests as a specific inclination which results in a corresponding rebirth, just as a tree which has grown in a certain direction will fall in that same direction when it is cut down (see Netti-Pakaraṇa 788). If, however, the mind and all actions originating in the mind become entirely free from greed, hatred and delusion, no further karmic consequences are generated (AN 3:34 and 10:174). Greed, hatred and delusion are thus understood as forms in which 'thirst' – the root of rebirth according to the Second Noble Truth (see above p. 32) – is manifested in the spiritual and moral inclinations of one's personality, and consequently in one's behaviour.

This understanding of the karma process allows for two different but related spiritual approaches. Firstly, one can attempt to improve one's karma in order to attain a better rebirth and avoid reincarnation's evil realms. This has certainly become a powerful motive in popular Buddhist morality. But since this motivation is still shaped by attachment – attachment to the more pleasant aspects of saṃsāric existence – it is not identical with the 'noble search'. The second approach is therefore to strive for ultimate liberation and hence for freedom from all karmic retribution, positive or negative, through a complete purification from even subtle forms of greed, hatred and delusion (see MN 117). Yet it must be said that because 'good karma' implies that the grosser forms of greed, hatred and delusion are avoided, the improvement of one's karma carries not only the promise of a better rebirth but also the prospect of coming closer to enlightenment through the attainment of a more favourable mental disposition.

The decisive point here according to the Buddhist understanding of karma is that the karmic dispositions – i.e., the specific mix of individual inclinations to greed, hatred and delusion or to their opposite – are transferred from one life into the next. Whether the character of a given individual is positively disposed for realising the *dharma* or is inflexibly set against it depends on the karmic formations and inclinations inherited from a former existence (see

Vism 3:83ff 17:271). In this light the idea of reincarnation acquires an encouraging aspect inasmuch as it allows for the possibility of a gradual progression towards final salvation over the course of several or, indeed, numerous successive lives. This idea of spiritual development over a potentially long series of existences has become a major feature in the Buddhist understanding of the spiritual careers of individual beings. And it has provided the otherwise grim reincarnation doctrine with an optimistic dimension.

In the first ring surrounding the hub of the *bhavacakra* the images underscore the basic message: If one is involved in the 'ignoble search' one is bound by 'Māra's fetter', i.e., by the sensual pleasures which trigger attachment, drawing the individual ever deeper into greed, hatred and delusion and therefore into the lower realms of rebirth. The alternative is depicted on the left half of the ring: One turns away from 'thirst' (symbolised by turning one's back to the offered cup) and listens to the word of the Buddha, thus proceeding upwards to better forms of reincarnation and ultimately towards the final liberation from *saṃsāra*.

With this in mind, let us now turn to the outermost ring which exhibits the principle of Dependent Origination.

The Principle of Dependent Origination

As a consequence of Enlightenment, according to the Buddha-legend (see Mv 1:1–4; Ud 1:1–4), the Buddha discerned the principle of 'Dependent Origination' (*pratītyasamutpāda*). The Pāli Canon offers several versions of this principle, but the one which enumerates twelve causally-connected members has become the most prominent, and it is this one which is depicted in the outer ring of the *bhavacakra*. Starting at the top and proceeding clockwise we find:

1) 'ignorance' or delusion (symbolised by a blind person with a crutch);
2) 'volitional formations' (here a potter);
3) 'consciousness' (a restless monkey);
4) 'name and form' or the individual composed of body and mind (two men in a boat);
5) the 'six senses' – i.e., the usual five senses plus mind as the sixth sense (a house with six windows);
6) 'contact' of the senses with their objects (a couple having intercourse);
7) 'feeling' (a man with an arrow piercing his eye);
8) 'thirst' (a person raising a cup);
9) 'attachment' or grasping (a monkey grasping for fruit);
10) 'becoming' (a pregnant woman);
11) 'birth' (a woman in delivery);
12) 'ageing – and death … and the whole mass of suffering' (a man walking through a field of corpses).

The point of the entire scheme lies in the relationship of causal dependency among the twelve members: Given (1) ignorance, volitional formation comes to be; given (2) volitional formations, name and form come to be – and so on until the twelfth member 'ageing-and-death' is reached. The causal dependency is further highlighted by the frequent repetition of the chain in its negative form: Through the cessation of (1) ignorance, volitional formations cease to be – and so on, up to the cessation of 'aging-and-death' … and the whole mass of suffering.

Already in the doctrinal scheme of the Four Noble Truths we find strong causal thinking at the bottom of Buddhist teaching: In order to become free from suffering one has to acknowledge the cause of suffering; once the cause is removed then the effect, suffering, will disappear as well. The formula employed in 'Dependent Origination' takes up and expands the same kind of causal thinking: Suffering is explained by the fact that we live a transitory life (12) which is the result of birth (11), which is the result of 'becoming' (10), i.e., the result of participating in the saṃsāric process, which in turn is the result of attachment (9) caused by 'thirst' (8). This is the point at which the analysis in the Four Noble Truths stops. Now the *pratītyasamutpāda* goes further, inquiring into the conditions for the arising of 'thirst'. First, it lists those factors which bring about the kind of feeling (7) that kindles thirst. Feeling presupposes sense-contact (6) activated by the respective faculties (5) belonging to an individual person (4). But this individual does not come into existence as a blank. It is itself conditioned by a consciousness (3) formed through karmic inclinations from a preceding existence (2) which are in operation because they are a manifestation of the basic existential 'ignorance' or 'delusion' (*avidyā*) (1).

Compared with the formula underlying the Four Noble Truths, the scheme of 'Dependent Origination' emphasises three particular considerations: First, 'thirst' is the root-cause of suffering and saṃsāric existence only in so far as it is the result of *ignorance*, illusion or delusion. To vanquish thirst one has to tackle ignorance. Second, everything within *saṃsāra* is not only impermanent (*anitya*) and unsatisfactory (*duḥkha*) but is also *causally conditioned* – indeed, it is impermanent precisely because its *origination depends* on certain causal conditions. Third, *reincarnation* itself, as indicated in the transition from the second to the third and from the tenth to the eleventh link, is to be understood *as a causal process*.

Particularly this last aspect opens up a way in which one can conceive of reincarnation without assuming transmigration – that is, without having to assume an unchangeable self or soul wandering from one existence to the next. The five aggregates constituting an individual are in fact a sequence of bodily particles and mental events (collectively called *dharmas*), each of which exists only for one moment. But in ceasing to exist it causes the origination of a similar, successive particle or event. The individual is thus constituted as a continuous process, as a stream of causally connected factors. This theory explains the various changes which each individual undergoes in the flow of time. Further, it neither presupposes nor needs any static unchangeable soul or self. And finally, it explains the process of reincarnation: The last mental events of a dying person cause the next life – that is, they constitute the origin of the consecutive mental phenomena and dispositions which form the beginning of the next existence. The new stream of events is not totally new; it is the continuation of the preceding one in another form, with all the corresponding karmic tendencies and inclinations. Hence, the transitional progression from the last moment of death to the first moment of new life is not entirely different from the transitional progression of the single successive moments within one lifetime. In the ultimate sense, says Buddhaghosa, each being lives only for one moment, dies and is reborn in the next moment, as a rolling wheel touches the ground only at one point every moment and is thereby moving on (see Vism 8:39); or, according to the Milindapañha, as the last flame of a burnt-out candle ignites a new one, or as milk ceases to be milk and turns into curd, and curd into butter and butter into ghee (cp. Mph 2:2:1).

This interpretation of reincarnation (and indeed of all change in time) as a chain of causally connected momentary events has important implications for the understanding of identity: The deceased person and the reborn person can neither be said to be entirely identical nor to be totally different – just as within one single lifetime the old man is neither entirely the same person he once was as a little baby nor is he a different person. Behind all this is simply the continuation of a causally connected process (see Mph 2:2:1).

But let us now turn to the goal in which this continuing process comes to an end, where all rebirth is stopped and ultimate bliss achieved.

Nirvāṇa

The literal meaning of '*nirvāṇa*' is 'extinction', the usual image being the extinction of a flame or fire. Nirvāṇa is the extinction of all the unwholesome factors: the extinction of thirst and ignorance, of attachment, greed, hatred and delusion, of any identification with the five constituents (see above p. 36f) as one's self, and of all the resulting evils: suffering and continual rebirth into the transitory existence of *saṃsāra*. After the Buddha had experienced Nirvāṇa in his enlightenment, he proclaimed: 'the deathless (*amṛta*) is found' (MN 26).

The insight connected with the doctrine of Dependent Origination, according to which everything conditioned is subject to decay, requires that Nirvāṇa, if it is truly deathless, must be an unconditioned (*asaṃskṛta*) reality. Only if there really is such an unconditioned reality, is liberation from the conditioned existence of *saṃsāra* possible. This is the logic of the following famous passage about Nirvāṇa:

> There is, bhikkhus, a not-born (*ajātaṃ*), a not-brought-to-being (*abhūtaṃ*), a not-made (*akataṃ*), a not-conditioned (*asaṅkhataṃ*). If, bhikkhus, there were no not-born, not-brought-to-being, not-made, not-conditioned, no escape would be discerned from what is born, brought-to-being, made, conditioned. But since there is a not-born, a not-brought-to-being, a not-made, a not-conditioned, therefore an escape is discerned from what is born, brought-to-being, made, conditioned.
>
> (Ud 8:3 and Itv 43; see Ireland, 1997, pp. 103 and 180)

Understanding Nirvāṇa as an unconditioned reality not only entails that it is truly deathless but implies as well that it is not simply a mental state. Two of the most influential classical Buddhist treatises, the Milindapañha (4:7:13–17) and the Visuddhimagga (16:67–74), present the following argument. If Nirvāṇa were merely the state of the enlightened person (his freedom from thirst and clinging, from the defilements and from suffering) then it would be conditioned – that is, its existence would depend upon the completion of the Noble Eightfold Path. But then, as a conditioned reality, it would cease to be the truly 'deathless'. Thus the state of the enlightened person must be understood as the attainment or perception of an unconditioned reality *which exists independently from this achievement.* It is the unconditioned reality of Nirvāṇa which makes enlightenment possible, not the other way around.

Having attained Nirvāṇa marks the end of *saṃsāra*. Hence Nirvāṇa should not be understood as everlasting life, for this would not be qualitatively different from the potentially endless continuation of saṃsāric existences. Nor should Nirvāṇa be understood as the kind of annihilation which the materialists assumed to occur at death. The mistaken conception of Nirvāṇa as annihilation is repeatedly rejected in the Pāli Canon (e.g. SN 22:85; Itv 49). But then what is the status of the enlightened person after his or her final death? As we already saw, the Buddha refused to answer the question as to whether an accomplished one, a Tathāgata, exists after death or not, or both, or neither (see above p. 40). Because the enlightened person has abandoned any attachment to the five transitory constituents that make up individual existence, because he no longer identifies his self with any of these constituents, he has become unidentifiable: 'he is profound, immeasurable, unfathomable like the ocean' (MN 72; Ñāṇamoli and Bodhi, 2001, p. 594). In a rather old section of the Pāli Canon the question is raised: '… has the man disappeared, does he simply not exist, or is he in some state of perpetual well-being?' And the Buddha replies:

> When a person has gone out, then there is nothing by which you can measure him. That by which he can be talked about is no longer there for him; you cannot say that he does not exist. When all ways

> of being, all phenomena are removed, then all ways of description have also been removed.
>
> (Sn 1075b–6; Saddhatissa, 1987, p. 123)

Nirvāṇa is ineffable (MN 44) and incomparable (Sn 1149). Nonetheless the Buddhist tradition has praised Nirvāṇa through numerous positive attributes and metaphors. It is 'ultimate bliss' (Dhp 203), highest peace, purity, freedom, shelter and release, infinite, secure, excellent, wonderful, etc. (see Chandrkaew, 1982, pp. 20–44; Collins, 1998, pp. 191–233). These attributes, as well as the many attractive metaphors, are based on the experience of Nirvāṇa by enlightened persons (Mph 4:8:61–75). How can we know that Nirvāṇa really is bliss?, asks King Milinda in the Milindapañha. By hearing the jubilant words of those who experienced it, says Nāgasena in reply (see Mph 3:4:8). Let me conclude this section by quoting one of Nirvāṇa's metaphors at some length:

> As food, o king, is the support of the life of all beings, so is Nirvāṇa, when it has been realised, the support of life, for it puts an end to old age and death. This is the first quality of food inherent in Nirvāṇa.
>
> And again, o king, as food increases the strength of all beings, so does Nirvāṇa … increase the higher power of all beings. This is the second quality of food inherent in Nirvāṇa.
>
> And again, o king, as food is the source of beauty of all beings, so is Nirvāṇa … the source to all beings of the beauty of holiness. This is the third quality of food inherent in Nirvāṇa.
>
> And again, o king, as food puts a stop to suffering in all beings, so does Nirvāṇa … put a stop in all beings to the suffering arising from every evil disposition. This is the fourth quality of food inherent in Nirvāṇa.
>
> And again, o king, as food overcomes in all beings the weakness of hunger, so does Nirvāṇa … overcome in all beings the weakness which arises from hunger and every sort of pain.
>
> (Mph 4:8:70; slightly modified after Rhys Davids, 1962b, p. 192)

A Religion Without God?

Frequently introductions to Buddhism assure their readers that Buddhism is a religion without God. But is this an adequate representation?

The answer to this question depends of course on what we understand by 'God'. As we have seen, traditional Buddhism reckons with the existence of many deities populating the heavenly realms. But these *devas* are as much saṃsāric beings as humans, animals, ghosts and denizens of the hells. In a broad sense they are still part of *this* world. They are certainly not transcendent. So if 'God' signifies a transcendent reality, a reality beyond that which is conditioned and transitory, the Buddhist *devas* are obviously the wrong place to look for a counterpart. Nirvāṇa however is indeed presented as a transcendent and ultimate reality; it is beyond *saṃsāra*, it is unconditioned and 'deathless'. If this is what we mean by 'God', Buddhism is by no means god-less (see Conze, 2001, p. 26).

However, Nirvāṇa is not related to the saṃsāric world as its creator. It is both the goal and condition of ultimate salvation, whereas 'God' in the so-called 'theistic' religions is usually understood as the redeemer and the creator of the world. The Buddha was critical of belief in a creator God (*īśvara*) if this implies a world where everything is predetermined by the creator, such that human beings are no longer responsible for their own spiritual development. This would undermine and in fact preclude any motivation to pursue the path of salvation (see AN 3:60). For the same reason, the Buddha rejected both a deterministic understanding of karma as well as the materialistic view that our deeds have no moral or spiritual consequences at all. Later, Buddhism developed its own doctrine of creation within the framework of a cyclical cosmology: Every world-system with its five or six realms of reincarnation is subject to decay. The reason why, after the cosmic collapse of a given world-system, a new world emerges is found in the collective karma of beings: If the karmic tendency of an individual being is responsible for the future destination of that particular being, then the collective karma of beings is responsible for the emergence of the respective realms to which they are inclined (see Abhidharmakośa 4:1). The implication here is that *saṃsāra* must be literally without beginning in time, inasmuch as each new world is the result of the karmic forces stemming from the beings of a preceding world. In the eyes of many traditional Buddhist philosophers this scenario guaranteed more cosmic justice than did the idea that a God created all the different beings with their vastly different life conditions, with no regard for any individual merit or demerit. Each individual fate would then entirely depend on the private deliberations and considerations of such a creator, which would make him, from a Buddhist point of view, a grossly unjust cosmic tyrant (see Schmidt-Leukel, 2006, pp. 127–141). But if the emergence of successive worlds is due to collective karma, and if the hidden force behind the karmic process is the real but obscured longing for Nirvāṇa, one could argue that ultimately Nirvāṇa does have some creative impact on the world, precisely by being its final salvific goal, the end for which all things strive (see AN 10:58). In later forms of Mahāyāna and Tantric Buddhism ultimate reality is explicitly seen as the eternal creative source of everything: Every world is not only the karmic product of deluded beings but, in a deeper sense, a Pure Land created by a supramundane Buddha in order to enable the liberation of beings, while all supramundane Buddhas themselves originate from and manifest the ultimate (see below pp. 108f, 112ff. 130).

As we have seen Buddhism clearly affirms an ultimate transcendent reality as the metaphysical precondition without which salvation would be impossible. In this regard there is even an aspect of 'grace'. The very fact that such an unconditioned reality exists is not the result of any human effort. That it is *really there* is the Buddha's great (re-)discovery, and it is also a kind of grace that this reality has been revealed through the Buddha's compassion. The Buddha is praised as 'the giver of the Deathless' (MN 18; Ñāṇamoli and Bodhi, 2001, p. 203) and his disciples – (so the Pāli Canon rejoices) have received the 'Deathless … for free' (Khuddaka-Pāṭha 6:7).

It has been further argued that Nirvāṇa and God are very different in that Nirvāṇa is no personal, loving being (e.g. Gowans, 2003, 151). Now whether the 'God' confessed by the great theistic traditions of Judaism, Christianity and Islam, or certain forms of Hinduism, can be characterised as a 'personal, loving being' without any further qualification is highly questionable. While the living theistic traditions certainly affirm that God is validly experienced and praised as relating to us *like* a loving person, it is equally affirmed that this expression is a human image or analogy and that God's being transcends everything that we can conceive or express. The God of the great theistic traditions is not less ineffable than the Nirvāṇa of traditional Buddhism. And how is Nirvāṇa in relation to us? The inconceivable Nirvāṇa becomes 'visible' through the loving, compassionate, self-less lives of the enlightened ones, through their fully developed and liberated personalities:

> In what way, … is Nibbāna directly visible …?
>
> … when lust, hatred and delusion have been abandoned, he neither plans for his own harm, nor for the harm of others, nor for the harm of both; and he does not experience in his mind suffering and grief. In this way … Nibbāna is directly visible, immediate, inviting one to come and see, worthy of application, to be personally experienced by the wise.
>
> (AN 3:55; Nyanaponika and Bodhi, 1999, p. 57)

By its visible presence in the enlightened persons, Nirvāṇa is not only utterly transcendent but also deeply immanent in the midst of the saṃsāra. The Buddha did not leave the world, as Māra had demanded, but remained present in it out of compassion. And those who follow in his footsteps, the Bodhisattvas (see chapter 10), do the same. The *bhavacakra* (Figure 6) shows a Bodhisattva in each of the saṃsāric realms bringing consolation, offering guidance and providing assistance on the way to overcome suffering. Is it not the case that transcendent reality acquires the face of a loving person through its manifestation in each enlightened being?

For further reading: Collins (1998); Gethin (1998); Halbfass (2000); Harvey (2004); Pandit (1993).

6

Buddhist Meditation

The popular image of Buddhism in the West almost always includes an association with meditative practice. Although there are in fact a few later forms of Buddhism in which meditation plays only a subordinate role or has even been abolished (as in some forms of Japanese Pure Land Buddhism), this image is not altogether incorrect. Together with insight and morality, meditation is one of the three principles which underlie the Noble Eightfold Path and is thus traditionally regarded as indispensable on one's road to salvation/liberation.

Early Buddhism had a wide range of meditative practices at its disposal, each with a different function. Despite their differences all were ways of training or cultivating one's mind and bringing about mental dispositions favourable to the realization of *morality* and to the attainment and internalisation of *insight*. Some of the practices are obviously of pre-Buddhist origin but were nonetheless adopted insofar as they were perceived to be particularly helpful in the realization of Buddhist goals.

Meditation and Morality

The sixth member of the Noble Eightfold Path, 'right effort', links those members of the path belonging to the principle of 'morality' (*śīla*) with those belonging to 'concentration' (*samādhi*) or 'meditation'. 'Right effort' is then explained rather formally as striving 'to prevent the arising of unarisen evil unwholesome mental states', 'to overcome evil unwholesome mental states that have arisen', 'to produce unarisen wholesome mental states', and 'to maintain wholesome mental states that have arisen, ... bring them to greater growth, to the full perfection of development' (see DN 22:21; Walshe, 1995, p. 348). This covers all facets and forms of religious striving but views them all under the aspect of cultivating one's mind. Therefore the persistent attempt to lead a morally good life is in itself already a kind of meditative practice, a form of mental training.

Morally good behaviour however should not only result from inner discipline and relevant efforts. The Buddhist ideal is that morality should flow from one's very nature. Hence there is a particular type of meditative practice which aims at developing a good and loving mind which would naturally manifest as good and loving behaviour. This practice is called the 'cultivation' (*bhāvanā*) of the four 'divine abidings' (*brahmavihāra*) or 'immeasurables' (*apramāṇas*). According to the standard canonical description the practitioner 'abides pervading' all four directions: 'so above, below, around, and everywhere, and to all as to himself, ... the all-encompassing world with a mind imbued with *loving-kindness*, ... with *compassion*, ... with *altruistic joy*, ... with *equanimity*, abundant, exalted, immeasurable, without hostility and without ill will' (see MN 7:13–16; Ñāṇamoli and Bodhi, 2001, p. 120; my emphasis). The relations among these four mental qualities and their impact on the Buddhist understanding of morality will be investigated more closely in the next chapter. (see below, pp. 68f). But it may be worth noting that this particular form of meditation (together with other aspects of Buddhist spirituality) found entry into one of the most influential Hindu texts of meditative practice, i.e. Patañjali's Yoga-Sūtra (1:33).

Various Contemplations

A large group of early Buddhist meditative practices is concerned with the consideration, recollection and visualisation of pivotal topics in the Buddhist religion and their respective symbols. Several different collections of such reflections exist, focussing upon subjects such as the Buddha, the Dharma, the Saṅgha ('community'), morality, generosity, heavenly beings, the body, death, the peace (of Nirvāṇa), etc. (see e.g. AN 1:26; 1:35; 5:57; 10:60, etc.). In serene and silent contemplation the practitioner is encouraged to reflect upon the excellent properties of the Buddha, the various benefits of the Dharma, the disadvantages connected to the body, and so on. Contemplation of this sort has a basically discursive character, not unlike the meditative recollection of the mysteries of Christ's life and death practiced by medieval Christian contemplatives. Yet in Buddhist practice such recollections could also take a less cognitive form in which the practitioner gazes at examples or symbolic representations of the *sujet* at hand, or keeps these before his mental eye by visualising them in his or her imagination. Later, visualisation techniques became particularly important in Mahāyānic and Tantric forms of meditation (see Chapter 13), where the meditator trains him- or herself in visualising mental images of Buddhas and Bodhisattvas or complex geometrical configurations *(maṇḍalas)* representing multifaceted aspects of the doctrine. There is strong evidence that meditative visualisation exerted a considerable influence on the origin and the further development of Buddhist art (see Schlingloff, 1987).

A typical example of early Buddhist contemplation is provided by the meditation on death. Buddhist scriptures take for granted that human beings have a deep-seated tendency to ignore or suppress the fact of their mortality (e.g. Dhp 286ff; Thag 276). Contemplation of death thus aims at cultivating the awareness that death is inevitable, that no one is exempt from it, that human life is rather short and that the time of death is unpredictable (see Vism 8:1–41). The practitioner should recollect that life is as a dewdrop vanishing at sunrise or as a bubble in water (AN 7:70).

The primary aim however is to transform general knowledge of the fact of death into personal awareness of one's own mortality. This is accomplished with the help of a fairly demanding visualisation: The practitioner imagines himself 'as though he were to see a corpse thrown aside in a charnel ground, one, two, or three days dead, bloated, livid, and oozing matter', or 'as though he were to see a corpse thrown aside in a charnel ground, being devoured by crows, hawks, vultures, dogs, jackals, or various kinds of worms'. A series of such visualisations is carried forward until finally only the image of the bare bones of the skeleton is left. At every single stage of the imagined decomposition process the practitioner is to think of his own body 'This body too is of the same nature, it will be like that, it is not exempt from that fate' (MN 10:14–30; Ñāṇamoli and Bodhi, 2001, p. 148). The meditation was carried out not only in the imagination. As places which offer illustrative material in abundance, 'charnel grounds' are regularly mentioned among the settings most suitable for meditation ('the forest, the root of a tree, a mountain, a ravine, a hillside cave, a charnel ground, a jungle thicket, an open space [or: empty room], a heap of straw', see MN 27:17; 38; DN 2; 3, etc.)

Several objectives are mentioned in connection with the contemplation of death. For one thing, a material consciousness of death's unpredictability will stimulate the practitioner to strive ever more seriously and diligently for spiritual advancement (see AN 8:73–4). For another, the full realization that the most beautiful body will inevitably end as a decomposing corpse is meant to provide a fast-working antidote for carnal lust (see MN 13:18–30). And the sober awareness that one's own bodily existence cannot escape the same fate will aid the practitioner in abandoning all self-identification with (see AN 6:29) and attachment to his or her own body: 'he abides independent, not clinging to anything in the world' (MN 10:15; Ñāṇamoli and Bodhi, 2001, p. 148).

The contemplation of corpses still belongs to the repertoire of currently practiced forms of meditation, particularly within Theravāda Buddhism. Santi Asoka, a radical Buddhist reformist group in Thailand, employs quite hideous photos of massive injuries, accident casualties and the like as a modern substitute. Other contemporary Buddhists have criticised this method as 'a sick obsession' coming dangerously close to 'pathological abnormalities' (Takeuchi, 1983, p. 18f). Even the Pāli Canon reports a wave of religiously motivated suicides stemming from the practice of this contemplation within the early Buddhist movement and relates that as a consequence the Buddha recommended that the monks change their meditative practice to mindful breathing (see SN 54:9).

The contemplation of specific facets of Buddhist doctrine took an interesting turn in the Zen practice of *kōan*-meditation (see Chapter 14). A *kōan* consists of a short story and/or question usually dealing with a certain aspect of Buddhist (in the case of Zen, Mahāyāna Buddhist) doctrine. In contrast to earlier forms of contemplation, the *kōan* method seeks to achieve the internalisation of insight on a level which is neither discursive nor imaginative. By means of insoluble dilemmas, paradoxes, etc., the practitioner should reach a point where he or she abandons all attempts to find a cognitive solution, discovering instead a spontaneous, existential response to the problem. To cite just one example which continues the theme of mortality:

> It is like a monk hanging by his teeth in a tree over a precipice. His hands grasp no branch, his feet rest on no limb, and under the tree another man asks him, 'Why did Bodhidharma come to China from the West?' If the man in the tree does not answer, he misses the question, and if he answers, he falls and loses his life. Now what shall he do?
>
> (Mumonkan 5)

Cultivating Mindfulness

The seventh member of the Noble Eightfold Path, 'right mindfulness' (*smṛti*, Pāli: *sati*, also meaning 'recollection' or 'close attention') is described in the standard explanation of the Path as one's full consciousness of the body, feelings, mind and mind-objects without any 'hankering and fretting for the world' (see MN 141:30; DN 22:21; Walshe, 1995, p. 349). The ancient narrative exposition of the Path describes this as follows:

> Here a monk acts with clear awareness in going forth and back, in looking ahead or behind him, in bending and stretching, in wearing his outer and inner robe and carrying his bowl, in eating, drinking, chewing and swallowing, in evacuating and urinating, in walking, standing, sitting, lying down, in waking, in speaking, and in keeping silent he acts with clear awareness.
>
> (DN 2:65; Walshe, 1995, p. 100)

Mindfulness here is closely linked to the 'guarding of the sense-doors', meaning that in view of all sensations of the five senses, all mental activities and all accompanying feelings the practitioner should be on guard against grasping or clinging to any of them – and that can only be done by maintaining constant mindfulness.

One can 'train' oneself to mindfulness, as it were, through particular forms of meditative exercise, the basic practice being mindful breathing. Sitting upright and with crossed legs (the famous lotus-position) the practitioner begins by mindfully observing the flow of breath: 'Breathing in long, he understands: "I breathe in long"; or breathing out long, he understands: "I breathe out long". Breathing in short, he understands: "I breathe in short"; or breathing out short, he understands "I breathe out short"' (MN 10:4; Ñāṇamoli and Bodhi, 2001, p. 146). It is most important not to regulate one's breath, not to intervene, but simply and mindfully to observe its coming and going, thus experiencing (and learning) for oneself what not-grasping, not-clinging is: 'he abides independent, not clinging to anything in the world' (ibid. p. 146). This mental attitude of calm and clear observation without intervention is then expanded to feelings: 'when feeling a pleasant feeling, a bhikkhu understands: "I feel a pleasant feeling"; when feeling a painful feeling, he understands: "I feel a painful feeling"' (ibid. p. 149), and so on. The practitioner mindfully observes how the pleasant, painful or indifferent feelings arise and vanish, and by merely *observing* them he or she avoids grasping them. The practice is then extended to the mind: Mental states arising in greed, hatred or delusion, as well as such states which are free from these negative qualities, are merely observed with no attempt to 'do' anything about them – for this mindful observing-without-intervening is already in itself the practicing of non-attachment, and will thus lead to the desired 'purification'. Hence it is praised in the Pāli Canon as the 'direct path for the disappearance of pain and grief, ... for the realization of Nirvāṇa' (see MN 10:2; DN 22:1).

Among the meditations on death is one which calls upon the practitioner to contemplate life's brevity with the thought: 'Oh, were I to live just for the time I breathe in after the out-breath or breathe out after the in-breath, I would direct my mind on the Blessed One's teaching. Much, indeed, could then be done by me!' (AN 8:73; Nyanaponika and Bodhi, 1999, p. 224f). But what is this 'much' that can be done in the briefness of one's last breath? What meaningful work can be done in one single moment? For Buddhism the answer is to take this one breath mindfully!

Meditation techniques for the cultivation of mindfulness, particularly through mindful breathing, have been widely revitalised in twentieth-century Theravāda Buddhism (see Kornfield, 1977; Nyanaponika, 1971). Moreover these techniques show a marked resemblance to *zazen*, the type of Zen meditation which is not based on *kōan* practice, but is 'sitting only' (literally: 'sitting in contemplation'). Other forms of religious activity, like recitation or the performance of certain rituals, are frequently seen as supports for the cultivation of mindfulness even if this is not their immediate purpose. And almost all Buddhist schools would agree that much of the art of living one's everyday life consists in combining mindfulness with equanimity.

Absorption and Nirvāṇa

According to the Buddha-legend, Siddhārtha Gautama experienced enlightenment in a particular state of meditative concentration. While there are some canonical records of people achieving enlightenment spontaneously (Thag 270, 274, 302, 410, 465), the standard expectation is that it occurs during meditation. The goal of meditation, or more precisely, of some specific forms of meditation to which we will now turn, is the creation in the practitioner of the right disposition for attaining Nirvāṇa. Such meditations have been appropriately described as 'enstatic practice' (see Griffith, 1997, pp. 36ff), inasmuch as they presuppose a withdrawal from external stimuli and a penetration into progressively deeper states of inner experience.

One of these enstatic meditations is known as the 'four *dhyānas*' (*dhyāna* = 'absorption') or '*rūpya dhyāna*' ('form-based absorption'). It is linked to the Buddha's own enlightenment and consists of four successive states: The *first* state or *dhyāna* is characterised by 'rapture and pleasure born of seclusion' and 'accompanied by applied and sustained thought'. In the *second* state the overwhelming joy remains but the discursive activity of the mind is stilled and transformed into 'singleness of mind'. During the *third dhyāna* rapture turns into a quieter form of pleasure, and the mind is in a state of mindful equanimity. In the *fourth dhyāna* there is no longer pleasure or pain, but only 'purity of mindfulness due to equanimity' (see MN 27:19–22; Ñāṇamoli and Bodhi, 2001, p. 275–6). In this state, the practitioner may acquire the same liberating insight as the Buddha, i.e., he or she may gain a recollection of previous lives, a full understanding of the law of karma and the Four Noble Truths, and may experience the complete and lasting liberation from thirst and all remnants of attachment.

Another kind of enstatic meditation is known as '*ārūpya dhyāna*' ('formless absorption'). It too consists of a series of progressive mental states, though these are quite different in nature from those of *rūpya dhyāna*. After some preliminary meditational exercises during which the practitioner first gazes at some visible coloured object (a blue or red disc, for instance) and then concentrates on an inner mental image of this, he or she reaches a point where all perception of 'form' or 'shape', external or internal, is left behind; only the awareness of the *infinity of space* or void remains. This is the *first ārūpya dhyāna*. This too is then left behind, and in the *second state* awareness is reduced to a sense of the *infinity of consciousness* or perception itself. Proceeding further, the *third ārūpya dhyāna* is characterised by the awareness '*there is nothing*'. But even this awareness can be further transcended, so that the *fourth state* is described as a state of 'neither-perception-nor-non-perception'. Yet this is still not the end. The practice culminates finally in a *fifth state*, the 'cessation of perception and feeling' (e.g. MN 77:22). The practitioner is now in a kind of catatonic state, seemingly dead. But there is still body heat, the senses are not operating but still intact, and so the practitioner can and will emerge from this trance (see MN 43:23–5).

Some canonical texts explain this state as the bodily experience of Nirvāṇa, as a direct perception of Nirvāṇa here and now (see AN 9:42–51; MN 121). Yet how can one speak of a perception at all if the state is characterised as the 'cessation of feeling and perception'? This question is explicitly raised (see AN 10:6f; 11:7:f). By way of response it is said that in this state nothing of this world or of any other world is perceived, but it is nevertheless the perception of 'the peaceful ... Nirvāṇa'. What has come to a complete standstill is the perception of the world of diverse impressions and concepts (*prapañca*) (AN 4,174) – and Nirvāṇa is a reality beyond this *prapañca* (AN 6:14). The very same terminology is also used by non-Buddhists – in the Māṇḍūkya Upaniṣad 1:7, for example – as indicative of the inexpressible experience of ultimate reality. Indeed, it may very well be the case that 'formless' meditation is of non- and pre-Buddhist origin.

At times, some texts in the Pāli Canon are rather critical of 'formless' meditation. They reject the claim that such 'formless' meditation leads to the experience of Nirvāṇa (see MN 26:15f), or they demand that this meditation be supplemented by thorough doctrinal instruction (see AN 9:36). The major difference between the two types of absorption practice, the 'form-based' and the 'formless', is that in the former the experience of Nirvāṇa is linked to a clear conceptual understanding of the Four Noble Truths while in the latter the experience of Nirvāṇa is linked to a complete cessation of all cognitive activity. There is some evidence that these two different approaches are representative of a conflict or tension in the early Buddhist movement between more doctrinally and more mystically minded groups (see AN 6:46; see also La Vallée Poussin, 1936–7; Schmithausen, 1981). Be that as it may, most of the traditional texts pursued a harmonising solution by including both form-based and formless states within one single chain of nine successive states, ending with the 'cessation of feeling and perception'.

A third type of absorption or trance technique is presumably underlying the doctrinal scheme of the 'higher' or 'supernatural powers' (*abhijñā*). This scheme is usually integrated into the standard description of the path to salvation where it appears as a list of special abilities acquired through meditation (see DN 2:85–98; MN 77:30–36). It seems however to represent an absorption practice in its own right which, in contrast to the other two, can be characterised as 'ecstatic', for it entails a classic 'out-of-body' experience. In and through meditation the practitioner inwardly creates 'another body having form, mind-made, with all its limbs'. With this ethereal body he departs from his material body as if he 'were to pull out a reed from its sheath' or 'a sword from its scabbard'. Having thus left his flesh-and-blood body behind (which is presumably still sitting in motionless meditation) he experiences the ability to multiply himself, appear and disappear, go through walls, dive into the earth, walk on water, and ascend cross-legged into space, touching the sun and the moon with his hands and even flying to the heavenly worlds of the gods. With the 'divine ear' he hears sounds whether near or far; with the 'divine eye' he sees into the hearts and minds of all beings. He then is able to recall previous lives, comprehends the law of karma and the Four Noble Truths and achieves final liberation. The production of an ethereal body able to levitate and transcend the limits of space, and possessed of telepathic capacities, thus constitutes another technique for attaining the experience of perfect enlightenment. It is a visionary, shamanistic form of meditation presented alongside the 'form-based' and 'formless' meditation as a third way to approach the ultimate goal of Nirvāṇa.

It appears that these three forms of absorption practices not only represent three paradigmatic forms of meditation but in fact anticipate three recurring models of Buddhist spirituality: The master of wisdom who approaches the goal of salvation via clear doctrinal insight, the contemplative mystic who approaches Nirvāṇa by transcending all conceptual understanding and finally the shamanic *siddha* who reaches the goal through his extraordinary visionary and magical capacities.

A Foretaste of Nirvāṇa

In early Buddhism, meditation was practiced primarily by the monastics. To a large extent this is explained through the concrete circumstances of their life. Serious meditation training required a considerable amount of time, conditions favourable to the daily practice and the presence of experienced guides or gūrus. For the majority of lay-followers intensive meditation was simply not a realistic option. Their days were filled with labour and care for their families, and they were encouraged (as we shall see in the next chapter) to perform such tasks in the Buddhist spirit to the best of their abilities. Nevertheless some of the more wealthy among Buddha's lay-followers must have been in a position to gain at least some experience with meditation, and thus they were urged to aim for the lower stages of 'form-based' absorption in the light of the overwhelming joy linked with these stages. In this way they would be able to experience a kind of happiness very different from the sensual pleasures they have hitherto known (see AN 5:176).

The joy and rapture of the first two stages of 'form-based' absorption arise from the temporary overcoming of the so-called 'five hindrances': (1) greed or covetousness, (2) ill will or hatred, (3) sloth and torpor, (4) restlessness and remorse and (5) doubt. These states are replaced by (1) inner freedom, (2) compassion for all beings, (3) mindfulness, (4) inner peace and (5) clarity. The result is the overflowing joy of the first stage of absorption. The Pāli Canon illustrates this with five short similes: The practitioner feels like a businessman whose business has become so successful that he can pay off his debts with enough left over to buy gifts for his wife. Or like a man who recovers from a long and severe sickness, regaining appetite and feeling new strength. Or like someone released from prison who discovers that his possessions are still intact, untouched. Or like a slave who is set free and is now his own master. Or like a trader who transported his goods on a long and very dangerous journey through desert areas, and now arrives safely at his goal (see DN 2:68–74). Experiencing the disappearance of the five hindrances, ‘it is as if he were freed from debt, from sickness, from bonds, from slavery, from the perils of the desert’ (DN 2:74; Walshe, 1995, p. 102).

The five hindrances are variants of the three root evils: greed, hatred and delusion, and only with the attainment of enlightenment is their disappearance complete and lasting. Yet this also implies that their temporary overcoming in meditation, and the joy of liberation associated with this, is in fact a foretaste of Nirvāṇa.

For further reading: Bronkhorst (1986); Griffiths (1987); Griffiths (1997); Kornfield (1977); Nyanaponika (1971); Vetter (1988).

7

Buddhist Ethics

Ethics and the Path to Salvation

After insight and meditation we now turn to morality, the third of the three principles structuring the Noble Eightfold Path (see above p. 38). And the first question to be addressed is: Why is a moral life seen as an integral, even indispensable part of the path to ultimate salvation? Before we look more closely at what Buddhism understands by morally good life, it is important to grasp the overall role of morality within the Buddhist religion.

The decisive point here has already been indicated: The experience of suffering *and* the infliction of suffering upon others have one and the same existential root: 'thirst', and its manifestation as 'attachment'. An important text from the Pāli Canon, the 'Greater *Sutta* on the Groups of Suffering' (MN 13) clearly underlines this point. Whether suffering arises from the transitoriness of life, the loss of what one likes or old age, illness and death, or whether suffering has been inflicted upon others through 'misconduct of body, speech and mind' (burglary and adultery, quarrelling, fighting and wars) – *both* forms of suffering are caused by 'thirst' and 'attachment', lured by the deceptive promises of sensual pleasures. That we experience our own suffering and that we inflict suffering upon others, both stems from the same root, the deluded striving for worldly enjoyment and the attachment to it. The great Mahāyāna philosopher Śāntideva (8th cent. CE) formulated this in the following aphorism:

> His the knife, and mine the body – the twofold cause of suffering.
> He grasped the knife, I my body.
>
> (BCA 6:43; Crosby and Skilton, 1995, p. 54)

In this imagined scene of suffering a violent attack we have two elements responsible for the ensuing suffering: the attack with the knife and the vulnerable body. Yet in the end just one root: 'grasping', 'attachment': The attack being carried out because of the attacker's attachment to his vicious goals, the suffering of the victim due to his attachment to his own life.

If 'thirst' and 'attachment' constitute the one root of suffering – both the suffering one undergoes oneself in saṃsāric existence, and the suffering one inflicts upon others – it follows that any successful attempt to reduce one's 'thirst' and to moderate one's 'attachment' will also result in a life causing less suffering (at least less deliberately-inflicted suffering) to others – and this is what morality basically means for Buddhism: reducing suffering, alleviating suffering, causing less suffering. Morality is an intrinsic part of the path to salvation because it is part and parcel of the salvific process of overcoming 'thirst' and 'attachment'.

Living a morally good life thus always brings a twofold benefit: Others are aided and one's own spiritual development or karmic disposition is positively affected. This point is captured in one of the central Buddhist virtues: *dāna*, which is 'giving' or 'generosity'. 'Giving' creates a win-win situation. Not only is the gift's recipient benefited but also the gift's donor – particularly from a Buddhist point of view, since through giving one counters attachment in its deep-seated form of greedy grasping, of not letting-go. A passage in the Pāli Canon describes the whole moral life with its twofold beneficial effect as a single great gift to the beings: By refraining from the destruction of life, from stealing, from sexual misconduct, from false speech and from the use of intoxicants:

> ... the noble disciple gives to immeasurable beings freedom from fear, freedom from hostility and freedom from oppression.... Thereby he himself will enjoy immeasurable freedom from fear, hostility and oppression. This is a great gift and a flood of merit.
> (AN 8:39; slightly modified after Nyanaponika & Bodhi, 1999, p. 216)

The twofold benefit of living a morally good life is linked to a twofold motivation: 'Protecting oneself, one protects others; protecting others, one protects oneself' – just as each acrobat in a balancing act protects his partner by concentrating on himself, and protects himself by concentrating on his partner (see SN 47:19). If we take care of our own spiritual development, we render a service to others; and if we develop love towards others, we thereby also help ourselves. Accordingly, it is explicitly stated, someone who pursues the path of salvation only for his or her own benefit is to be censured, while the one who follows the path for one's own benefit *and* for the benefit of others is to be commended (see AN 7:64).

Two further points must be mentioned in connection with the fact that morality forms an integral part of the Buddhist path to salvation. Firstly, morality stands in a relationship of reciprocal influence with the other two central principles of the path: wisdom and meditation. Morality is 'purified by wisdom' and conversely 'wisdom is purified by morality' (see DN 4; Walshe, 1995, p. 131); furthermore, moral effort is viewed as a precondition for right meditative practice. (e.g. in the sequence of the Noble Eightfold Path as well as in the ancient scheme of the path mentioned earlier, see above p. 38). Indeed, as we have seen, there are particular forms of meditative practice which aim directly at the development of a morally good mind.

Secondly, as an integral part of the path, morality contributes to the final achievement of enlightenment. Reaching the goal however does not make morality irrelevant: With enlightenment the roots of immoral behaviour are entirely eradicated and the virtue of the enlightened one has become perfect. The enlightened one will act in a good way because of having become good himself.

Abstaining from Evil and Doing the Good

Three segments of the Noble Eightfold Path (3 – 5) are traditionally subsumed under the principle of morality (*śīla*): 'right speech' (3), 'right action' (4) and 'right livelihood' (5). In standardised canonical descriptions (DN 22, MN 141, etc.) these are frequently explained indirectly – by stating which behaviour should be avoided. 'Right speech' means to abstain from lying, from malicious, divisive, or harsh speech and from frivolous or idle talk. 'Right action' is explained as abstaining from harming and killing sentient beings – including animals (!), and further as abstaining from 'taking what is not given' and from sexual misconduct, which means avoiding sexual relations with women who are still under the protection of their families, or with those who are married, betrothed, or celibate for religious reasons. From monks and nuns complete sexual abstention is demanded. 'Right livelihood' means abstaining from those sources of income which involve harming other beings: trading in weapons for instance, or trading in living beings, meat, intoxicants or poison; also included is the avoidance of fraud and avarice. Striking here is the listing of 'right livelihood' as a separate and distinct element of the Noble Eightfold Path, for from a purely logical point of view it could of course be subsumed under 'right action'. That it is specifically mentioned reflects the Buddha's sharp awareness of the importance of the economic dimension in a person's life.

The exposition of right moral conduct in terms of what one should *not* do is grounded in the basic Buddhist idea that morality is part of overcoming the sources of those kind of actions which cause suffering. Unfortunately this has led a number of Western interpreters to the false conclusion that Buddhist ethics merely entails a passive morality of avoidance. Buddhist texts, however, generally assert that an effective opposition to the roots of evil consists in practicing the opposite behaviour (e.g. AN 6:107–116; NP 244) – and thus Buddhist morality involves positive and active forms of conduct as well.

'Right speech', for example, involves speaking the truth, speaking words which promote reconciliation, friendship and concord, words which are gentle, loveable, reasonable and helpful, words which elucidate the Dharma (see MN 114; AN 10:176). 'Right action' basically means to act gently and kindly and to be 'compassionate to all living beings'. What 'right action' and 'right livelihood' positively involve becomes clearer in the numerous practical guidelines for dealing with one's parents, teachers, spouse, children, friends, one's master and servant, Brahmans and Śramaṇas. So, for example, in the very popular Sigālovāda Sutta (DN 31): Children should honour their parents, be grateful and support them when they are in need or grow old; parents should show their love to their children by teaching them virtue, training them for a profession and passing on their inheritance when it is due; pupils should be attentive and supportive to their teachers, and teachers should not only instruct but also praise, recommend and protect their pupils; a husband should minister to his wife 'by honouring her, by not disparaging her, by not being unfaithful to her, by giving authority to her, by providing her with adornments'. A wife will reciprocate 'by properly organising her work, by being kind to the servants, by not being unfaithful, by protecting stores, and by being skilful and diligent in all she has to do'. Friends are encouraged to trust and help one another, to point out what is good for the other and to be 'the same in happy and unhappy times'. Very humane are the rules for the treatment of one's servants: 'arranging their work according to their strength, … supplying them with food and wages, … looking after them when they are ill, … sharing special delicacies with them, and … letting them off work at the right time.' Conversely, servants and workpeople should be diligent, not betray their masters or steal from them, and care for their good reputation. Religious mendicants should be supported by the gifts from the lay people and in return they will give instruction in living a good life (see Walshe, 1995, 461–9). The best among those who enjoy sensual pleasures and wealth is praised as the one who earns his possessions lawfully, who is ready to share them and who uses his wealth without greed and craving because he is aware of the dangers of attachment (see AN 10:91).

Leading a moral life is seen as having a wider social dimension as well. Establishing public parks, constructing bridges, digging wells and providing a residence for the homeless (see SN 1:1:47; similarly Jat 31) – all these are commended. In addition there are instructions for kings concerning the virtues he should practice and the principles of good governing; these give precedence to the common good of the people, enjoin support for the needy and even demand the protection of animals (see DN 26:5). I will take this up again in more detail when considering Buddhist politics (see Chapter 9).

Many of the afore mentioned moral counsels are directed to Buddhist lay-followers, while among monks and nuns, in light of their distinct lifestyle and calling, different practical moral demands prevail. The greatest gift the monastics can offer is the gift of the Buddhist Dharma (see e.g. AN 9:5; Dhp 354), and through their own serious religious efforts they contribute to passing this gift on. There are also some moral demands upon the monks and nuns, specific to their monastic way of life but comparable in principle to those for the laity, as for example the injunction to care for fellow monastics who are ailing (Mhv 8:26:1–4) or to serve one another in a quiet and loving manner (see DN 16:1:11; MN 31; AN 5:105).

The minimal moral requirements for both laypeople and monastics are summarised in the famous 'five precepts' (*pañca śīla*):

1) abstention from the destruction of life,
2) abstention from taking what is not given,
3) abstention from sexual misconduct,
4) abstention from false speech,
5) abstention from 'wines, liquor and intoxicants which are a basis for negligence'.

(see AN 8:25; Nyanaponika and Bodhi, 1999, p. 207)

For monks and nuns the third precept translates as celibacy. In addition to the numerous and detailed regulations of their monastic life they are further obliged to observe the following supplementary precepts: (6) abstention from solid food after noon, (7) avoidance of events with dancing, musical performance, etc., (8) abstention from all perfumes or personal adornments, (9) non-usage of high, luxury beds, (10) non-acceptance of any gold or silver. It became a widespread tradition that, on Buddhist festival days, lay people as well should observe parts of these additional precepts (usually with the exception of the last one).

The first four of the 'five precepts' cover more or less the same territory as the third and fourth members of the Noble Eightfold Path: 'right speech' and 'right action'. It may be worth noting that these four minimal moral injunctions find many parallels in all the major world religions – a fact which has been recognised in the contemporary effort to formulate a global ethic (see Küng, 1996). Nor is the fifth of the 'five precepts' without counterparts in other religious traditions, though in the Buddhist context the precept points up the specific connection between morality and meditation, the training of one's mind, which can only be done if the mind is kept clear.

Before we look more closely at the Buddhist approach to developing a morally good mind, a final remark should be made on the principle of *epikeia*, of choosing the lesser evil. Does Buddhist ethics allow for such a principle, or are the moral rules seen as uncompromising, inviolable laws? While there is a certain tendency towards the latter, Buddhism also affirms that as far as the karmic consequences of our behaviour are concerned, the motivation behind a deed is more decisive than the deed itself. Therefore Buddhism tends to agree that in some situations the morally good intention permits, or even demands, an action which violates certain moral rules. Particularly when it comes to issues of governing a state in accordance with Buddhist morality, questions like the legitimacy of punishing evil-doers (thereby doing harm to them) or defending the country (thereby killing living beings) had to be addressed. Even the relatively early treatise *Milanda Pañha* asserts that deeds cannot be morally wrong if they are done with a benevolent intent and for the benefit of the people – even if they involve pain-causing actions, as for example in the case of a necessary but painful medical treatment (see Mph 4:1:33). This emphasis on the priority of the good intention has wide ranging implications for social and political ethics to which I will later return. For the moment let us see what Buddhism says about a good intention and how it can be developed.

Developing a Morally Good Mind

'All things proceed from the mind' is axiomatically stated in the two famous opening verses of the *Dhammapada*, one of the most popular of all Buddhist scriptures. Bad words and bad deeds stem from a wicked mind; good words and good deeds stem from a pure mind (see Dhp 1–2). In consequence, much of Buddhist moral discourse focuses on the development of a morally good mind – once again leading some interpreters to the erroneous conclusion that Buddhism is not interested in practical deeds. Yet it is precisely because of the deeds that Buddhism starts with the mind, the source from which the deeds spring.

The good mind or the 'right intention', the second member of the Noble Eightfold Path (see above p. 38), links the principle of insight with the field of morality, for right behaviour flows from the right intentions formed under the influence of the 'right view', the first component of the path. The canonical texts explain 'right intention' as the 'intention of renunciation, intention of non-ill will, and intention of non-cruelty' (MN 141:25 or DN 22:21; Ñāṇamoli and Bodhi, 2001, p. 1100). The related classification of the tenfold wholesome and unwholesome conduct explains the wholesome mind as being free from covetousness, ill will and hate (see MN 114; AN 10:206). So while the first member of the Noble Eightfold Path is directed against the evil of delusion or ignorance, the second counters greed and hatred. The latter are the two basic forms in which attachment manifests itself and as such they constitute the mental roots of morally wrong behaviour. Since the focal point of attachment is one's own self, immorality is intrinsically linked to self-centredness: 'May what belongs to another be mine!' is the structural subtext of greed or covetousness (MN 114), as causing pain to others for one's own benefit or satisfaction forms the structural foundation of hatred (see Dhp 291). Accordingly, the good mind is one which is free (or relatively free) from these negative attitudes and shaped by their opposites: by generosity, sympathetic joy and equanimity instead of greed, by loving-kindness and compassion instead of hatred, by non-discrimination between self and others and by selflessness instead of self-centredness.

Against all immoral forms of self-centredness Buddhism affirms the so-called 'Golden Rule': 'What is displeasing and disagreeable to me is displeasing and disagreeable to the other too. How can I inflict upon another what is displeasing and disagreeable to me?' (SN 55:7; see also Sn 705). Greed is seen as an evil which is hard to overcome (AN 3:68) and can only be defeated through thoroughgoing insight into the unsatisfactory character of saṃsāric existence; nevertheless greed can be moderated through the development of equanimity. Hatred, however, can be tackled more directly by developing loving-kindness (*maitri*, Pāli: *metta*). Once again, the key is to overcome the discrimination between self and others.

As mentioned before, the development of a loving mind towards all beings, whether friend or foe, is the aim of one of the meditative practices of early Buddhism (see above p. 53f). In his instructions for this kind of meditation, Buddhaghosa recommends starting with a wish for one's own happiness: 'May I be happy and free from suffering.' Only if one is able to love oneself will one be capable of extending the same love to others. And so Buddhaghosa then suggests directing this loving mental attitude to a dear friend, then to a neutral person and finally towards a hostile person until it becomes possible to bear love towards all beings indiscriminately, such that one sincerely wishes that 'all may be happy and free from suffering' (see Vism 9:1–12). Buddhaghosa is realistic enough to expect some difficulties: If someone is unable to overcome ill feelings against a particular person, one should imagine that in a former reincarnation the person in question has been one's own beloved mother, father, brother, sister, son, daughter or friend. For, as Buddhaghosa quotes the canonical scriptures, within the unfathomable length of saṃsāric existence 'it is not easy to find a being who has not formerly been your mother ... your father ...' (SN 15:14–19), etc. (see Vism 9:36; Ñāṇamoli, 1999, p. 297f). Making oneself aware of the universal kinship of all beings should aid in becoming free of negative feelings. The crucial importance of overcoming every form of hatred or ill will was emphasised by the Buddha himself in his parable of the saw, which Buddhaghosa recalls: Even if bandits would cut one literally to pieces with a sharp saw, one should not develop any hatred or hostility against them, but encompass them with loving-kindness (see MN 21).

The Buddhist attempt to develop a good and loving mind is, however, beset with a profound problem, one which is not peculiar to Buddhist ethics but surfaces in every serious ethic: the interrelationship of self-interest and altruism. What motivates the effort to become loving and kind? Does one want to become a morally good person *in order to* improve one's own karma – whether with the prospect of a better rebirth or (as on the Noble Eight-fold Path) with the prospect of ultimate salvation? If so, then the motivation behind the development of a loving mind would still (or even primarily) be an egoistic, self-centred one. This could hardly qualify as an altruistic motivation and to see it as such would simply be one more form of self-deception. The attempt to develop other-directed love for the sake of one's own spiritual progress seems to suffer from a structural failure: If it is for one's own progress, it is not real love, and if it is not real love, no spiritual or moral progress is made.

Buddhaghosa does not explicitly discuss this problem but he does make an interesting remark which seems to indicate his own solution. He cites the canonical statement that love must be developed 'equally to all' and comments: 'Equally ... to all classed as inferior, medium, superior, friendly, hostile, neutral, etc., just as to oneself'. He even suggests the reading 'equality with oneself' and explains: '... without making the distinction "This is another being", is what is meant' (Vism 9:47; Ñāṇamoli, 1999, p. 301). The problem that love does not seem to be real love if it is cultivated out of spiritual self-interest appears to dissolve once the distinction between self and others is overcome.

Another solution (seemingly similar but in the end markedly different) is presented by Śāntideva in his exposition of the Bodhisattva path (see Chapter 10). The paradox is faced quite clearly: 'Those who suffer in the world do so because of their desire for their own happiness. All those happy in the world are so because of their desire for the happiness of others' (BCA 8:129). Not unlike Buddhaghosa, Śāntideva first recommends making oneself aware that all are equally experiencing suffering and happiness, and thus one should help others in the same way as one helps oneself (BCA 8:90–6). This means accepting others as oneself or as one's self (8:136). However, Śāntideva continues, this can be realised only by means of an 'exchange of self and other' (8:120). To overcome suffering – both one's own as well as that of others – 'one must have no other concern than the welfare of all beings' (8:137; see Crosby and Skilton, 1995, pp. 96–104). Only through genuine selflessness can there be any spiritual progress for oneself, and genuine selflessness is possible only if one forgets one's self and puts the others in its place by being concerned exclusively for them. This is precisely the point where Mahāyāna ethics goes beyond the Theravāda standpoint as represented by Buddhaghosa.

Detachment and Involvement

The question however persists: Is not love, or true caring for others, always a form of attachment? If the true goal of Buddhism is the severance of all attachments, must not one ultimately aim at abandoning all motions of love? Here we confront another widespread misunderstanding of Buddhist ethics – one which leads us however to what we might consider the heart of Buddhist spirituality, namely, the compatibility of loving involvement and non-attachment.

A number of sayings in the Pāli Canon seem, at first glance, to confirm the incompatibility of love and detachment. There is, for example, Buddha's exclamation when faced with a father mourning the death of his only son: 'Sorrow, lamentation, pain, grief, and despair are born from those who are dear, arise from those who are dear' (MN 87; Ñāṇamoli and Bodhi, 2001, p. 718), or his saying on a similar occasion that those 'who abandon whatever is dear … they dig up the root of grief' (Ud 2,7; Ireland, 1997, p. 29). Furthermore, the sage is said to be free from any sort of likes and dislikes (see Sn 811), etc. On the other hand, 'loving-kindness' (*maitrī*, Pāli: *mettā*) is frequently called 'mind-releasing' (Pāli: *cettovimutti*), and this is clearly related to the release from attachment. A song in praise of loving-kindness (Itv 27 and AN 8:1) says:

> For one who mindfully develops
> Boundless loving-kindness
> Seeing the destruction of clinging,
> The fetters are worn away.
>
> (Itv 27; Ireland, 1997, 169)

Buddhism distinguishes between forms of love which are but another variety of attachment and a kind of love which has the potential to overcome attachment and is fully compatible with complete non-attachment. If early Buddhists had not been convinced of the latter, they would not have been able to present the Buddha as someone who abandoned all forms of attachment but was nevertheless perfected in loving-kindness and compassion!

The distinction between clinging and non-clinging forms of love apparently rests on two essential criteria. True loving-kindness which accompanies detachment will 1) be selfless, i.e. concerned with the benefit of the other and not one's own; and 2) it will be non-differentiating, that is, it is directed towards friend and foe alike. As long as love is discriminative, as long as one loves the one and hates the other, attachment is involved: The one is loved because of the benefit deriving from him or her, and the other is rejected because of the opposite – so that there is attachment in both its positive and negative modes (see above p. 35). But even this discriminating, differentiating love can have a liberating aspect if and inasmuch a genuine element of selfless caring is present in it. The song just quoted above continues:

> If with an uncorrupted mind
> He pervades just one being
> With loving kindly thoughts,
> He makes some merit thereby.
>
> (Ireland, 1997, p. 169)

The ideal, however, remains the development of 'a compassionate mind towards all living beings' (ibid, p. 170). This is also expressed in the most famous among the early Buddhist songs in praise of love, the Mettā-Sutta (Sn 143–152):

> Just as a mother would protect her only child at the risk of her own life,
> Even so, let him cultivate a boundless heart towards all beings.
> Let his thoughts of boundless love pervade the whole world:
> Above, below and across without any obstruction, without any hatred, without any enmity.
>
> (Sn 149–150; Saddhatissa,1987, p. 16)

Here both of the criteria for non-attached love are combined: It should be as selfless as the love of a mother who would give her life for her child and it should be directed indiscriminately towards all beings. Not infrequently Buddhist scriptures stress the spiritual value of sacrificing ones life out of love for others. Particularly the stories about the Buddha's previous lives, the so-called Jātakas, relate that the 'Bodhisattva', that is, the person who is on the way to become a Buddha, has sacrificed his life several times and thereby developed his selfless compassion and love (e.g. Jat 12; 316, 407). Sacrificing one's life is seen as the culmination of the virtue of 'giving' (*dāna*) (see BCV 7:25).

There is however even more to say: Not only is there a form of love fully compatible with non-attachment, but indeed love and detachment need each other and modulate each other in a crucial way. They are more than merely compatible, they are complementary. Once more the point can be illustrated by Buddhaghosa's reflections on the development of a loving mind.

Loving-kindness, as we saw, belongs to a set of four mental qualities, called the four 'divine abidings' or the four 'immeasurables': 'loving-kindness', 'compassion', 'sympathetic joy' and 'equanimity'. Buddhaghosa explains that for each of these states or qualities there is a 'near enemy' and a 'far enemy'. The 'far enemy' is simply the diametrical opposite; the 'near enemy', on the other hand, is a state which on first sight resembles the genuine quality in some respects; in fact however it is still an 'enemy', a very different and no less opposing attitude. In the case of loving-kindness, for instance, Buddhaghosa identifies the 'far enemy' as 'ill will'. Its 'near enemy', however, is 'greed', which at times can indeed look like genuine love but in fact pursues a very different interest. Equanimity's 'far enemy' is comprised of greed and resentment – the two forms of attachment which at the same time are the near and far enemies of 'loving-kindness'. Equanimity thus protects loving-kindness against both its enemies, and it follows then that loving-kindness needs to be accompanied by equanimity. Equanimity's near enemy is worldly indifference: the unconcerned mind of someone unaware of what distinguishes merit from demerit, someone insensitive to both good and evil. Clearly loving-kindness, together with insight, protects equanimity against this blasé, self-satisfied attitude – its 'near enemy'. Hence loving-kindness and equanimity are dependent upon each other so as to prevent their degeneration into greed or indifference respectively. This one mental attitude

– of love tempered with equanimity or equanimity amplified by love – is concretely expressed in the two complementary qualities of compassion and sympathetic joy: compassion in face of others' suffering (and more specifically: one's wish to expunge it) and sympathetic joy in the face of their (spiritual) wellbeing (see Vism 9:94–5).

Buddhaghosa sums up the complementarity of loving-kindness and equanimity with the following description of 'Great Beings':

> They are unshakably resolute upon beings' welfare and happiness. Through unshakeable loving-kindness they place them first (before themselves). Through equanimity they expect no reward.
>
> (Vism 9:124, Ñāṇamoli, 1999, p. 318)

The 'Great Beings' he has in mind are of course the Buddha and all who follow in his footsteps. Buddha's perfection in non-attachment and compassion proves that loving involvement and detachment complement each other and also demonstrates how this complementarity works. The Buddha functions as the great example of Buddhism's attempt to take up the fundamental insight of the Śramaṇas, that is, the need to become free from attachment, and make it fruitful for a spirituality which is at the same time lovingly involved with this world for the benefit of all beings.

For further reading: Aronson (1980); Dharmasiri (1989); Harris (1997); Harvey (2000); Küng (1996); Runzo and Martin (2001).

8

The Buddhist Community

The Fourfold Community

The standard formula a Buddhist uses in declaring him- or herself a Buddhist is the so-called 'triple refuge' (see Mv 1:12:4 and AN 8:25):

> I take my refuge in the Buddha,
> I take my refuge in the Dharma,
> I take my refuge in the Saṅgha.

Now what precisely is this 'Saṅgha' to which the Buddhist turns for 'refuge'? The literal meaning of *saṅgha* is simply 'group'. But as used in the Buddhist tradition the term has at least three meanings: In a *broad sense* the term designates the 'fourfold community' (*catuṣ pariṣad*), which is to say: monks (*bhikṣus*; Pāli: *bhikkhus*), nuns (*bhikṣunīs*; Pāli: *bhikkhuṇīs*), laymen (*upāsaka*) and laywomen (*upāsikā*). The Buddha-legend relates that when the Buddha resisted Māra's temptation to leave the world, he declared that he would not pass away before the Dharma was well proclaimed, firmly established and flourishing together with this fourfold community, a community which would follow the Path and competently instruct others (see DN 16:3:34–5; see also DN 29:14–5, see above page 23f).

One important canonical text (AN 4:7) explicitly uses the term '*saṅgha*' in this broad sense, while at the same time calling attention to those virtues which make 'monks' or 'nuns', 'laymen' or 'laywomen', true disciples: If they are 'wise, disciplined, experienced (or: confident), deeply learned, bearers of the Dharma, who live in accordance with the Dharma', then they are an 'ornament' and 'light of the Saṅgha'.

At least in the early Buddhist scriptures, however, the term '*saṅgha*' more often than not refers in a more *specific sense* only to the ordained members of the institutionalised orders: the monks and nuns. In this sense, the term can designate either a particular local monastic community or the universal community of monks and nuns of all times and all places.

Yet there is a *third meaning* in which the term refers to something like the 'ideal Saṅgha', sometimes called the 'Noble Saṅgha' (*ārya-saṅgha*). This Saṅgha includes everyone who has attained one of the four stages of saintliness, from the lowest stage of the 'stream-enterer', who will definitely achieve enlightenment within a maximum of seven more lives, up to the *arhat* (Pāli: *arahat*) who is already enlightened. In some sense this ideal Saṅgha is smaller than the institutionalised monastic Saṅgha, for not every monk or nun was regarded as belonging to the group of saints. At the same time however the ideal Saṅgha is larger than the institutional order, for lay-people too can achieve all four stages of saintliness – and perhaps the ideal Saṅgha is not even limited to those who are nominally 'Buddhists' (depending on how Buddhists assess other religions; see below Chapter 15). Probably it is the Saṅgha in this third sense to which a Buddhist goes for 'refuge' and in which he or she puts his confidence (see Gombrich, 1988, p. 2; Prebish, 1996, p. 3).

Whether in its broadest or in its ideal sense, the purpose of the Saṅgha is twofold: to live in accordance with the Dharma for one's own salvation, and to spread the Dharma for the benefit of all others. The purpose of the Saṅgha in its institutionalised monastic form is to provide the optimal conditions for both purposes: for the inner spiritual progress of each individual member and for the propagation of Buddha's message for the welfare of the world. This double purpose is also reflected in the somewhat surprising self-designation of the monastics as both, 'Śramaṇas and Brāhmaṇas'. But from the Buddhist perspective they pursue the śramaṇic ideal of an individual search for salvation via an ascetic lifestyle (which, however, they tempered considerably). And by presenting themselves as the 'true Brahmans' they bolster their claim to be custodians and teachers of the Dharma via an association with the brahmanical tradition.

The twofold purpose of the Saṅgha is also clearly expressed in the narratives surrounding its foundation. After his first sermon the Buddha encouraged his disciples to live the 'holy life for the complete extinction of suffering' (Mv 1:6:32–4) and not long afterwards he commissioned his disciples to spread the Dharma:

> Go ye now, O Bhikkhus, and wander, for the gain of the many, for the welfare of the many, out of compassion for the world, for the good, for the gain, and for the welfare of gods and men. Let not two of you go the same way. Preach, O Bhikkhus, the doctrine which is glorious in the beginning, glorious in the middle, glorious in the end, in the spirit and in the letter; proclaim a consummate, perfect, and pure life of holiness.
>
> (Mv 1:11:1; Rhys Davids and Oldenberg, 1881, p. 112f)

The lay-followers participate in this twofold purpose of the Saṅgha to the extent that the conditions of their lives permit. That is, they focus on the cultivation of morality, thereby helping themselves as much as their neighbours, and they are encouraged to practice *dāna:* 'giving' or 'generosity'. Through giving they train themselves in non-attachment; through giving to the order they indirectly participate in the promotion of the Dharma – the order's principal obligation. Lay-followers however are meant not only to finance the spread of the Dharma but also to spread the Dharma themselves, encouraging others to live in accordance with it (see AN 8:25). At times some were even teaching the Dharma to monks (see AN 8:21).

The life of the order is governed by the *vinaya*, the 'rule' or 'discipline'. Through these regulations the order was provided with the institutionalised framework which should secure its effective survival beyond the lifetime of the Buddha, which, according to the canonical scriptures, had been the Buddha's own intention. Living in conformity with the monastic rule was seen as ensuring that 'this holy life may continue and be established for a long time for the profit and happiness of the many out of compassion for the world ...' (DN 29:17; Walshe, 1995 p. 432). Shortly before his death the Buddha reminded his disciples that the Dharma and the monastic discipline will be their 'teacher' after his passing (see DN 16:6:1), and if the monks live accordingly, the world will not lack in enlightened persons (see DN 16:5:27). A decisive step towards the institutional autonomy of the order was taken when the Buddha transferred the authority to ordain new monks to the order itself, a step which he took at a very early stage (see Mv 1:12:1–4).

The concern for the order's future survival and prosperity testifies to the awareness that success of this kind cannot be taken for granted. Indeed, there are a number of passages which directly express the expectation that the order will, or might, decline as a consequence of spiritual deterioration: The number of rules will increase (as in fact they did) but the number of those who attain enlightenment will decrease; heresies will endanger the knowledge of the true Dharma; the fourfold community will lose their reverence for the Buddha, for the Dharma, for the Saṅgha, for training and meditation (SN 16:13; AN 1:19; 4:116) and will lack in mutual respect (AN 5:201; 7:56). Usually these concerns are expressed as a warning together with the pledge that the opposite attitudes will surely guarantee the Dharma's flourishing and the Saṅgha's survival.

There is, though, another tradition which asserts that the decline of the Saṅgha and therefore of the (understanding and teaching of the) Dharma are consequences of the establishment of the nuns' order. According to this tradition, Buddha's disciple Ananda, on behalf of Buddha's aunt Mahāprajāpatī, persuaded the Buddha to admit women to the order despite the Buddha's initial reluctance. Ananda had asked him if women were able to attain the four stages of saintliness, a question which implies that if so, then they would thereby become members of the ideal Saṅgha. After the Buddha confirmed that this is possible, Ananda argued that women should then also be admitted to formal ordination. The Buddha consented but prophesied that the order would become weaker as a result, and would now endure only five hundred rather than one thousand years (see Cv 10:1–2).

This narrative illustrates just how revolutionary the establishment of the female order was. An equivalent did exist among the Jains, but within official Brahmanism women played no significant religious role. On one occasion, when King Pasenadi, a supporter of the Buddha, was displeased with the birth of a daughter, the Buddha told him that a woman may turn out to be better than a man, more wise and more virtuous (see SN 3:16). But as an obvious concession to the patriarchal spirit of the time, the female order was ranked below the order of monks and burdened with additional rules (some of these rules, however, undoubtedly worked to protect the women). Nevertheless, the life and function of the nuns' order were basically the same as the monks'. Some nuns (though not very many) were regarded as excellent teachers of the Dharma and their words recorded in the canon (see MN 44; SN 5:10). Several testimonies from among the early nuns reveal how much they experienced their monastic life as a personal liberation, at times from quite ordinary forms of *duḥkha*:

> O free, indeed! O gloriously free
> Am I in freedom from three crooked things: –
> From quern, from mortar, from my crookback'd lord!
> (Thig 11, Rhys Davids, 1909, p. 15; see also Thig 23)

Life in the Order

Buddhist monastic life runs on a few simple principles which follow from the twofold purpose of the Saṅgha: On the one hand, it provides an opportunity to the individual member for learning, studying and exploring the Dharma, for perfecting morality even in minor and inconspicuous aspects of one's conduct, and for practicing intensely and persistently the various forms of meditation. In short, monastic life should help to realise the three basic principles of the Noble Eightfold Path: insight, morality, concentration. These are regarded as the three fields of monastic 'training' (*śikṣā*), and according to one text all the monastic rules are contained within these three principles (see AN 3:85). It is for the purpose of this training that the monk or nun lives a life of (relative) poverty and moderation, of chastity and a binding commitment to the rules of the community. On the other hand, the life of the order is organised in such a way that its members have to maintain contact with the Buddhist laity and, in fact, with the world, thus ensuring ample opportunities for preaching and teaching and thereby spreading the Dharma.

To enter the order one must be at least seven or eight years old, though at such a young age only a lower form of ordination can be received. Full ordination requires a minimum age of twenty (counted from conception). Children need the consent of their families, and some groups of people were excluded from ordination, as for example active soldiers, slaves who were not set free by their lords, or thieves and people in debt. It appears that these regulations were meant to prevent the order from becoming an easy escape for such persons. Other groups excluded from ordination include persons with contagious diseases, severe handicaps or no clearly identifiable sex. Caste, however, was irrelevant and according to Buddhist understanding one's caste was discarded with the entry into the order (see AN 8:19) – a feature of tremendous significance in a society where religion was almost entirely dependent on caste and where official Brahmanism excluded people of the lowest caste from the study of the Dharma.

When entering the order the postulant makes no lifelong vows but commits him- or herself to live by the monastic rules so long as he or she has not formally 'disrobed', that is, left the order. Practically, however, the expectation in early Buddhism was that one would spend the rest of one's life within the order. As an exterior sign of renouncing one's former life in the world, the head hair is shaved off and the monastic robe taken on. Originally the robe was meant to be made from old, cast-off pieces of cloth, but this custom fell into disuse rather early on. Usually the lay-followers donate the robes – but in order to commemorate the early practice the fabric is cut up into pieces and then stitched together again!

The number and kind of personal belongings was confined to a few items: a three-piece robe (for nuns: five-piece), a begging bowl, razor, needle, belt, water-strainer and, if needed, medicine. Occasionally a few more items were added (a toothpick and a staff, for instance), and in more recent times such articles as sandals, an umbrella, a bag, towel, books, a watch, mobile phone, etc. Nonetheless the monk or nun had and has to learn being 'content with little' (see Gombrich, 1988, p. 88). Yet compared to more radical Śramaṇa-groups who sometimes had no belongings at all, not even clothing, this represented a fairly moderate form of asceticism.

In the early days of the order, the monks and nuns spent most of their time without any permanent lodging, wandering from village to village and sleeping outside, thereby pursuing the śramaṇic ideal of 'homelessness' while at the same time spreading the Dharma. Only during the rainy season should they stay in one place for a three-month retreat. The buildings for these retreats were donated by wealthy lay-supporters and soon developed into permanent monasteries, where monks and nuns could dwell in simple rooms or huts.

Food had to be received from the lay-supporters. Originally the monks went to a nearby village, collected what was given and consumed it before noon, because after noon no more solid food was permitted. Soon though it became the custom to invite monks and nuns for meals. The monks were not permitted to decline these invitations, for they were regarded as excellent opportunities for the religious instruction of the laity. With the emergence of permanent monasteries, lay-followers either brought food to the monasteries or set up annexed kitchens where they prepared meals for the monastics (though the traditional alms-round is still frequently practiced, particularly in Theravāda-Buddhist countries). The strict dependence of the monastics on the laity drew both parts of the Buddhist community closely together: Laypeople were given the opportunity to sustain the life and mission of the order through their donation of food, clothing, lodging, medicine – of everything that the order needed to exist; monks and nuns were given the opportunity to fulfil their duty to and in society by preaching the Dharma and serving as spiritual counsellors in all fundamental issues of life.

The Buddha permitted the practice of some more rigorous forms of ascetic austerities without making them obligatory (see MN 5; 113; AN 5:181–190). Most of these practices involve a stricter interpretation and performance of the usual monastic discipline regarding food, clothing and sleep – eating only one single meal per day, for example, or living exclusively on self-collected food, wearing only a robe made of old rags, sleeping only outside, sleeping only in a sitting position, etc. Practicing these austerities was generally restricted to a limited period of special training, and the Buddhist texts bluntly warn that those who undertake them might possibly do so only in order to impress people, or out of folly and foolishness (see MN 113; AN 5:118). In any event, even these rather exceptional exercises were modest compared with the various forms of self-mortification common among Śramaṇas.

The organisation of monastic life was able to get by with an astonishingly minimal hierarchy. Local groups of the order more or less administered themselves. The Buddhist scriptures frequently affirm the principle that the monks should act and make decisions 'in harmony' or unanimously (see DN 16:1:6). Disrupting that harmony, deliberately instigating division, or even merely calling attention to a matter which could cause division is treated by the rule as a serious offence. Any work which was necessary and yet prohibited for monastics (in particular anything that involved the handling of money) was carried out by lay-assistants associated with the monastery. The basic hierarchical principle among the monastics was age – not in terms of biological years but in terms of the years one has been in the order! The only other hierarchical principle was that the order of the monks was ranked in every regard as superior to the order of the nuns. A crucial element within the monastic structure was the office of the preceptor. Every new member of the order had to become the disciple of a particular preceptor who functioned as an overall teacher and supervisor, not only instructing the disciples as to all aspects of the monastic life but also introducing them to meditation practice. Generally, communal interaction among the members of the order was to be characterised by 'showing loving-kindness to their fellows in acts of body, speech and thought, both in public and in private' (DN 16:1:11; see Walshe, 1995, p. 234, modified) and by sharing the little they have, even that which is put into their alms bowl (see MN 104:21)

The rules and regulations structuring the details of monastic life were collected in so-called *prātimokṣa-sūtras* which display slight differences in content and number among the various early Buddhist schools. Theravāda-Buddhism counts 227 rules for monks and 311 for nuns. These were grouped into classes according to their gravity, which in practical terms meant the violation of rules of different classes led to different types of sanctions. While the transgression of the lesser or minor rules only requires confession, there are four cardinal rules whose violation leads to lifelong expulsion from the order: (1) sexual intercourse, also with an animal; (2) stealing; (3) the killing or encouraging the killing of a human being, also suicide; (4) falsely claiming the possession of supernatural powers (even an authentic claim of that sort was prohibited, though its violation is seen as a lesser offence). These four grave offences are identical in all the monastic codes of the different Buddhist schools. They represent the most serious violations of the first four of the ten monastic precepts (*śīlas*; compare above p. 66), a false claim to higher spiritual attainments constituting the grossest form of mendaciousness for a monk or nun, whose whole life should be a testimony to the truth of the Dharma. Other serious transgressions of the rules lead to temporary suspension or demotion of various duration. Most of the rules are concerned with appropriate, decent and peaceful moral behaviour, with limiting one's private possessions, adhering to the monastic lifestyle as regards eating, dressing, sleeping, etc., and particularly avoiding even the faintest impression of sexual relations. On all full- and half-moon days the local monastic Saṅgha was to assemble for the ceremonial profession of the 'purity of the order'. On these occasions the rules were read out and the Saṅgha asserted that none of its members was currently violating any of the rules, which of course presupposes that all the actual violations had already been dealt with.

Development and Transformations

By and large the institution of the monastic Saṅgha stood the test of history and fulfilled its twofold purpose. But it also underwent some significant and in part drastic transformations. The reasons for these developments vary, and may reflect doctrinal changes and/or built-in structural problems. Only a few of them can be indicated here (for a good overview see Harvey, 1998, pp. 217–243).

All forms of Buddhism have retained some kind of clergy which in one way or another can be traced back to the ancient monastic order. At least the ideal of a lifelong, celibate monastic existence under the rules of the *vinaya* has been preserved in Theravāda countries, as well as in parts of Tibetan, Chinese, Vietnamese and Korean Buddhism. But even under these more traditional circumstances, monasticism underwent considerable changes, which are, however, even more drastic in other parts of the Buddhist world.

The division of the Buddhist community into laity and monastics was not without its generic problems. There are texts in the Pāli Canon which testify to the awareness that some of those who took up 'homelessness' were inwardly still clinging to the world, while others who still lived in the world nevertheless achieved a remarkable state of inner freedom (see AN 4:138). Though monastic life was generally regarded as more conducive towards enlightenment, the canon did not deny that lay-followers too could achieve all four stages of saintliness, including the enlightened state of an *arhat* (see AN 6:119–139). In the Milindapañha however this is explained as the fruit of rigorous monastic training in their previous lives (see Mph 6:9f). And should a layperson achieve enlightenment he/she will either enter the order immediately or die on that same day (see Mph 4:7:7)! Of course the conclusions to be drawn from all this are that there are no enlightened lay-followers and that monastic life is the only way to enlightenment. Yet how plausible were such claims in the face of unmistakeable signs of decadence among the monastics, and outstanding examples of Buddhist spirituality among the lay-people? Moreover, does not the heart of Buddhism, the spiritual fusion of wisdom and compassion, of inner detachment and loving involvement, almost necessarily imply the overcoming of the distinction between laypeople and monastics, at least in so far as this would entail a two-class religious system?

As a matter of historical fact, this overcoming of distinctions did indeed occur in a number of instances. Particularly under the influence of Mahāyāna Buddhism several features which strikingly highlighted the difference between monastics and laity – celibacy for instance, or the banning of agricultural and other forms of manual labour or work, including even martial activity – were dropped in branches of Tibetan, Chinese, Korean and Japanese Buddhism. Often the monastic rules were liberalised and simplified with the argument that in the current era of marked decline strict observance is no longer possible. Other arguments were of a doctrinal nature, such as the idea that all dualistic distinctions are only of relative value, or Shinran's (1173–1262; see below p. 149ff) conviction that the limitlessly gracious nature of ultimate reality not only transcends but necessarily removes any form of religious segregation. Such ideas played an important role in the transformation of the Buddhist monk or nun into a kind of cleric who still fulfils certain religious functions but is no longer viewed as essentially different and no longer lives essentially differently from a lay-person. In Japanese Zen Buddhism the monasteries have become seminaries, as it were, preparing the 'monks' for their profession as temple priests. Their monastic, celibate lifestyle is obligatory only during the limited period of their training in the monastery.

Even in Theravāda-Buddhist countries there are developments which have narrowed the gap between monastics and laity. The Buddhist revival of the 19th and 20th centuries, sometimes referred to as 'Buddhist Modernism' or 'Protestant Buddhism', particularly inspired the laity to incorporate the study of doctrine and the practice of meditation into their own spiritual lives, making this thereby less different from that of the monastics. In some

Theravāda countries it has become a tradition for lay-persons to spend a certain period of their lives (usually when they are either very young or rather old) in a monastery. Today temporary monkhood is becoming increasingly popular among practicing lay-Buddhists (Eastern as well as Western) who want to enrich their spirituality through an intense period of monastic training without having to give up their lay-status entirely.

A somewhat contrary development, however, can be observed with regard to the nuns' order. The regulations of the *vinaya* stipulate that the valid ordination of a nun can be carried out only by a group of fully ordained nuns with the consent of fully ordained monks (whereas male ordination is performed by monks alone). In all Theravāda countries the lines of succession which were to guarantee valid ordinations have collapsed several times. Yet while it has always been possible to reintroduce the full ordination for monks, it has not been possible for nuns. This is not to say that there can be no nuns in Theravāda countries. There are, in fact, several thousands. However they live their monastic life without a full, valid ordination. On the one hand, this gives them more freedom to establish and creatively modify those rules they regard as meaningful in the present world. On the other hand, their 'incomplete' status deprives them of the full public recognition and numerous privileges and legal protections which are accorded the monks. The status of Tibetan nuns is also controversial since it seems that in Tibet the order of nuns was established by monks alone, which would invalidate the female ordination – hence the current efforts to ensure a valid, recognised ordination for the existing female orders within Tibetan and Theravāda Buddhism via ordination ceremonies performed with the help of nuns from Taiwan and Korea whose ordination is largely unquestioned. Whether these attempts to introduce (in the case of the Tibetan nuns) or reintroduce (in the case of the Theravāda nuns) a fully ordained status will find the unreserved endorsement of their male counterparts remains to be seen.

The more the Buddhist order succeeded in spreading the Dharma (and thereby transforming societies into Buddhist civilisations), the more powerful it became. In a number of Asian countries Buddhist monasteries developed into centres of learning and education, of culture and art. But they also developed into places of tremendous economical power and political influence. Through the donations of the laity and, not infrequently, royal patronage monasteries became wealthy landlords, owning large estates including whole villages which had to work for them. In some countries the monasteries became centres of wide-ranging commercial activities. In Tibet, China, Korea, and Japan monasteries even maintained their own armies at times in order to defend their economical and political interests or those of their royal patrons. In Theravāda countries the major monasteries were often closely tied to the reigning monarchs by direct family links. In Sri Lanka a royal decree even set up a quasi caste system for determining who was to be admitted to which order.

Many of these developments certainly had a corrupting impact on the more ascetic aspects of the Buddhist monastic ideal and contributed to a gradual flattening of the difference between monastics and laity. This process however cannot be properly understood as simply a form of decadence. In a sense, some of the afore mentioned developments were the result of the order's genuine success. The Saṅgha became influential, wealthy, powerful (and therefore susceptible to corruption) precisely because it had succeeded so well in focussing the attention of whole societies on the Buddha's Dharma. That this process is inevitably accompanied by its own challenges and ambiguities is also quite evident when we look at the relation between Buddhism and politics.

For further reading: Gard (1961); Gombrich (1988); Dhirasekera (1982); Prebish (1996); Wijayaratna (1990).

9

Buddhism and Politics

Early Buddhist Concepts of Political Rule

The Buddhist canon contains the following mythological account of the origin of political rule (see DN 27). In primordial times, when the preceding world-system had collapsed and the new world was about to emerge (see above p. 51), all beings were alike and dwelled as luminous, mind-made spirits in a heavenly realm. The earth was simply a vast sea without any light. After a long time some earth-like substance appeared on the water, as skin forms on hot milk cooling down. It smelled and tasted delicious. One being, of a greedy nature, sampled the substance and soon all other beings followed suit; they ate and ate and craved ever more. As a result they lost their luminous appearance, while sun, moon and stars emerged. Over a long period the beings became coarser and coarser, developing bodies, some of beautiful, others of ugly appearance; the beautiful ones grew proud and arrogant. Other types of food came into being and the bodies changed even more. With the appearance of wild rice, the beings developed male and female bodies, leading to passion and lust. Now they started living in houses so that they could conceal their sexual activities. And whereas they used to live on just the amount of rice they gathered for the day, they now began gathering more, storing and finally cultivating it. With the development of privately owned rice-fields, stealing arose and as a result of that, lying, quarrels and violence.

> Then those beings came together and lamented the arising of these evil things among them: taking what was not given, censuring, lying and punishment. And they thought: 'Suppose we were to appoint a certain being who would show anger where anger was due, censure those who deserve it, and banish those who deserve banishment! And in return, we would grant him a share of the rice.' So they went to the one among them who was the handsomest, the best looking, the most pleasant and capable, and asked him to do this for them in return for a share of the rice, and he agreed.
>
> (DN 27:20; Walshe, 1995, p. 413)

Some other beings however decided to 'put aside evil and unwholesome things' within themselves. They left the villages, lived on alms-food, dwelt in simple forest huts, and began to meditate. This was the origin of the Brahmans, while those among them who did not succeed in meditation went back to the villages and composed the Vedas.

This myth (often called the Aggañña Myth, after the name of the Pāli Sutta which includes it) points up central elements of the early Buddhist concept of society. The problem of violence stems from human craving, the root of all evil, and there are two basic responses to the problem: On the social level, the response takes the form of the human – not divine (!) – institution of a ruler who is given a monopoly on the use of force so as to contain violence and guarantee peace and justice. On the individual level, the response lies in the personal determination to eradicate the roots of evil within oneself, a religious ideal which the Buddhists see realised in their own version of the Śramaṇa life and which they regard as betrayed in the institutionalised Brahman caste. These two responses to the problem of evil indicate the two focal points of all further developments in Buddhist political reflection: How should the political ruler ideally accomplish his task of suppressing social evil? And how does the Buddhist community, as the 'true Brahmans', relate to the political authority?

Causal thinking – which we find in the Four Noble Truths as well as in the principle of Dependent Origination (see above pp. 31ff and 36ff) and according to which suffering can be eradicated by removing its causes – was also applied in early Buddhist reflections on politics. An important text explains social discord and unrest as the result not simply of greed or craving but also of poverty. The king had failed to provide for the needy, and thus 'from the not giving of property to the needy, poverty became rife, from the growth of poverty, the taking of what was not given increased, from the increase of theft, the use of weapons increased, from the use of weapons, the taking of life increased …' (DN 26:14; Walshe, 1995, p. 399f). Accordingly, another text explicitly recommends that a king should not react to growing criminality and social unrest by increasing punishments, but by improving the economy through sensible investments:

> Suppose Your Majesty were to think: 'I will get rid of this plague of robbers by executions and imprisonment, or by confiscation, threats and banishment', the plague would not be properly ended. … To those in the kingdom who are engaged in cultivating crops and raising cattle, let your Majesty distribute grain and fodder; to those in trade, give capital; to those in government service assign proper living wages. Then those people, being intent on their own occupations, will not harm the kingdom. Your Majesty's revenues will be great, the land will be tranquil and not beset by thieves, and the people, with joy in their hearts, will play with their children, and will dwell in open houses.
>
> (DN 5:11; Walshe, 1995, p. 135f)

Once again the text takes a polemical swipe at Brahmanism: Supporting the needy is a far better thing for a king to do than financing the costly – and sanguinary – sacrifices prescribed by the brahmanical tradition.

Combating criminality and other social problems by removing their causes is not only the task of the ruler. One of the Jātakas (stories about the Buddha's former lives) tells how the Buddha, during his life as the young man Magha, became the leading figure of a social development movement. Stirred by the desolate social situation of the local community he encouraged the people to build a community house, construct roads and irrigation systems and support those who were in need. As a result both the consumption of liquor and the overall crime-rate decreased – a development which brought the social activists into conflict with the local authorities, who had hitherto profited handsomely from the various fines they were accustomed to impose. Under false charges Magha and his companions were imprisoned and sentenced: They were to be trampled to death by an elephant. The elephant, however, sensed the good spirit of the delinquents and refused to kill them. Thus the king wanted to know what spell they had used to bewitch the elephant. Magha replied that their only 'spell' was to keep the precepts, develop a loving mind and put it to use in practical social work (see Jat 31). In this story the Buddha, alias Magha, acts as an exemplary Buddhist layman. And the Buddhist expectation – or should we say 'hope' – was that rulers would behave in the same way. In other words the ideal ruler should live and act as a pious Buddhist layman.

Of course Buddhists were fully aware that this is not what one would generally expect from a king. Indeed, kings are often included in standard lists of serious threats, together with fire and water, robbers, enemies and unscrupulous heirs (e.g. AN 5:41, MN 13:10). Yet precisely in light of the potentially dangerous nature of kings, Buddhism proclaimed the ideal of the '*cakravartin*' – the 'universal ruler' who is at the same time a 'Dharma-King': a 'just and righteous ruler' who honours the Dharma and manages his government in accordance with the Dharma (see AN 3:14; 5:133). His righteousness as both king and Buddhist lay-follower is described by the following stereotypical list of ten virtues: generosity, morality, spirit of sacrifice, honesty, mildness, spiritual discipline, peaceableness, non-violence, forbearance, and non-offensiveness (see also Collins, 1998, pp. 460–6).

The Buddhist ideal of kingship is summarised in the following instruction given by a king to his heir concerning the duties of a *cakravartin*:

> Well then, my dear: depend on the Dharma, honour and respect it, praise it, revere and venerate it, have Dharma as your flag, Dharma as your banner, govern by Dharma, and arrange rightful shelter, protection and defense for your family, for the army, for your noble warriors, for Brahmin householders, for town dwellers and countryfolk, for Śramaṇas and Brāhmaṇas, for animals and birds. Let no wrongdoing

> take place in your territory, if there are poor people in your territory, give them money. The Śramaṇas and Brāhmaṇas in your territory, my dear, who abstain from drunkenness and negligence, who practice forbearance and gentleness, each one conquering himself, calming himself, quenching himself – you should go to them from time to time and ask 'What, sir, is good? What is not good? What is blameworthy, what blameless? What is to be practiced, what not? Doing what would lead to suffering and harm for me in the long run? Doing what would lead to happiness and benefit for me in the long run?' You should listen to them, and avoid what is bad; you should take up what is good and do that.
>
> (DN 26:8; transl. modified after Collins, 1998, p. 604)

All the major themes of Buddhist kingship are addressed here: The king should honour the Dharma and govern in accordance with it. To do this he needs to seek the advice of the 'Śramaṇas and Brāhmaṇas' – i.e. the Buddhist Saṅgha. He has to protect all people in his country and also all animals. He must not tolerate any wrongdoing. He must support the poor. This will, at least in the long run, be of great benefit to him.

For centuries these points have formed the foundation for Buddhist political ideas. Buddhist kings strove (with more or less seriousness) to follow the ideal of the *cakravartin,* and were encouraged by the Saṅgha to do so (see Bechert, 1966ff; Tambiah, 1976). Two Mahāyāna scriptures, particularly influential in China, Korea and Japan: the 'Sūtra of the Golden Light' (*Suvarṇaprabhāsa*) and the 'Sūtra for the Humane Kings' (*Jên-wang Ching*), promise that honouring the Dharma, observing its ideals and protecting the Saṅgha will be the best means for a king to protect his state against all calamities, whether natural disasters, wars, plundering or whatever (see Orzech, 1998). The king's religious status was generally seen as that of the leading lay-follower, the first among the faithful laity. Under Mahāyāna influence – though by no means only in Mahāyāna-Buddhist countries – he was accorded the status of a Bodhisattva, that is, one who is on his way to becoming a Buddha and acts only for the welfare of all others (see Chapter 10). In cases of serious conflict between the Buddhist order and the king, the strongest (though rarely used) way for the Saṅgha to express its discontent consisted in the formal act of 'overturning the alms bowl', thereby symbolically demonstrating that they no longer accepted the king as a lay-follower. In Tibet the fusion of Buddhism and politics went so far that worldly rule remained no longer in the hands of the first among the laity but became instead an office assigned to a monk – the Dalai Lama.

The question of whether Buddhism can or should have any genuine interest in politics, or whether this runs counter to its true or original nature, is a subject of ever-recurring debate among Western scholars. I believe this to be a more or less artificial problem. Buddhism is and has always been interested in politics for the same reasons and to the same extent as it is interested in ethics. Morally good behaviour, whether in the private or in the social realm, is beneficial to one's own spiritual development and to the welfare of one's fellow beings. And behaviour is morally good if, in line with the Dharma, it contributes to the reduction or containment of suffering.

The idea that mundane rule should be administered in accordance with the Dharma is, of course, fairly vague. What precisely does this mean when it comes to crucial political questions concerning the use of violence, the economic system, the rights of citizens and – quite fundamentally – the form of government? For the remainder of this chapter I will touch briefly upon some of these issues.

Buddhism and Violence

As we saw in the chapter on Buddhist Ethics (see Chapter 7) right conduct in thought, word and deed is characterised as peaceful and non-harming behaviour. That violence cannot be ended by violence but only by its opposite, non-violence, is moreover a deeply-rooted Buddhist conviction. Hence we read in the Dhammapada:

> Victory breeds hatred, for the conquered is unhappy. He who has given up both victory and defeat, he, the contented, is happy.
>
> For hatred does not cease by hatred at any time: hatred ceases by love – this is an old rule.
>
> (Dhp 201; 5; Müller, 2000, pp. 24 and 1)

The classical commentary on the last verse underlines the point:

> A spot smeared with impurities like spit and nasal mucous cannot be cleaned and freed of smells (by) washing it with the same impurities; on the contrary, (thereby) that spot will be all the more unclean and foul-smelling. In the same way, one who reviles the reviler, one who strikes back at the striker, is not able to pacify hatred with hatred. On the contrary, one (thereby) creates more hatred still.
>
> (Carter and Palihawadana, 1987, p. 95f)

Reacting to violence non-violently is not the same as remaining passive. It is indeed a form of active involvement, but one that refrains from violent means. The Buddha-legend offers the famous example of how the Buddha 'tamed' the fierce bandit Aṅgulimāla 'without force and weapons' whereas the king with all his troops had been unable to get hold of him (see above p. 30f). Another narrative from the life of the Buddha recalls how the Buddha once managed, through active but non-violent intervention, to prevent a war over rare water resources by preaching the supreme value of human life, the disadvantages of war and the advantages of peace to the hostile parties (see Jat 536). Although several of the texts on the *cakravartin*, the ideal Buddhist monarch, describe him as having an army, Buddhists nevertheless fantasized the *cakravartin* skilfully ruling the country without any force other than the convincing power of the Dharma (e.g. DN 3:1:5; 14:1:31). Presumably however the Buddhists were fully aware of the utopian nature of this vision. In sub-ideal reality, a king can hardly refrain from using violent means in fighting crime, upholding law and order or defending the country. To declare that the only possible Buddhist view on right governance entails an across-the-board abstention from all physical force would ultimately mean the wholesale surrender of political power to those who do not care about Buddhist moral values. Many Buddhists then take a more realistic approach: The use of violence may be justified if not excessive, if restricted to unavoidable situations and motivated by benevolent intentions.

The *Sūtra of the Golden Light* lists several arguments as to why a king who rules in accordance with the Dharma must punish evil-doers and reward the good: In doing so, he demonstrates the basic principle of *karma:* good deeds lead to good results and bad deeds to bad ones. In this way the king establishes his subjects in good conduct. Moreover, if a king would overlook evil acts and leave the evil-doers unpunished, lawless conduct would become rife and the use of violence increase. By refraining from punishment, a king would thus support the evil-doers and become directly responsible for the growth of violence in his country. Ultimately, then, non-violence is not really an option, for non-violent rule would in fact lead to even more violence. Nevertheless the king's motives in employing force must be selfless and lawful, his judgements impartial and the punishment measured to the crime (see Emmerick, 1970, pp. 57–73).

Another Buddhist scripture addresses the issue of war. If a king is threatened by a foreign army he should first try to prevent the conflict with every conceivable non-violent strategy – showing kindness to the enemy, for instance, or even granting certain favours. He might also attempt to deter the enemy with a display of the strength of his own army. Should all peaceful means fail however he is justified in declaring war, but should do so with the sole motive of protecting his own people and should do his utmost to spare the lives of the hostile soldiers (see Zimmermann, 2000). The notion of Buddhism's 'state-protecting' function was carried so far that Buddhists not only supported and encouraged wars of national defence but even became actively involved in them. The entanglement of Zen Buddhism with Japanese militarism is by no means the only example of this, but a particularly prominent and recent one (see Victoria, 1997).

In questions of rebellion or tyrannicide right motivation is decisive. The history of Buddhism bears witness to a number of cases in which faithful Buddhists resorted to rebellious acts for diverse reasons. Well known are the examples of the Buddhist king Harṣavardhana (606–47) who could only come to power by overthrowing the unlawful ruler Śaśāṅka, or of the assassination of the Tibetan king Glang Dar-ma who had persecuted Buddhism grievously and was shot in 842 by a Buddhist monk. In China a number of rebellions were inspired by Buddhist ideas and sometimes even led by Buddhist monks. Justification for Buddhist involvement in violent upheavals and similar forms of political struggle was drawn from the basic conviction that there can be cases of 'compassionate killing' – certain situations in which the exercise of compassion requires the killing of an evil-doer, either to protect others from him or – more frequently – to protect him from accumulating even more bad karma (see Tatz, 1994, pp. 73–77).

If the defence of societal security, of law and order, of a country against foreign invaders or its own unrighteous rulers legitimises the use of violence – particularly when combined with an honest, compassionate, self-less motivation, seeking only the higher good – the same argumentation could also be extended to cases of religious wars or conflicts. There are indeed cases where major Buddhist scriptures or prominent figures have justified the use of violence for the defence of the true Dharma against any threat, real or imagined, coming from other religious communities or other Buddhist groups. For instance, the use of violence in the Sri Lankan ethnic conflict between the Buddhist Singhalese and the Hindu Tamils was, and still is, justified by the need to protect the true Dharma of Theravāda Buddhism (see Bartholomeusz, 2002). One might also cite the example of Nichiren (1222–82), the great Japanese propagator of the Lotus Sūtra, who declared that a monk unwilling to fight actively against those who would destroy the Dharma is himself an enemy of the Buddha's teaching. The protection of the true Dharma may require the use of 'swords, bows and arrows, and halberds and lances' (see Nichiren, 2003, pp. 282–287).

Although Buddhists have legitimised the conditional use of violence the emphasis has always been on acting as non-violently and peacefully as possible. As we saw, even the early texts on kingship teach that a king should not combat crime by increasing punishment but by eradicating its social and economic roots. One can point to examples in Buddhist history where Buddhist rulers refrained from the use of violence even when their country was attacked or usurped by hostile forces – the most prominent recent example being the Dalai Lama's non-violent stance in face of the Chinese occupation of Tibet. There are also cases where Buddhists did not kill a tyrant but protested non-violently against unjust rule even at the cost of their own lives, as in the case of the Burmese monk U Wisara who was imprisoned under British colonial rule in 1929 and died after more than a hundred days of a hunger strike protesting against the colonial government's treatment of Buddhists. Working non-violently towards peace is certainly a major concern of socially and politically engaged Buddhists (see Chappell, 1999).

Buddhism and Economy

In his widely read book *Small is Beautiful* (first published in 1973) the economist Ernst F. Schumacher opened the chapter on 'Buddhist Economics' with a statement as simple as it is remarkable: '"Right livelihood" is one of the requirements of the Buddha's Noble Eightfold Path. It is clear, therefore, that there must be such a thing as Buddhist economics' (Schumacher, 1993, p. 38).

Indeed, Buddhism from its inception has devoted special attention to economic issues – not only by making 'right livelihood' an indispensable element of the path to salvation, but also by assigning the support of the needy a prominent place among the fundamental tasks of the ideal ruler. As we have seen, 'right livelihood' is primarily defined as the avoidance of those sources of income which would entail the harming of sentient beings or suggest malicious intentions. Profit-making in itself, on the other hand, is not condemned as evil or unwholesome. Buddhist texts (see AN 5:41 or 10:91) assume that one can turn a handsome profit without necessarily being greedy. Wealth can be beneficial if the money is used for the well-being of one's family, employees, friends and, last but not least, the order. Members of the order, however, must themselves refrain from profit-making work, living a life of voluntary poverty (at least as individuals) and sharing what they and the community possess.

These two approaches, the monastic and the non-monastic, to the issue of profit and possessions have had a powerful impact on recent Buddhist discussions of economic issues. On the one hand, there is a tendency to view the monastic order as a kind of ideal community which can serve as a model for society-at-large. This is the view taken by the Sri Lankan Buddhist Vijayavardhana, for example, in his influential 1953 book, *The Revolt in the Temple:* The order, at least in principle, forms a classless society where all are equal and where communal ownership has replaced private property – in short, the order is a truly communist society. Vijayavardhana thus concludes that orthodox Communist theory (as distinct from some forms of its political realization) and ideal Buddhism are compatible. This was the position of many Buddhist reformers and activists in South- and Southeast Asia during the twentieth century, and a certain fellow-feeling between Buddhists and Communists based on supposedly common values underlay many of the political developments in that region. On the other hand, Buddhists have also sharply criticised the purely materialistic basis of Marxism together with the corresponding Communist attempts to wipe out all religions, including Buddhism. This is not however to imply that Buddhists would feel quite comfortable with the capitalist alternative, which meets with much scepticism or even open rejection, as fostering a consumerist and avaricious attitude. Frequently Buddhists are looking for a third way, a Buddhist 'Middle Way' in economics. Is such a way feasible?

Bhikkhu Buddhadāsa (1906–93), an eminent figure in Thailand's reform Buddhism, suggested a political model which he called 'Dictatorial Dharmic Socialism' (see Swearer, 1989, pp. 182–193). Both capitalism and communism according to Buddhadāsa are based on materialist greed, and the proper goal of a Buddhist political system must be to tackle this root-problem. Contentment and moderation, 'using only what is necessary', embody for Buddhadāsa the ideals of both the monastic and the non-monastic approaches to material possessions and must therefore be the guiding principles of Buddhist economic thought (see ibid. p. 172f). For Buddhadāsa, any system fostering greed and attachment, whether in the individual or in the collective, cannot gain Buddhist approval. The principle goal of politics needs to be the welfare of the *community*, the 'good of the whole', and not the personal interests of individuals – and therefore, he holds, a socialist system is preferable to any form of political or economic liberalism: Such a socialist system 'would not allow for class distinctions based on wealth. Nor would it permit anyone to accumulate private wealth at the expense of others' (ibid. p. 189). The government needs to be dictatorial in order to restrict the selfish interests of individuals, but the ruler must be someone who follows the ideal of the Buddhist king, exemplifying the ten royal virtues.

It is evident that Buddhadāsa's ideas are deeply rooted in the Buddhist tradition – in its basic soteriological beliefs, its ancient ideals of governance in accordance with Dharma and in its understanding of the Saṅgha as an ideal community. Hence it is not surprising that his ideas are influential among contemporary socially-engaged Buddhists. Further, they indicate what is perhaps the greatest challenge for Buddhist political reasoning: the confrontation with liberalism and its accompanying values.

Buddhism and Liberalism

For Buddhadāsa, a 'political system must first address the problem of defilement', that is, greed, hatred, delusion (see Swearer, 1989, p. 185). The critical question, of course, is how this is to be accomplished. Should politics be based on the insight that people *are* 'defiled', and thus seek forms of accommodation and adjustment through which the negative social effects of 'defilements' can be controlled and minimised? Or should politics be based on the attempt to *overcome* the defilements and educate people towards some form of ideal society? Buddhadāsa favoured the latter, holding that liberal democracy is to be rejected, as it not only fails to account for the defilements, but indeed rather fosters them. But Buddhadāsa's 'dharmic dictator' can address the problem of defilement only through intensified methods of public control and collective education. For Buddhadāsa these methods can be compared with those of a good parent. But could these methods actually be put into practice without considerable coercion and violence? This seems more than doubtful. (For a concrete scenario of such a society see the sketch by Buddhadāsa's coworker Bhikkhu Santikaro in Watts *et al.*, 1988, pp. 89–161.) The monks and nuns of the Buddhist order choose monastic life voluntarily, but if a political authority were to view Buddhist monastic life as a more or less exemplary model which should be obligatory for the whole of society, then the ideal would have to be imposed on all members of the society. What would then to be done about those who do not want to follow the Buddhist ideal or do not even see it as 'ideal'? This throws up three interrelated questions: How does Buddhism relate to democracy? Can Buddhism support the idea of human rights? Does Buddhism share the value of religious freedom?

These issues are by no means abstract. In Myanmar (Burma), for example, the democratic movement must continually defend itself against the allegation that democracy is not suited to the traditional standards of a Buddhist culture. In Sri Lanka the Buddhist 'National Heritage Party' pursues an anti-conversion legislation which is seen by many as a serious threat to religious freedom. The classical Buddhist political ideal of a monarchy under the Dharma does not tend to be compatible with democracy nor with the concept of a secular state in which no religion is prioritised. Yet it is also true that classical Buddhism does not understand monarchy as a divine institution: According to the Aggañña myth it is based on social convention and the first king is, in a sense, 'elected'. In principle, then, there is no reason why the task of upholding law and order could not be fulfilled by a democratically constituted body instead of a king. And presumably some Buddhists could accept the idea that the laws by which such a government rules must not be based exclusively in the Buddhist Dharma but could also rest upon a social consensus as long as certain indispensable ethical standards are guaranteed.

In this context the question of human rights emerges as the key issue: The right to freely choose one's political representatives as well as one's religion are non-negotiable points on the human rights agenda – an agenda serving to protect the individual, or more precisely: to protect individual self-determination and free agency against the powerful institutions of the collective – whether that be a state or a religion or even the family. Not only in its historical origins but also in its innermost core, the human-rights idea is inseparably bound to individualism, or better: to 'moral individualism' – and that is exactly what makes many Buddhists deeply suspicious. In light of its intrinsic connection with individualism the human-rights idea is seen as 'an incitement to clinging' (Junger, in Keown *et al.*, 1998, p. 61) and as 'strengthening the illusion of self' (Ihara, in ibid. p. 51). Liberalism, together with its concept of individual freedom, 'promotes selfish, egoistic interests', as Buddhadāsa says (Swearer, 1989, p. 184). Like-minded Buddhists offer an alternative view, a 'holistic' view, where everyone 'is playing one's part in a cooperative enterprise' (Ihara, in Keown *et al.*, 1998, p. 51) and where freedom means not free individual agency or self-determination, but 'in the most fundamental sense to be free from defilements' (Buddhadāsa in Swearer, 1989, 186).

Probably the most convincing response on the part of Buddhists supportive of the human rights idea recalls the strong Buddhist tradition of individual responsibility (see various contributions to Keown *et. al.*, 1998, and Perera, 1991). According to the law of karma each individual is responsible for his or her deeds and is heir to their consequences (see AN 5:161 and 10:48). Spiritual progress requires that one freely follow one's own insight (see AN 3:66). Of course this does not imply that one's own 'insight' is always right, but genuine insight is, by definition, individually appropriated and cannot be imposed. Hence the groundwork is already in place for a Buddhist endorsement of the ideas of individual self-determination and free agency – the very ideas found at the heart of the human rights concept. This means then that personal freedom must be respected even – and particularly – when the individual chooses not to follow Buddhist ideas or opts for a government not guided by the Buddhist Dharma. Thus the appropriate reaction to such a situation from a Buddhist perspective should be to use the classical means of teaching and expounding the Dharma so that it may disclose its persuasive power, while rejecting the temptation to use coercive force which would only deny the individual's right to self-determination.

Buddhists unanimously emphasise that the Dharma is not primarily about rights but about responsibilities, both individual and collective. This however must not contravene the idea of individual rights. The responsibility – actually the duty – to respect the rights of others is an essential component of the human rights idea. With this in mind, a recent attempt to arrive at a kind of declaration on Buddhism and Human Rights suggested the following basic statement:

> Those who have the good fortune to have a 'rare and precious human rebirth', with all its potential for awareness, sensitivity, and freedom, have a duty to not abuse the rights of others to partake of the possibilities of moral and spiritual flourishing offered by human existence. Such flourishing is only possible when certain conditions relating to physical existence and social freedom are maintained. Human beings, furthermore, have the obligation to treat other forms of life with the respect commensurate to their natures.
>
> (Keown *et. al.* 1998, p. 221)

That last sentence recalls one of the classical duties of a *cakravartin,* i.e. his obligation to protect not only the citizens of his country but also the 'animals and birds'. Surely a particularly Buddhist contribution to the human rights debate has been to insist that that the rights of individuals are limited not only by the rights of other humans, but also by the respect that we owe to other sentient beings.

For further reading: Benz (1966); Harvey (2000); Jones (1989); Keown et al. (1998); Schmidt-Leukel (2004a, 2004b); Schmithausen (1999); Tambiah (1976).

10

The Bodhisattva Ideal

The Mahāyāna

The second period in Buddhist history (0–500 CE; see above pp. 2f) saw the development of a movement calling itself 'Mahāyāna', the 'great' or 'eminent vehicle' on the path to salvation, which gradually introduced new doctrines and religious practices. The origins of the Mahāyāna 'are obscure in the extreme' (Williams, 1989, p. 25) and have generated much scholarly debate: Did the Mahāyāna emerge first and foremost among Buddhist lay-people – as a vehicle, fuelled by some anti-clerical sentiments, for their own religious interests and preferred cultic practices? Or did it grow out of the protests of the more ascetic followers of the Buddha, the forest-monks, against his less zealous followers in the cities and villages? Was it based on a devotional practice closely associated with the stūpa-cult, i.e. the veneration of Buddhist relics at the sacred sites of symbolic tombs, the stūpas? Or was it centred on the veneration of certain new scriptures, the great Mahāyāna sūtras? Did it develop from doctrinal positions of some pre-Mahāyāna schools – for example, the Mahāsaṅghikas or Sarvāstivādins? Or was it rather the result of persistent influence from and interaction with Hinduism (which was and still is the major allegation levelled by Theravādins)? To what extent can it be seen as an expansion of pre-Mahāyāna motifs? Or does it rather mark an essential break with 'original' Buddhism – a break of such magnitude that it can only be explained through foreign, non-Indian religious influence: from Zoroastrianism, for example, or other Western religions?

All these questions have been and still are the subject of much discussion. It seems that a case can be made for several of the proposed explanations – which is to say that the Mahāyāna may have various, even heterogeneous roots. In any event recent research appears to justify at least two important observations:

First, in the beginning the term 'Mahāyāna' did not signify a new sect or religious institution but rather a specific persuasion within the fourfold Saṅgha. Only after several centuries, and largely outside of India, did this new persuasion develop its own religious institutions and 'sects'. While it is true that some Mahāyāna scriptures even testify to violent tensions between followers of the Mahāyāna- and non-Mahāyāna teachings (see for example Lotus Sūtra 12; chapter 13 in the Kumārajīva-version); and while we know about fierce struggles between Mahāyāna- and Theravāda-oriented monasteries in Sri Lanka during the fourth century CE, there is also evidence that at times followers of both lines lived together side by side in the same monasteries under the same monastic rules.

Second, initially the term 'Mahāyāna' seems to have been 'nothing more and nothing less than a synonym for the "Bodhisattva path"' (Nattier, 2003, p. 195). The 'eminent vehicle' was simply the 'vehicle of the Bodhisattva', and thus to be a follower of the Mahāyāna did not mean that one belonged to a new form of Buddhism or some new Buddhist institution, but that one pursued the path of a Bodhisattva. Nevertheless this did indeed imply a changed understanding of the goal of the Buddhist path, a shift from the ideal of the enlightened Arhat to the ideal of becoming a Buddha. This was accompanied by wide-ranging developments in the idea of what a 'Buddha' really is and therefore of what the nature of all reality ultimately is. The Bodhisattva ideal together with the new understanding of the Buddha and ultimate reality is therefore the topic of this and the two subsequent chapters.

The Bodhisattva Career: Becoming a Buddha

Before his enlightenment, Siddhārtha Gautama was, technically speaking, not yet *a* or *the* Buddha. The Pāli canon speaks of Siddhārtha before his enlightenment not as the 'Buddha', but calls him the '*Bodhisattva*' (Pāli: '*Bodhisatta*'). While the etymology is not entirely clear, the most likely explanation presents the term as a composite of '*bodhi*' ('enlightenment') and '*sattva*' ('being'), that is, the 'enlightenment being' or perhaps the 'enlightenment hero'. In keeping with the Buddhist belief in rebirth, the Buddha's life as Siddhārtha Gautama was only the last in a long series of preceding existences. Both inside and outside the canonical scriptures a special genre of Buddhist writings, the Jātakas, developed in which stories from the Buddha's previous lives were recounted – not just his lives as a human being but also those as an animal or a celestial *deva*. Since 'Siddhārtha Gautama' was the name of the Buddha only in his final existence, a fixed term was needed indicating which of the figures in a given Jātaka was that particular person who in the future would become Gautama, the Buddha. The term '*Bodhisattva*' accomplished this nicely, thereby becoming the standard designation for a being on its way to becoming a Buddha. Thus the 'path of the *Bodhisattva*' is simply the path leading to Buddhahood. And the Jātakas – that rich corpus of vivid and highly popular tales so often depicted in early Buddhist art – provided the 'script' for the Bodhisattva path (see Nattier, 2003, pp. 144f, 186).

To embark on the Bodhisattva path then meant to strive for Buddhahood. The belief that this was at all possible was grounded in the pre-Mahāyāna conviction that Siddhārtha was only *one* Buddha, preceded by a number of previous Buddhas and succeeded by future Buddhas, the next one being Buddha Maitreya. While it was indeed claimed that in each world system there can be only one Buddha (AN 1:15), there were held to be countless world systems throughout both space and time. Accordingly, Mahāyāna texts repeatedly assert that there are 'more Buddhas as grains of sand at the Ganges'. Yet if there will be many more Buddhas in the future there must also be beings on the way to becoming those Buddhas – that is, there must be Bodhisattvas. Thus, it must, at least in principle, be possible to embark on the Bodhisattva path and strive to become a Buddha oneself.

The belief in a plurality of Buddhas makes Buddhahood a conceivable religious goal, yet a key question remains: Why were some Buddhists no longer satisfied with the idea of becoming an enlightened Arhat? What made Buddhahood a special, preferable goal?

In pre-Mahāyāna Buddhism we find the conviction that there is no qualitative difference between 'one liberation and the other' (AN 5:31; Nyanaponika and Bodhi, 1999, p. 134). The difference between an Arhat and a Buddha is that the Arhat attains enlightenment as a result of instruction from a Buddha, whereas a Buddha finds enlightenment in a situation where the true Dharma has long been lost: In a previous life he too had been instructed by a former Buddha, but when he finally becomes a Buddha himself, he achieves this goal without hearing the proclamation of the Dharma. Further, while an Arhat, as a member of the Saṅgha, does participate in the proclamation of the Dharma for the benefit of unenlightened beings, he does not himself establish a Saṅgha at a time and in a land where the Dharma is no longer known – whereas a Buddha does just this. Thus an Arhat is not of the same maximum benefit to others as a Buddha is.

In addition to the Arhat and the fully enlightened Buddha (*samyaksaṃbuddha*), early Buddhism also recognized a third category of enlightened persons: the Pratyekabuddhas. A Pratyekabuddha ('Solitary Buddha') resembles a full Buddha inasmuch as he too attains enlightenment without hearing the proclamation of the Dharma, but he differs from a full Buddha in that he does not himself establish a Saṅgha. It is often said that Pratyekabuddhas do not teach at all, but this does not accord with what we find in the scriptures. They do teach, but generally they teach only *śīla*, Buddhist morality. Hence they do offer help and assistance to others, though not to the fullest extent: Because they do not found a Saṅgha, they do not re-establish the basis for an enduring and competent proclamation of the Dharma. They don't, in short, guide others to their own enlightenment and thus do not provide the same optimal help to suffering beings as do fully enlightened Buddhas.

Mahāyāna texts speak of three different *yānas* – which are the 'vehicles' (we could also say the careers) of these three types of Buddhist saints: The *śrāvakayāna* is the 'vehicle of the hearers', and refers to those who heard the Dharma from a Buddha; their 'vehicle', or career, takes them to the goal of

Arhatship. Then there is the *pratyekabuddhayāna*, i.e. the career or 'vehicle of the Pratyekabuddhas', which would be the religious pursuit leading to the status of a Pratyekabuddha. The third and last *yāna* is the *buddhayāna* or *Bodhisattvayāna*, the vehicle of and for those who strive to become fully enlightened Buddhas.

From a Mahāyāna perspective, the decisive difference between these three *yānas* lies in the spiritual motivation behind them. If one strives to become an Arhat, or if one is satisfied with being a Pratyekabuddha, one is only of limited help to one's suffering fellow beings. Striving for Buddhahood on the other hand means to strive for a spiritual state in which one is of maximum benefit to others. From this point of view those who strive for Arhatship (the 'hearers', or *śrāvakas*) and those who are content with being Pratyekabuddhas do not exhibit the same quality of altruism as those who strive to become Buddhas, i.e. those who choose the Bodhisattva path. From a Mahāyāna perspective Śravakas and Pratyekabuddhas seem preoccupied chiefly with their own salvation (or at least they do not accord first place to the salvation of others), whereas those who follow the Bodhisattva path strive for Buddhahood entirely for altruistic motives, seeking their own enlightenment only so as to be of the utmost benefit to all others. For this reason they want to become Buddhas.

If the spiritual motivation of those who choose the Bodhisattva path is completely altruistic, then, by implication, the motivation of those on the other two *yānas* is to some extent still egoistic or self-centred. In this light the very premises underlying the two other paths bespeak an inferior understanding of the Buddhist ideal which, in the highest sense, as understood by the Mahāyānins, is selflessness in every respect. The other two *yānas* are thus regarded as 'lesser vehicles' (*hīnayāna*) compared to the 'great' or 'eminent vehicle' (*mahāyāna*) of the Bodhisattva path. The influential *Lotus Sūtra* concluded from this that there is ultimately only one 'single vehicle' (*ekayāna*) – and this is the Bodhisattva path. In the end everyone should arrive at the same realization of perfect altruism, everyone should enter upon the Boddhisattva path and strive to become a Buddha. The other, 'lesser', vehicles were and are only taught as provisional, skilful means for those who are not yet sufficiently advanced on the spiritual path. For deluded, self-centred beings the idea of striving primarily for one's own salvation is the appropriate and attractive goal; only gradually, with further spiritual progress, will one be able to develop the fully altruistic motivation of striving wholly for the salvation of all other beings.

Embarking on the Bodhisattva path begins therefore with a genuinely altruistic motivation behind one's spiritual striving – a motivation which in later Mahāyāna became known as the *bodhicitta*, the 'enlightenment mind' or the mind truly set for enlightenment, that is, 'a concern for the welfare of others such as others have not even for themselves…, the Mind, which is the seed of pure happiness in the world and the remedy for the suffering of the world' (BCA 1:25f; Crosby and Skilton, 1995, p. 7). *Bodhicitta* is expressed – and indeed confessed – in the formal Bodhisattva vows (*praṇidhāna*), wherein a Bodhisattva publicly commits him- or herself to pursue enlightenment for the sake of all other beings.

There are numerous versions of Bodhisattva vows in the early Mahāyāna scriptures. In 'The Inquiry of Ugra', for example, we find the formula:

> The unrescued I will rescue.
> The unliberated I will liberate.
> The uncomforted I will comfort.
> Those who have not yet reached *parinirvāṇa*
> I will cause to attain *parinirvāṇa*.
> (Ugraparipṛcchā 2; Nattier, 2003, p. 213)

Or another formula, quoted in the *Aṣṭasāhasrikā Prajñāpāramitā* (15:2), reads:

> We will become a shelter for the world, a refuge, the place of rest, the final relief, islands, lights and leaders of the world.
>
> We will win full enlightenment, and become the resort of the world.
>
> (Conze, 1995, p. 188)

A number of other formulas emphasise the endless task to which the Bodhisattva is committed. The best known and most widespread of these is the so-called four-fold vow:

> However innumerable sentient beings are, I vow to save them.
> However inexhaustible the defilements are, I vow to extinguish them.
> However immeasurable the dharmas are, I vow to master them.
> However incomparable the enlightenment is, I vow to attain it.
> (Conze, 1959, pp. 183f)

The commitment to the salvation of *all* sentient beings means that the Bodhisattva does not leave *saṃsāra*, the cycle of rebirth, but voluntarily remains in it until his vows are completed – and this might well mean forever. However, this by no means implies that the Bodhisattva should defer his enlightenment or refrain from becoming a Buddha. (That would be quite absurd, for above all else the Bodhisattva wants to become a Buddha: *Only as a Buddha* can he render the best service to all others!) It is rather that the Bodhisattva-ideal led to a change in the understanding of the nature of enlightenment and, correspondingly, of Buddhahood, as we shall see in the next chapter. It is a 'private' or 'static *nirvāṇa*' which the Bodhisattva declines: His realization of Nirvāṇa does not imply to leave *saṃsāra*, but is instead wholly compatible with his ongoing presence in it. In that sense his realization is called the realization of a 'dynamic' or 'non-abiding *nirvāṇa*' (*apratiṣṭhita nirvāṇa*) (see Williams, pp. 52f, 211ff; Nagao, 1991, pp. 23–34). As Vasubandhu (and with him many other classical Mahāyāna thinkers) explains:

> Since he possesses compassion, a Bodhisattva ... does not dwell in nirvāṇa. Again, since he possesses the highest wisdom, ... he does not dwell in saṃsāra.
>
> (Nagao, 1991, p. 27)

Through his perfection of wisdom the Bodhisattva is free from all attachment to *saṃsāra*, and through his perfection of compassion he is also free from any attachment to a kind of 'private' peace. Once more, we see the complementarity of detachment and loving involvement at the heart of Buddhist spirituality.

The Virtues of a Bodhisattva

The path of the Bodhisattva is described in many traditional Mahāyāna scriptures as the gradual development of six virtues or 'perfections' (*pāramitās*), a process which encompasses innumerable rebirths before it is brought to completion. The scheme of the 'six perfections' provided the structure for some of the most remarkable classical expositions of the Bodhisattva path: Ārya-Śūra's *Pāramitāsamāsa* (= 'Compendium of the Perfections'; see Meadows, 1986) or Śāntideva's *Bodhicāryāvatāra* (= 'Introduction to the Conduct which leads to Enlightenment'; see Crosby and Skilton, 1995), the latter certainly belonging to the jewels of the world's religious literature. In a fairly old Mahāyāna scripture (*Aṣṭasāhasrikā Prajñāpāramitā* 15) we read:

> Doers of what is hard are the Bodhisattvas who have set out to win full enlightenment. Thanks to the practice of the six perfections – *giving* a gift, guarding *morality*, perfecting oneself in *patience*, exertion of *vigour*, entering into *concentration*, and mastery in *wisdom* – they do not wish to attain release in a private Nirvāṇa of their own. They survey the highly painful world of beings. They want to win full enlightenment, and yet they do not tremble at birth and death. (...) Doers of what is hard are the Bodhisattvas who have set out for the benefit and happiness of the world, out of pity for it.
>
> (slightly modified after Conze, 1995, p. 188)

The meaning of the six perfections becomes clearer if we compare them with the structure of the Noble Eightfold Path, the traditional Buddhist path to enlightenment (see above p. 38).

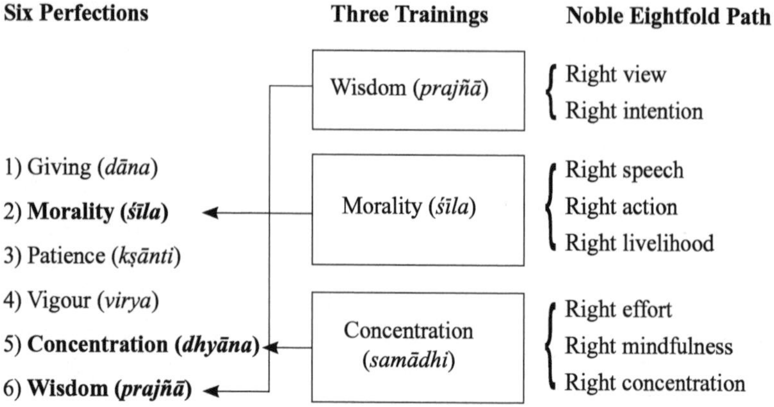

8. The six perfections in relation to the Noble Eighfold Path.

Three of the Bodhisattva's six perfections are not in fact different from the three principles or 'trainings' (*śikṣā*) which traditionally summarise the Noble Eightfold Path. Wisdom (*prajñā*) rightly appears at the end, for its final perfection is reached in enlightenment. *Śīla* ('morality') marks the basis and *samādhi* ('concentration' or 'meditation') is signified by the *dhyānas*, the absorption practices which stand at the pinnacle of Buddhist meditation techniques. Thus it is the remaining three virtues that give the list of the six perfections its distinctive flavour. Again, none of them is really new. All three are well known in pre-Mahāyāna expositions of spiritual striving. Here however they are highlighted because they are so closely related to the specific task of a Bodhisattva. *Dāna*, 'giving', sets the tone of the whole scheme: The Bodhisattva dedicates his/her religious efforts entirely to the well-being of others, thus realising pro-existence in the most comprehensive sense, making his whole life a gift to others. And given the immensity of the Bodhisattva's task – the salvation of all suffering beings – the Bodhisattva needs infinite *kṣānti* (= 'patience', with the strong connotation of 'forbearance' in face of hostility) and *virya* ('vigour' or 'energy').

The scheme of the six perfections thus turns out to be another way of emphasising the nature of the Bodhisattva career: one undertakes the Buddhist path for the sake of all others. It is therefore quite consistent when Śāntideva, quoting the *Dharmasaṅghīti Sūtra*, asserts that in the end the Bodhisattva should focus on one virtue only: great compassion (*mahākaruṇā*). 'In great compassion, … all the virtues of the Bodhisattva are included' (SS 16:286; Bendall and Rouse, 1971, p. 261). And Śāntideva takes this quite seriously: If the other's well-being requires that the Bodhisattva violate one of the Buddhist rules, he is not only allowed, but – in the name of compassion – even obliged to do so (see BCA 5:83f; SS 8:167f). Compassion is thus the ultimate criterion.

The emphasis on compassion as the cardinal virtue of a Bodhisattva underscores the point that the assistance provided by the Bodhisattva culminates in spiritual support, but is not at all restricted to spiritual support. Rather, the assistance involves a holistic effort to alleviate the suffering of the beings. The famous *Vimalakīrtinirdeśa Sūtra* praises the Bodhisattvas for their skill in combining spiritual with material help:

> During the short aeons of maladies,
> They become the best holy medicine;
> They make beings well and happy,
> And bring about their liberation.
>
> During the short aeons of famine,
> They become food and drink.
> Having first alleviated thirst and hunger,
> They teach the Dharma to living beings.
>
> During the short aeons of swords,
> They meditate on love,
> Introducing to non-violence
> Hundreds of millions of living beings.
>
> In the middle of great battles
> They remain impartial to both sides;
> For bodhisattvas of great strength
> Delight in reconciliation of conflict.
> (...)
>
> They intentionally become courtesans
> In order to win men over,
> And having caught them with the hook of desire,
> They establish them in the Buddha-gnosis.
>
> In order to help living beings,
> They always become chieftains,
> Captains, priests, and ministers,
> Or even prime ministers.
>
> For the sake of the poor,
> They become inexhaustible treasures,
> Causing those to whom they give their gifts.
> To conceive the spirit of enlightenment.
>
> (Vn 8; Thurman, 1976, pp. 70f)

Supramundane Bodhisattvas

According to common Mahāyāna belief the perfection of the Bodhisattva virtues is a very long process extending over countless successive lives. In the context of this belief more systematic views as to the developmental structure of this maturing process gradually emerged. A number of Mahāyāna scriptures put forward the idea of ten successive stages (*bhūmis*): On each stage a Bodhisattva is to bring to perfection another virtue, until at last he is ready for full Buddhahood. The traditional list of the 'six *pāramitās*' was expanded by an additional four, thus allowing an exact correlation of each stage with one perfection. These four additional *pāramitās* (numbers seven to ten) are: (7) skill in means (*upāya*), (8) firmness in the vow (*praṇidhāna*), (9) spiritual power or strength (*bala*), and (10) insight or knowledge (*jñāna*). If one thinks in terms of progressive achievements, the listing of these further virtues makes little sense; rather, they indicate general qualities linked to the Bodhisattva career. It is often assumed that the major reason for their introduction was the purely formal one of completing the correlation of the ten stages with the respective number of virtues/perfections.

The idea of successive stages carries a further implication, however – one with great significance for Mahāyāna belief and practice. With the completion of the first six stages, i.e. with the perfection of the six *pāramitās*, the Bodhisattva is considered capable of leaving *saṃsāra* and entering a private *nirvāṇa* should he or she wish to do so. Thus from the seventh stage onwards the Bodhisattva, having chosen to remain in *saṃsāra,* takes on a very different status. The place and form of rebirth can now be deliberately chosen, and progress on the further stages brings with it other extraordinary powers employed for the salvation of all beings. Among these higher faculties are, for example, the power to multiply and manifest oneself in various forms. The Bodhisattva can then appear in all saṃsāric realms, voluntarily descend to the hells or assume the form of animals or human beings in miserable conditions. The world – as seen through Buddhist eyes – is filled with Bodhisattvas in disguise.

One specific way in which Bodhisattvas can serve other beings involves the transfer of their own karmic merit to those who, left to themselves, have not produced anything meritorious. From the Bodhisattva perspective this is simply a follow-up on the practice of selfless compassion. From the perspective of the spiritually and morally less perfect recipients it is a most welcome substitutional act. From a more traditional point of view however the idea that a deficit of good karma can be offset by the merits of another is not easily reconciled with the original Buddhist understanding of karma. It can be argued though that already the assistance granted by Buddha Gautama enabled others to achieve a kind of spiritual progress and even liberation which they would have never managed out of their own karmic merits alone. The seed of the idea of grace is embedded in the idea of the Buddha's compassionate activity in the world, and this is, as we saw, the root and archetype of the entire Bodhisattva ideal.

Several Buddhist scriptures acquaint us with particular Bodhisattvas who have become extremely prominent figures, highly venerated throughout the Mahāyāna world, often depicted in Buddhist art and called upon as divine helpers and even saviours. Bodhisattva Maitreya, popular in both Theravāda and Mahāyāna, is venerated as the next Buddha who is presently residing in Tuṣita heaven and easily contacted through prayer and visionary meditational practice. His future coming is frequently linked to apocalyptic-messianic expectations, and at times has inspired chiliastic, revolutionary movements. Other very popular supramundane Bodhisattvas – usually believed to be at the highest stage of their spiritual career – are Mañjuśrī, Kṣitigarbha, Vajrapāṇi, Samantabhadra and many others. Sometimes their cult is confined to certain regions or branches of Buddhism, and often they have slightly different symbolic functions depending on the scriptures or schools in which they play an important part. One famous female Bodhisattva, venerated in the various branches of Tibetan Buddhism, is Tārā. She is said to have been born from the compassionate tears shed by Avalokiteśvara – by far the most popular and significant Bodhisattva, whose name means one 'who hears the cries of the world'. More than all others he is seen as the perfectly compassionate one, as 'compassion incarnate' (Williams, 1989, p. 232). Chinese Buddhist culture knows and venerates him in female form under the name Kuan-yin (in Japan: Kwannon or Kannon. His or her name even stands behind the label 'Canon', for the first camera the company produced was called 'Kwanon' which later became, in its anglicised form, the company's name.)

Already the Lotus Sūtra praises Avalokiteśvara as the great refuge and helper in all worldly needs. He is the redeemer of the shipwrecked, of the imprisoned, of those being led to execution, of those threatened by their enemies with death. He is the protector against goblins and demons, dangerous beasts and snakes, thunderstorms. He 'beholds all creatures who are beset with many hundreds of troubles and afflicted by many sorrows, and thereby is a saviour in the world, including the gods' (SpS 25; Kern, 1963, p. 414)

The praise of the great supramundane Bodhisattvas is at times so extraordinary that the boundaries between them and the fully developed Buddhas blur. This is particularly evident when we look at their role as cosmic Bodhisattvas.

The Cosmic Bodhisattva

The *Kāraṇḍavyūha Sūtra*, dedicated to the praise of Avalokiteśvara, takes up the ancient Vedic *puruṣa* myth (see above, p. 12) and presents Bodhisattva Avalokiteśvara as the true *puruṣa* from which the cosmos is created:

> From his eyes arose the moon and sun, from his forehead Maheśvara (Śiva), from his shoulders Brahmā, from his heart Nārāyaṇa, from his teeth Sarasvatī, from his mouth the winds, from his feet the earth, from his belly Varuṇa. (…) Thou shalt be called Ādideva (the primal god), the creator, the maker.
>
> (Kāraṇḍavyūha Sūtra 16; Thomas, 1952, p. 76f; see also Studholm, 2002, pp. 37–59)

This is not at all as unusual as it might appear. The Vimalakīrtinirdeśa Sūtra obviously alludes to passages like this when it says of the supramundane Bodhisattvas:

> They may become suns or moons,
> Indras, Brahmās, or lords of creatures,
> They may become fire or water
> Or earth or wind.
>
> (Vn 8; Thurman, 1976, p. 69)

Many Mahāyāna scriptures put forward a conception of the Bodhisattva as a cosmic, all pervasive reality. This is usually expressed with the image that the Bodhisattva manifests countless world systems in a single atom of his body while being present at the same time within these worlds.

How should we interpret these ideas? In the classical Indian context the reference to the *puruṣa* myth was certainly plain symbolic language: The Bodhisattva appears as the one from whom the cosmos and the cosmic order (including the Hindu deities) come into being and which continue to bear his features. Noteworthy however is the fact that there is no reference here to the caste system which in Hinduism was so closely associated with the *puruṣa* myth and which was the target of early Buddhist polemic. If Mahāyāna Buddhists, when looking at the cosmos, recognised in it Avalokiteśvara – 'compassion incarnate', the great saviour – as the divine *puruṣa,* the message seems to be that the world bears, at its heart, the character of the Bodhisattva. In other words, the world, as it is, is conducive to enlightenment; the world in itself is already a manifestation of cosmic compassion or liberating grace.

The Mahāyānic view of the Buddha further confirms this.

For further reading: Dayal (1932); Huong (2004); Kawamura (1981); Nattier (2003); Williams (1989).

11

The New Understanding of the Buddha

The Supramundane Buddha of the Lotus Sūtra

One of the thirty-two bodily marks ascribed to a Buddha by the Buddhist tradition is the sign of a 'wheel with thousand spokes' on the soles of his feet. The Pāli Canon relates that once, when the Brahman Doṇa spotted the Buddha's footprints and noticed the wheel marks, he wonderingly exclaimed: 'these certainly cannot be the footprints of a human being!' (AN 4:61; Nyanaponika and Bodhi, 1999, p. 87). Having followed the traces and caught up with the Buddha, Doṇa asked him what sort of being he is and what he will be in his next life. In responding the Buddha made clear that he had left all forms of saṃsāric existence behind and thus can be properly understood neither as a human being nor as a *deva* or a celestial being. Having overcome the world he is a 'Buddha'.

Among the early Buddhist schools it was undisputed that the Buddha cannot be interpreted within the categories of saṃsāric beings. Thus it would entirely miss the mark to regard the Buddha as *merely* or *simply* a human being. As one who transcended *saṃsāra* the Buddha is beyond gods and humans. One disputed point however among early Buddhist schools was whether the Buddha could nevertheless be viewed as a real human or whether his human existence should be understood rather as a kind of apparition, the manifestation in human shape of an essentially suprahuman reality. While the Theravāda School defended the former, other early Buddhist schools, particularly among the Mahāsaṅghika Schools, held the latter view (see Kv 18:1–4). This latter view is also put forth by one of the early Mahāyāna scriptures, the Lotus Sūtra, which later came to exert decisive influence in East Asian Buddhism.

One of the major focal points in the Lotus Sūtra is the revelation (in Chapter 16; or 15 in the Sanskrit version) that the Buddha had only feigned his birth, his death and his enlightenment, whereas in truth, he is 'unlimited in the duration of his life, he is everlasting' (Kern, 1963, p. 302), and his real enlightenment 'happened' in an immeasurable past – or in a sense: before all time. He only appeared as a limited human being for the sake of teaching and educating the deluded. He pretended to die so that his disciples, having lost their teacher, may stick more seriously to his teachings. When however their longing for their teacher has become strong enough the Buddha finally shows them that he never really disappeared revealing his true eternal nature as the 'Father of the World' – a term used by the Lotus Sūtra but also appearing in the Bhagavadgītā (an important Hindu text of roughly the same age) as an epithet for the highest God. (For further parallels between the Lotus and the Gītā see Kern, 1963, pp. XXVf):

> So am I the father of the world, the Selfborn, the Healer, the Protector of all creatures. Knowing them to be perverted, infatuated, and ignorant I teach my final rest, myself not being at rest.
>
> What reason should I have to continually manifest myself? When men become unbelieving, unwise, ignorant, careless, fond of sensual pleasures, and from thoughtlessness run into misfortune,
>
> Then I, who know the course of the world, declare: I am so and so, (and consider): How can I incline them to enlightenment? How can they become partakers of the Buddha-laws?
>
> (Lotus Sūtra 15, Kern, 1963, pp. 309f)

Now was the Buddha lying when he presented himself as a mortal human being? No, says the Lotus Sūtra, addressing this question. He was simply employing 'skilful means' for pedagogical purposes, so as to gradually prepare his followers for a fuller understanding of the truth.

The message of the Lotus Sūtra has always been controversial. The Lotus Sūtra itself, as already mentioned, even records the violent opposition it encountered from fellow Buddhists (see Lotus Sūtra 12/13). Even today the Lotus Sūtra is at times charged with an illegitimate 'deification' of the Buddha – a deification supposedly at variance with earlier or authentic Buddhist principles. Particularly the idea of an eternal nature of the Buddha – or perhaps more accurately: of a status beyond time – seems to contradict the Buddhist principle that everything is transitory. Paul Williams (1989, pp. 151f) argues that the attribution of eternity to the Buddha in the Lotus Sūtra should be seen as merely a form of literary hyperbole, though Williams admits that the Sūtra's adherents did in fact interpret it literally. Actually, however, traditional Buddhism never taught that *everything* is transitory. To be sure, every saṃsāric 'thing' or 'being' is *anitya*, impermanent, but Nirvāṇa was always regarded as a reality which is beyond and free from transitoriness: the 'Deathless'. Moreover, the nature of the Buddha cannot be understood in saṃsāric terms. The early view that the Buddha's enlightenment had 'nirvāṇised' him, such that he became the 'visible Nirvāṇa' (see above p. 52), could have easily given rise to the corresponding motif of 'Buddha-ising' Nirvāṇa. In other words if transcendent Nirvāṇa is manifested in the Buddha, Buddhahood can be – and in a sense needs to be – projected back into transcendent Nirvāṇa itself.

Something similar holds for the relationship between Buddha and Dharma. Even before Mahāyāna Buddhism the Buddha had been identified with the Dharma (see above pp. 19f) and understood as the 'visible Dharma'. But the Dharma, in the highest sense, can not simply be identified with the proclaimed teaching. The proclaimed Dharma *is* transitory: It is subject to corruption; it can and will be forgotten, whereas the cosmic Dharma, on which the taught Dharma is based and which the taught Dharma proclaims, is eternal. Therefore it can be rediscovered, like an old city overgrown by jungle, and subsequently re-established. Hence the identification of Buddha and Dharma may be valid not only on the human, transitory level, but on the suprahuman level as well. This would imply that there is an eternal Buddha behind or beyond his transitory human form, just as there is the eternal Dharma behind or beyond its perishable proclaimed form. The true Buddha would not be different from the true Dharma, and he would be 'eternal' in the sense in which the Dharma is eternal: as a cosmic reality beyond all time. Thus the Buddha of the Lotus Sūtra discloses his true nature by referring to his perpetual teaching of the Dharma:

> An inconceivable number of ... aeons, never to be measured, is it since I reached superior (or first) enlightenment and never ceased to teach the law
>
> (Kern, 1963, p. 307)

But if the Buddha's real being is eternal or timeless, how is it possible to *become* a Buddha at all (see Williams with Tribe, 2000, p. 171)? In this light, the Lotus Sūtra can be seen as threatening the very core of the Bodhisattva-ideal. Moreover the Lotus Sūtra appears to be violating its own intentions, for one of the other startling messages of the Lotus Sūtra is that everyone can and should become a Buddha.

One possible solution to this problem lies in distinguishing more clearly between the eternal or timeless nature of the Dharma and the way in which the supranatural Buddha participates in it. To some extent this distinction is achieved in the so-called doctrine of the *Three Buddha-Bodies* (*trikāya*). Another solution might consist in the assertion that one does not really 'become' a Buddha but that each of us already *is* a Buddha so that we 'become' what we truly are. 'To become a Buddha' then is merely to uncover our true *Buddha-Nature*. Neither solution is explicitly present in the Lotus Sūtra itself, but some scholars believe that the doctrine of the universal 'Buddha-Nature' is implicit in some passages concerning the 'originally pure mind' (see Hirakawa, 1990, p. 284). The 'originally pure mind' is essentially a pre-Mahāyāna teaching (see above p. 37) and certainly one of the roots of the Buddha-Nature doctrine. In later forms of Mahāyāna Buddhism, both doctrines, the general Buddha-Nature and Three Buddha-Bodies, came to play a major role, and to these we shall now turn.

The Three Buddha-Bodies

The Lotus Sūtra was not the only Mahāyāna scripture to introduce the idea of supramundane or suprahuman Buddhas. The need thus arose to bring the relationship between human Buddhas, suprahuman Buddhas and the cosmic or eternal Dharma into a coherent systematic relationship. This gradually took the form of the so-called *trikāya doctrine*, the doctrine of the 'three bodies' of the Buddha. Initially it seems to have been closely linked with the Yogācāra school of Buddhist philosophy (see below, pp. 124f), though with time it became a more or less generally accepted Mahāyāna conception.

At the beginning of this development stands the bifurcation just discussed: the Buddha in his physical, human form or 'body', and the Buddha as identical with the Dharma, i.e. the Buddha as 'Dharma-body' (*dharmakāya*). Recent research indicates that the term 'Dharma-body', even in Mahāyāna-Buddhism, initially referred either to the Dharma in the sense of the Buddha's teachings – and to the Buddha then as one who incarnates these teachings – or to that particular 'body' of *dharmas* – i.e. set of 'qualities' – characterising a Buddha (see Harrison, 1992). This has led some scholars to the conclusion that the later Mahāyāna usage of *dharmakāya* to refer to ultimate or absolute reality represents a break with the original meaning. It should not however be overlooked that already in the classical Buddhist understanding Dharma is far more than merely the proclaimed teaching, and certainly not a mere invention of the Buddha. Rather it is an eternal cosmic law. In this respect it is quite significant that the first reference to the Buddha's *dharmakāya* in the Pāli canon is made in parallel with the *puruṣa* myth (DN 27:9; see above p. 27). And the 'qualities' of a Buddha do not merely reflect outstanding personal characteristics but rather the Buddha's nirvāṇised status. It is therefore not surprising but indeed quite logical that '*dharmakāya*' finally developed into a term signifying that ultimate reality is the true body or (as it is also called) the 'essence' body of a Buddha.

In so far as the *dharmakāya* refers to the ultimate it is said to be inconceivable or 'formless'. It is 'beyond' any shape or conceptual form which would permit it to be conceived as one reality among others. In consequence the *dharmakāya* was ranked even above the concept of the Buddha as a supramundane figure, for the various supramundane Buddhas of which the Mahāyāna scriptures speak do have their particular form, their individual names, their typical attributes, their special spheres or realms of influence, and they can even be seen or visualized in meditation. Hence the elaborate *trikāya doctrine* distinguishes three 'bodies': (1) one 'formless body' (the *dharmakāya*) and two 'form bodies' (*rūpa-kāya*): (2) the supramundane Buddha (of the *saṃbhogakāya*) who manifests himself in (3) the physical appearance of a Buddha (*nirmāṇakāya*) as a transitory human being.

The second of the two form bodies is usually called the 'transformation body' (*nirmāṇakāya*), probably because of its status as a kind of 'magical'

formless body	dharma body (*dharmakāya*)
form bodies	enjoyment body (*saṃbhogakāya*)
	transformation body (*nirmāṇakāya*)

9. The Three Buddha-Bodies (*trikāya*).

transformation of a supramundane Buddha into a transitory human manifestation. The form body of the supramundane Buddha is called the 'enjoyment body' (*saṃbhogakāya*) or 'body of communal enjoyment' (depending on how the prefix *sam-* is translated), presumably because it stands for the kind of being or status that a former Bodhisattva 'enjoys' after having reached his goal, the Buddhahood. Therefore the *saṃbhogakāya* is sometimes also referred to as 'reward body' – being the reward of the Bodhisattva's striving.

The *trikāya doctrine* offers a solution to the problem posed by the Lotus Sūtra: Strictly speaking, only the *dharmakāya* is eternal. One can attain Buddhahood and *become* a Buddha on the levels of the 'transformation body' and 'enjoyment body', or – strictly speaking – only on the level of the 'enjoyment body' and then bring about its manifestation as a 'transformation body'. The eternal or timeless *dharmakāya* on the other hand is nothing that 'becomes'. It is the ultimate ground and support of the two form-bodies which could never themselves come into existence without the unconditioned existence of the ultimate 'behind' them. (See the classical account of the *trikāya doctrine* in Ms 10.) Itself inconceivable and unconditioned, the formless *dharmakāya* is thus 'manifesting itself in conditioned images' (Ms 10; Keenan, 1992, p. 106), such that the form-bodies of a Buddha are in a sense 'the spontaneous compassionate "overflow" of the *dharmakāya*' (Williams, with Tribe, 2000, p. 176).

At times it is discussed in Mahāyāna texts as to whether the *dharmakāya* should be regarded as one singular reality or whether there is a plurality of *dharmakāyas* – as many as there are Buddhas. According to the Mahāyānasaṃgraha (Ms 10:8) the *dharmakāya* can indeed be seen as differentiated in relation to the innumerable beings who attain perfect enlightenment on its basis. At the same time however it is undifferentiated because of its formlessness: It is the one single support of all its diverse manifestations. Thus both aspects are affirmed, and there is a non-duality of unity and differentiation (Ms 10:3). The form-bodies are on the one hand different from the *dharmakāya,* but on the other hand they are not separate from it as their ultimate ground (see Ms 10:36–7). In the end their relation to the ultimate can only be described paradoxical: 'The unborn Buddha is born, abides in non-abiding…' (Ms 10:28; Keenan, 1992, p. 112).

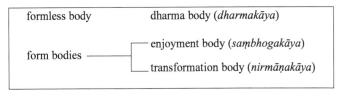

The Buddha-Nature

Apparently in early Mahāyāna the Bodhisattva career was viewed as a rather elitist path. Only a few followers of the Buddha choose to strive for the highest of all possible goals, Buddhahood. However, one of the startling messages of the Lotus Sūtra was that everyone should and could become a Buddha. Of course this implies that everyone has the potential to become a Buddha. This potential is generally called *tathāgatagharba*, which may mean the 'germ', or 'embryo', or 'womb' of the Tathāgata, i.e. the Buddha. But how is this potential to be understood?

As we saw above (p. 37), the Pāli Canon already speaks of the original luminosity of the mind, in light of which the defilements of greed, hatred and delusion are merely adventitious. The process of advancing towards enlightenment could therefore be seen as the gradual removal of these defilements so that the mind's original luminosity is uncovered. Since Buddhist cosmology does not assume that there was some sort of initial state of purity in the past, the 'originality' of this luminosity should perhaps be understood as a natural inclination towards enlightenment or Nirvāṇa. But does this exhaust the implications of 'original luminosity'? Would not such a natural inclination towards Nirvāṇa also entail some metaphysical presuppositions, a kind of essential relatedness between the seed (however we view the seed's 'nature') and the fruit of full Buddhahood?

In its most modest form the Buddha-Nature doctrine understands the Buddha-germ, the *tathāgatagarbha*, as a potential only, as the mere possibility of the radical transformation from delusion to full enlightenment. Yet this does not explain the relation between, on the one hand, the unconditioned Nirvāṇa or Dharma or *dharmakāya* (which as such cannot come into being or undergo changes) and the transformation of a deluded being into an enlightened one, on the other.

Another version of the *tathāgatagarbha* doctrine holds that such a transformation is only possible if there is a kind of metaphysical resemblance, or better: identity, between the Buddha-germ and the full fruit of Buddhahood. This would mean that that reality which is essential for a Buddha's Buddhahood, is *in nuce*, already there in the deluded being: It is the *dharmakāya* itself, the highest and the most essential of the three Buddha-bodies, present in every sentient being but obscured by the defilements. As soon as the defilements are removed – which is what it means to become a Buddha – it will shine forth of itself. Hence it is not the Buddha-Nature or *dharmakāya* that is changed; rather, our non-awareness of it is changed into full awareness. Every sentient being then is in some sense already 'enlightened' – its original or inherent nature *is* enlightenment – though it is usually unaware of this. Some of the scriptures which teach the *tathāgatagarbha* doctrine do not hesitate to call the Buddha-Nature our 'true self', the *ātman*.

In a third version (of Indian origin though particularly popular in East-Asian Buddhism) the *dharmakāya* is seen not only as the essence-body of a Buddha but as the ultimate reality or true nature of everything. Not only sentient beings but all beings whatsoever participate in the Buddha-Nature – including plants and stones (regardless of the fact that only sentient beings can realize this participation to such an extent as to be fully aware of their original enlightenment or Buddhahood). *Tathāgatagarbha* and *dharmakāya* become equivalent with *dharmadhātu*, the true nature of all things. Obviously, this is reminiscent of the upaniṣadic Brahman-Ātman teaching, wherein the true ultimate self of a being or thing is at the same time identical with Brahman as the one ultimate reality beyond and within everything.

There is no doubt that the Buddha-Nature doctrine has a number of advantages, which may account for its enormous popularity. First of all it provides powerful consolation and encouragement on the Bodhisattva path, for no one should think of him- or herself as incapable of reaching the high goal of Buddhahood. This is the message of the short and very widely-known *Tathāgatagarbha Sūtra*: People think of themselves as (spiritually) impoverished, but in fact there is a treasure hidden in their poor huts of which they are unaware – 'the treasure-store of wisdom, and the great wealth of widely caring for one another' (Tathāgatagarbha Sūtra; Grosnick, 1995, p. 99). If a person becomes aware of this and develops confidence he or she will achieve the highest goal.

Furthermore, the Buddha-Nature doctrine provides an explanation of how the ultimate, despite its eternal, immutable and motionless nature, is nevertheless the driving agent of the entire process of spiritual transformation. It is efficacious; it 'acts' simply by means of its universal presence – very much like Aristotle's 'unmoved mover' who, being unmoved, moves everything else by the irresistible power of its attraction. Why do deluded people feel dissatisfaction with saṃsāric existence? Why is it that even the pleasures of *saṃsāra* cannot provide lasting satisfaction? Does not this bear witness to a deep, but obscured knowledge of Nirvāṇa as being that which we really long for? – thus the argument of the *Ratnagotravibhāga* (or *Uttaratantra*, as it is also called), another important scripture proclaiming the Buddha-Nature:

> If the Buddha element were not present,
> There would be no remorse over suffering.
> There would be no longing for nirvana,
> Nor striving and devotion towards this aim.
> (Ratnagotravibhāga 1:40; Fuchs, 2000, p. 25)

Finally, the idea that everything participates in the ultimate Buddha-Nature made possible a more balanced view of the negative and positive aspects of natural life. While there was no question that attachment to perishable existence needs to be overcome in order to overcome suffering, the transitory world could also be seen as making its own specific contribution to the achievement of liberation. This world not only has a 'Bodhisattva-Nature', as we saw in the preceding chapter; it also testifies – in truly sacramental form – to ultimate Buddhahood. As Malcolm David Eckel (1997, p. 339) so pointedly states: '"Nature" in the Indian tradition was a world to be transcended, while in East Asia it took on the capacity to symbolize transcendence itself.'

On the other hand, the Buddha-Nature teaching has been and still is viewed with deep suspicion, the major allegation being its nearness to the Hindu Brahman-Ātman doctrine. The classical Buddhist treatises promulgating the Buddha-Nature seem to be aware of such actual or potential accusations, and make various attempts to distinguish the *tathāgatagarbha* from the upaniṣadic *ātman* in an effort to defend the teaching. Sometimes however they were bold enough to seize the opportunity – inherent in this teaching – of flouting the ordinary clichéd opposition between the Hindu insistence on *ātman* and the Buddhist insistence on *anātman* (Not-Self). Already the great Nāgārjuna had argued the need to go beyond the affirmation of both *ātman* and *anātman* alike (see above p. 37). And now the Ratnagotravibhāga declared with regard to the Buddha-Nature:

> It is true self, since all conceptual elaboration
> In terms of self and non-self is totally stilled.
> (Ratnagotravibhāga 1:37; Fuchs, 2000, p. 24)

Buddha-Lands

As Buddhaghosa, the eminent Theravāda commentator of the fifth century CE, explains, 'purity' or 'purification' is used in Buddhist scriptures as a synonym for Nirvāṇa, and the 'path of purification' refers to the path leading to this transcendent goal (see Vism 1:5). A 'Buddha-field' (*buddhakṣetra*) is the technical term for the 'environment' in which a Buddha exerts his influence, and a Buddha's activity is thus described as 'purifying' the Buddha-field. This is to say that the beings under the Buddha's influence are purified of suffering and its roots: the defilements of greed, hatred and delusion. As the Vimalakīrtinirdeśa explains, 'purifying the Buddha-field' means bringing about the spiritual development of the sentient beings, increasing their spiritual faculties so as to guide them towards enlightenment. How efficaciously a Buddha purifies his field is a reflection of his own spiritual achievement (see Vn 1).

At a quite early stage Mahāyāna scriptures developed the idea that Buddhas not only 'purify their fields' in the conventional manner of preaching the Dharma and establishing the Saṅgha, but are capable of creating their own Buddha-fields, which are 'pure lands' right from the start. According to the classical Mahāyāna treatises a Buddha has 'the quality of manifesting pure Buddha lands in accord with the aspirations of sentient beings' (Ms 2:33; Keenan, 1992, p. 58).

The meaning of 'manifesting' in this context is multilayered. Frequently it is understood quite literally: as an act of creation. The underlying concept here is the traditional cosmological view that new worlds are the 'creation' of collective karmic impulses; worlds emerge because there are sentient beings with karmic tendencies which bring forth a corresponding material environment (see above p. 51). During his long spiritual career as a Bodhisattva, a Buddha accumulated such tremendous stores of karmic merit that he is able to produce from this good karma a correspondingly good or pure world. Moreover, by transferring his karmic merit to other beings, he can cause them to be reborn into this pure Buddha-land. Yet there are also passages in the Mahāyāna scriptures which understand the construction of pure lands in a more sophisticated way: as the 'magical' production of a collective apparition. In any event, for those who enjoy being reborn into such a pure Buddha-land this does not make the slightest difference.

Pure Buddha-lands are paradisal worlds – or better: *Buddhist* types of paradise. In the most famous among the pure lands, Sukhāvatī ('Land of Happiness') situated in the far West and created by Buddha Amitābha (Jap.: Amida), suffering is unknown. Physical settings and also trees are made of jewels and other precious materials. The light is soft and colourful. There are lovely little lakes with clear water surrounded by most beautiful flowers. Diverse birds sing their charming melodies – yet these birds are only apparitions: the lower forms of rebirth (as animals, ghosts or hellish beings) do not exist in Sukhāvatī. The songs of the magical birds of Sukhāvatī remind people of the truths of the Buddhist teachings, and everyone in Amitābha's 'Pure Land' can quickly and easily reach the highest enlightenment.

The Buddhas preside over their pure lands in form of their *saṃbhogakāya*, their 'reward body' or 'body of communal enjoyment'. They create these worlds out of their boundless compassion so as to offer an easy route to salvation for a large number of beings. Through the veneration of a particular Buddha, through meditating upon him, through having faith in him and cultivating the wish to be reborn into his land, the beings can – thanks to the merit of the respective Buddha – find their way into his land where they will attain their own enlightenment. The creation of a pure Buddha-land is thus the climax of a Buddha's Bodhisattva career, the fulfilment of his vow to employ all his striving solely for the benefit of others. This is why the marvel of a Buddha-land reflects the spiritual perfection of its creator. But what does this say about our world, which is hardly a paradise, and about its Buddha, Siddhārtha Gautama?

The Vimalakīrtinirdeśa tells of a delegation of Bodhisattvas who once visited the Buddhist layman Vimalakīrti. The Bodhisattvas have come from a remote Buddha-land where the presiding Buddha teaches the Dharma entirely through the exquisite scents of various perfumes. With no little surprise they learn of the harsh conditions of life on earth and how Siddhārtha teaches the beings here. But then Vimalakīrti explains to the baffled Bodhisattvas that in a single lifetime on earth more benefit for living beings can be accomplished than in a hundred thousand aeons in their world. For only in a world like this, a world with genuine hardship and real evil, can the virtues of a Bodhisattva be developed. These, says Vimalakīrti, 'do not exist in any other buddha-field':

> ... to win the poor by generosity; to win the immoral by morality; to win the hateful by means of tolerance; to win the lazy by means of effort; to win the mentally troubled by means of concentration; to win the falsely wise by means of true wisdom ...
>
> (Vn 10; Thurman, 1976, p. 83)

This world too, then, is a pure Buddha-land, and it is even an exceptional one for it genuinely fulfils the real purpose of pure lands: to multiply and intensify the spiritual qualities of sentient beings. It only seems to be an impure field to those who in their ignorance and delusion do not recognize its true character as an ideal environment for the development of Bodhisattva qualities (see Vn 1). Already the Lotus Sūtra (15:11–14; see Kern, 1963, p. 308) had declared that the true character of this world as a pure Buddha-land is unknown to the deluded people, as is the true nature of the Buddha.

This understanding of a 'pure land' ties in well with other crucial Mahāyāna ideas: the idea of the 'dynamic *nirvāṇa*' which the Bodhisattva realises without leaving *saṃsāra*; the idea of a common Buddha-Nature being obscured by the defilements; the idea of the cosmic Bodhisattva and even of a cosmic Buddha-Nature as the true reality in and of everything. All these concepts are variations on one motif – that *saṃsāra*, with all its suffering and evil, is permeated by an unconditioned absolute reality whose ultimate goodness is manifested as wisdom and compassion. Only existential ignorance and delusion prevent us from recognising the true character of reality.

For further reading: Gōmez (1996), Griffiths (1994), Hookham (1991), King (1991), Makransky (1997), Nagao (1991, pp. 103–122), Williams (1989).

12

Concept, Language and Reality

From its inception Buddhism assumes that our habitual view of life is deluded. We do not see things as they really are. The Buddha is called a 'Buddha' ('Awakened One') precisely because he awakened from delusion or ignorance (*avidyā*) to the insight into the true nature of reality. The understanding of salvation/liberation as the transition from delusion to insight is an ancient legacy from the Śramaṇas. As we saw in the last two chapters, Mahāyāna Buddhism speaks of these two states, delusion and insight, in a variety of ways: Deluded, one thinks of the Buddha as a mortal being, though in truth he is always present; deluded, one sees the world as a place of misery and evil, though in truth it is a pure Buddha Land; deluded, one does not see that the defilements are merely hiding one's true Buddha Nature, nor that the cosmos bears the features of the Bodhisattva and that everything participates in the ultimate reality of the *dharmakāya*, the highest of the three Buddha-bodies.

The *dharmakāya* however is also said to be 'formless' and therefore cannot possibly be 'captured' in our conceptual moulds and categories. Even the traditional records of the Buddha's enlightenment declare that the insight he had found was 'sublime, unattainable by mere reasoning' (MN 26) and that Nirvāṇa is ineffable (MN 44) and incomparable (Sn 1149). If that is the case, must not the difference between ignorance and insight be understood in a far more radical sense – namely, as the difference between the illusion of living in a describable, conceptually graspable world and the experience of its indescribable, inconceivable true nature? Mahāyāna Buddhism did indeed take that position and expressed it powerfully in its teaching of universal 'emptiness' (*śūnyatā*).

Universal Emptiness in the 'Perfection of Wisdom' Sūtras

Among the crucial early Mahāyāna texts is a group of scriptures called the 'Perfection of Wisdom Sūtras' (*Prajñāpāramitā Sūtras*). In length and age these texts vary considerably – from the voluminous Sūtra in Hundred-Thousand Verses to the very brief and highly revered Heart Sūtra, for example. The so-called Diamond-Sūtra (*Vajracchedikā Sūtra*) came to be particularly influential. One of the oldest texts in this group is presumably the 'Perfection of Wisdom Sūtra in Eight Thousand Verses' (*Aṣṭasāhasrikā Prajñāpāramitā Sūtra*), perhaps composed between the first century BCE and the first century CE. As this text addresses all the major themes of the Perfection of Wisdom Sūtras, we can concentrate here on this one scripture. (For a full translation see Conze, 1995.)

Basically, the Perfection of Wisdom Sūtras deal with the Bodhisattva career as characterised by the six Bodhisattva 'virtues' or 'perfections' (*pāramitās*) (see above pp. 99ff) though the main focus is on the sixth perfection: the 'perfection of wisdom' (*prajñā pāramitā*). According to these texts the 'perfection of wisdom' consists in the insight into universal 'emptiness' (*śūnyatā*). Now what does that mean?

The term 'emptiness' already appears in pre-Mahāyāna Buddhism. Though the term as such is not included among the principal early Buddhist concepts, the contexts in which it appears are indeed central. Firstly, 'emptiness' is employed in connection with the not-self teaching: The world is 'empty' inasmuch as it is lacking a substantial self (see Sn 1119). None of the five constituents (see above p. 36) possesses a 'self' and therefore all of them are 'void, hollow, insubstantial'. They are 'like a lump of foam, ... a water bubble, ... a mirage, ... a plantain trunk, ... an illusion'. Having recognised their 'voidness' or 'emptiness' one should give up all attachment to them and yearn for the 'imperishable state' (see SN 22:95; Bodhi, 2000, pp. 951ff). Secondly, the term 'emptiness' appears in connection with absorption meditation (MN 121 and 122): Entering 'supreme, unsurpassed voidness' is here equated with the gradual transcendence of all cognition and perception until finally full enlightenment is achieved (MN 121, Ñāṇamoli and Bodhi, 2001, p. 969f). These two features: lack of a substantial self and the transcending of conceptual perception, are also present in the 'Perfection of Wisdom' literature, but here, as distinct from early Buddhism, wide-ranging conclusions are drawn.

In pre-Mahāyāna doctrinal development it had become common to analyse all reality into various groups of '*dharmas*', i.e. material and mental, conditioned and unconditioned entities. The conditioned *dharmas* were often believed to exist only for a brief moment, and the existence of each conditioned *dharma* is caused by a preceding, similar *dharma*, such that streams or chains of consecutive *dharmas* are constituted. It is the continuity of these chains which accounts for the impression of a persistent, identical entity or being, while the fact that it is a chain of different, rapidly succeeding *dharmas* accounts for the mutability and transitoriness of everything, whether material or mental or both (see the explanation of rebirth in terms of the *dharma*-theory, above p. 47f). Thus, what customarily appears as one being or thing is here understood as a conglomerate of different *dharmas*. It is like watching a film: We have the impression of seeing self-identical yet nevertheless constantly changing persons and things, but in fact what is there is just a lightning-quick series of many different single pictures, one after another after another (see Stcherbatsky, 1988).

All *dharmas* are empty – this is the central and radical message of the 'Perfection of Wisdom' Sūtras. They lack any 'own being', any substantial nature, and therefore they also lack any essential 'mark' which would identify them:

> A mark does not possess the own-being of a mark. The marked does not possess the own-being of being marked, and own-being does not possess the mark of (being) own-being.
>
> (AP 1:11; Conze, 1995, p. 86).

Hence, it is not only the beings or composite entities which lack any substantiality (since they are constituted by conglomerates of successive *dharmas*) but the *dharmas* themselves lack any substantial basis or substantial features. This makes their being 'like a magical illusion, like a dream' (AP 2:40; ibid. p. 98f). Moreover, the 'Perfection of Wisdom' Sūtras do not confine this view to the conditioned *dharmas*, but extend it to all *dharmas*, including the unconditioned ones:

> Even Nirvana, I say, is like a magical illusion, like a dream. How much more so anything else!
>
> (AP 2:41; ibid. p. 99).

Is this a denial of ultimate reality, of the 'Deathless' which constitutes the original goal and basis of Buddhism? Thus have the 'Perfection of Wisdom' Sūtras at times been understood – or better: misunderstood, for the texts themselves point to a different answer. Their claim that everything, including Nirvāṇa, is empty is based on the conviction that everything is as inconceivable and ineffable as Nirvāṇa. The illusion or dream consists in our assuming that the definable and discrete entities we construct with our concepts and mental images show us reality as it really is:

> Foolish, untaught, common people have constructed all the dharmas. … But while they construct all dharmas which yet do not exist, they neither know nor see the path which is that which truly is. In consequence they do not go forth from the triple world, and do not wake up to the reality-limit.
>
> (AP 1:16, Conze, 1995, p. 87f)

All *dharmas* are just 'mere words' (AP 1:26), while true reality, or 'suchness' (*tathatā*), is 'immeasurable' (AP 18:348–52). 'Nirvāṇa' – so the conclusion of the 'Perfection of Wisdom Sūtra in Eight Thousand Verses' – cannot be conceived as merely one *dharma* among others. Rather, we approach it by going beyond all our limited, i.e. definable and defining, concepts:

> 'Islands' are pieces of land limited by water, in rivers or great lakes. Just so form, etc., is limited at its beginning and end, and so are all dharmas. But the limitation of all dharmas is the same as the Calm Quiet, the Sublime, as Nirvana, as the Really Existing, the Unperverted.
>
> (AP 15:297; Conze, 1995, p. 189)

Hence 'perfect wisdom' is realised when 'all constructions and discriminations' are forsaken, when every notion is given up, including the notion of 'perfect wisdom' or 'being near to Enlightenment' (AP 26:441f).

Yet what is the connection between the Bodhisattva ideal and the realization of universal emptiness? Why does a Bodhisattva need that particular 'perfection of wisdom'? The 'Perfection of Wisdom Sūtra in Eight Thousand Verses' offers two reasons: First: The realization of emptiness 'detaches' him from both conditioned and unconditioned *dharmas* – that is, from both *saṃsāra* and *nirvāṇa* – and this is exactly what a Bodhisattva needs to fulfil his vocation of becoming enlightened while remaining in this world (see AP 2:37–8; 8:195–6). Second: The insight into universal emptiness enables the Bodhisattva to maintain the correct perception of himself and of other beings. Because of his vow to work for the liberation of all beings the Bodhisattva is in danger of entertaining the illusory idea of 'selves' – the 'selves' of the beings to be liberated and the 'self' of the being who liberates them (AP 7:175f), whereas the perfection of wisdom involves a paradox: '… a Bodhisattva … leads countless beings to Nirvana, and yet there is not any being that has been led to Nirvana, nor that has led others to it' (AP 1:22; Conze, 1995, p. 90). On the one hand then the Bodhisattva, in cultivating compassion, should 'identify all beings with his own self' and thus strive to liberate them from suffering, and on the other hand he should cultivate the insight that 'in each and every way a self does not exist' (AP 1:29f; ibid. p. 93). He neither abandons any being, nor does he forsake the insight into universal emptiness (AP 22:449). Thereby the Bodhisattva combines detachment with loving involvement, thus uniting compassion (*karuṇā*) with wisdom (*prajñā*) (see AP 22:403–6).

Emptiness and the Philosophy of Nāgārjuna

While the Perfection of Wisdom Sūtras proclaim the teaching of universal emptiness (*śūnyatā*) as the Buddha's own word (or at least as the ultimate meaning of the Buddha's word) they offer almost nothing which could establish or justify this teaching on rational/philosophical grounds. That task was performed by Nāgārjuna (2nd–3rd cent. CE). Numerous works have been ascribed to him (a good many of which, however, are spurious – for a discussion of their authenticity see Lindtner, 1982, pp. 9–18, and Ruegg, 1981, pp. 4–33). These writings constitute the foundation of the so-called Madhyamaka school ('Middle Way' School) of Indian philosophical Buddhism, though Nāgārjuna's ideas also exerted a considerable influence on the Yogācāra school, the second major philosophical branch of Mahāyāna Buddhism, as well as on a number of further philosophical and doctrinal developments outside India, particularly in Chinese, Japanese and Korean Buddhism. It is almost impossible to overestimate the impact Nāgārjuna had on Mahāyāna Buddhism in general.

In his explanation and justification of universal emptiness Nāgārjuna employs a two-step reasoning. First he tries to show that all our concepts depend for their definition – and thus for their significance – upon each other. For example, a cause is a cause not in itself but only in relation to an effect, and an effect is an effect only in relation to (and hence in dependence upon) a cause. Or if something is defined as the bearer of certain properties it is obviously dependent upon these properties in order to be what it is; conversely, something is a property only in relation to that of which it is a property, i.e. its bearer. Or something is regarded as future or past only in relation to the present, yet the present can be defined only as the intersection of the past and the future. According to Nāgārjuna this mutual interdependency holds for all our concepts and categories. In a second step, he sets out to show that our concepts have meaning solely in relation to each other; any attempt to anchor their meaning in reality itself inevitably fails. Our concepts are comparable then to empty stencils or templates. They are empty of any sort of 'own-being' (*svabhāva*), that is, they lack substantial reality. In and through their interrelatedness they constitute an artificial gridwork which is imposed on reality by our mind.

To illustrate this rather abstract argument consider the following: Imagine an apple which develops out of a first little bud into a nice ripe fruit, and then begins shrivelling until it finally rots and totally decomposes. But is there any self-identical entity underlying the whole process? Which 'apple' underwent this transformation: the little bud? or the nice ripe fruit? or the rotten remains? None of these 'apples' was continuously present. The ripe one is not identical with the initial bud nor with that which is shrivelled or that which has decomposed. Neither however are they totally different entities. 'Neither the same nor another' – that was the famous answer given in the Milindapañha (Mph 2:2:1) to the question of whether the reborn person is the same as or different from the deceased (see above p. 48). Our way of determining and delineating identities turns out to be static and artificial, and not in line with the fleeting nature of reality.

As we saw, pre-Mahāyāna Buddhist philosophy attempted an explanation via the theory of consecutive *dharmas,* all causally connected, all existing only for the space of a single moment. For Nāgārjuna this theory does not solve the problem but only defers it, for however short the existence of such consecutive *dharmas* is supposed to be, there will always be a beginning, an end and something in between. Yet how is one to account for this process of origination, duration and cessation which each single *dharma* undergoes? To attempt an account by introducing further chains of successive *dharmas* only leads to infinite regress; a substantial reality underlying any such process is simply not to be found. The origination, duration and cessation of anything is therefore like 'a magical trick, a dream or a fairy castle' (MMK 7:34).

Moreover, how should a past *dharma*, which has already perished, be able to cause the successive *dharma* to exist? If the past *dharma* has already come to an end it cannot effect anything, for it no longer exists. And if it is still there, it cannot have any effect either, for how could it have any influence upon the next *dharma* if this latter is not yet existent? Furthermore, when we look at the postulated *dharmas* not under their aspect as temporal entities but as spatial ones, similar problems arise. Can we assume that there is really something like an ultimately indivisible unit? According to Nāgārjuna this is not possible (see Ratnāvalī 1:71), and subsequent Madhyamaka philosophers supported this view with the following argument: If a *dharma* is understood to be connected to other *dharmas* in space (thus forming a conglomerate of larger 'entities'), the *dharma* would have to have six directions (the classical four plus upwards and downwards). Yet if we can distinguish six sides of a *dharma*, then it is not indivisible. But without the six directions it would have no spatial existence at all (see, for example, BCA.9:86, 94).

So whether the investigation explores the dimension of time or the dimension of space, we end up in infinite regress. We never arrive at a smallest unit in time nor in space, and thus the *dharmas* are empty of any 'own-being' or 'substantial reality' – and empty *dharmas* as such can have neither real relations nor functions such as causing other *dharmas* to come into existence. It follows then that any supposed relations between *dharmas* are empty as well. The whole idea of 'real entities', as units which are demarcated in time and space and defined by their mutual relations, is an artificial construct of the human mind.

The identity of a being (i.e. its 'own-being') is conceptually defined by distinguishing it from other beings and by allocating to it certain properties, relations, functions, etc. Indeed, to define something entails the setting up of boundaries or limits – and precisely these limits turn out to be artificial. They can never be rooted in reality itself and their supposed substantiality is always questionable. We can always postulate smaller constituents, whether in time or in space, without arriving anywhere. And we can always question the boundary between a property and the bearer of the property, for how can we delineate the bearer without the property or the property without the bearer? The problems which traditional Buddhism addresses as the ten 'unanswerable questions' (whether the world is eternal or not eternal, finite or infinite, whether body and soul are the same or different, whether after death a Tathāgata exists, does not exist, both exists and not exists, or neither exists nor does not exist, (see above pp. 39f and 49f) are therefore not exceptional problems; rather, they exemplify the general aporetic structure underlying every attempt to provide a description of reality, for the ten unanswerable questions are simply the inevitable consequence of constructed and artificial conceptual delineations. In that sense Nāgārjuna says:

> That which is produced and its cause, as well as the characteristic and that which is characterized.
> The sensation and the one who senses, and whatever other things there are –
> Not only is the former limit of existence-in-flux (*saṃsāra*) not to be found,
> But the former limit of all those things is not to be found.
> (MMK 11:8; Streng, 1967, p. 196)

Or:

> The views (regarding) whether that which is beyond death is limited by a beginning or an end or some other alternative
> Depend on a *nirvāṇa* limited by a beginning (…) and an end (…).
> Since all *dharmas* are empty, what is finite? What is infinite?
> Is there anything which is this or something else, which is permanent or impermanent,
> Which is both permanent and impermanent, or which is neither?
> (MMK 25:21–3; Streng, 1967, p. 217)

'Eternity', 'non-eternity', 'both' or 'neither' – these terms are utterly inapplicable to ultimate bliss, says Nāgārjuna, for such designations depend upon descriptive ideas and demarcated concepts (see MMK 22:12–5; 25:1–18). Understanding the emptiness of everything means understanding that not only is Nirvāṇa indescribable, inconceivable and ineffable, but so is all reality. In that regard there is no difference between Nirvāṇa and Saṃsāra:

> There is nothing whatever which differentiates the existence-in-flux (*saṃsāra*) from *nirvāṇa*;
> And there is nothing whatever which differentiates *nirvāṇa* from existence-in-flux.
> (MMK 25:19; Streng, 1967, p. 217)

Yet this is not to imply a reduction of Nirvāṇa to the level of Saṃsāra, as some contemporary secularized interpreters of Buddhism seem to suggest. Rather it is Saṃsāra which is lifted up, in a sense, to the level of Nirvāṇa. For the emptiness of everything means not only that Nirvāṇa is unconditioned, unoriginated and unterminated, but that all reality is (see MMK 25:9). However, this is not to be taken as a back-door affirmation of a monistic metaphysical system, but rather as the front-door affirmation that everything – without exception – is inconceivable and indescribable:

> When the domain of thought has been dissipated, 'that which can be stated' is dissipated.
>
> Those things which are unoriginated and not terminated, like *nirvāṇa*, constitute the Truth (*dharmatā*) …
>
> 'Not caused by something else', 'peaceful', 'not elaborated by discursive thought',
>
> 'Indeterminate', 'undifferentiated': such are the characteristics of true reality (*tattva*).
>
> (MMK 18:7 & 9; Streng, 1967, p. 204)

Two Truths

Nāgārjuna's philosophy thus supports the idea put forward in the Perfection of Wisdom Sūtras that all conceptual apprehension of reality is an illusion. At the same time, however, the idea of a mind constructing an illusory image of reality equally fails the critical test, for 'the mind' can be analysed in the same critical manner as everything else and shown to be empty and illusory as well (see MMK 23). The teaching of 'emptiness', says Nāgārjuna, must therefore not be taken as the 'correct' view of reality as opposed to and distinct from false views. Instead, 'emptiness' is no viewpoint at all but an antidote to all views: 'Emptiness is proclaimed by the victorious one (that is the Buddha) as the refutation of all viewpoints' (MMK 13:18; modified following Streng, 1967, p. 198; see also MMK 22:11). This has decisive consequences for Nāgārjuna's understanding of the Buddhist doctrine.

Nāgārjuna declares that the Buddha's teaching should not be seen as a true description of reality. 'Emptiness' is the real point of the teaching, and thus the teaching in its entirety must be understood as an instrument to overcome *all* views and doctrines which present themselves as an adequate representation of reality. 'Out of compassion' the teaching has been promulgated by the Buddha 'for the destruction of all views' (see MMK 27:30). And for Nāgārjuna this includes the Buddhist teaching itself – should this itself be mistaken for a 'view'. The teaching of 'emptiness', as the true consummation of the Buddhist doctrine, resembles a medicine that must leave the body together with the sickening substances it is intended to remove (an image used in Ratnakūṭa, Kāśyapaparivarta 65, and referred to by Nāgārjuna in MMK 13:8).

For Nāgārjuna the most comprehensive summary of the Buddha's teaching is found in the doctrine of 'Dependent Origination' (*pratītyasamutpāda*, see above p. 46ff). For him this doctrine expresses most clearly the connectedness and dependency of all *dharmas,* in the light of which their 'emptiness' and lack of 'own-being' is but the logical conclusion. In this understanding of 'Dependent Origination' Nāgārjuna, of course, extends the dependency of conditioned origination to the logical inter-dependency of all concepts, so that even concepts like '*nirvāṇa*' appear as 'dependent' in so far as their meaning depends on other concepts. This is the reason why Nāgārjuna identifies the principle of Dependent Origination with the teaching of universal emptiness (MMK 24:18f). Ultimately however the insight into universal emptiness implies that there are not really any 'things' which dependently originate and disappear nor 'things' which are causally connected, for if there are no real entities there are neither any causal or other relations between them. In other words, the principle of Dependent Origination leads to the insight into emptiness, but then the insight into emptiness leads to the refutation of the principle of Dependent Origination itself:

> Origination and disappearance does not obtain for that which is empty. Origination and disappearance does not obtain for that which is non-empty.
>
> (MMK 21:9; Streng, 1967, p. 208. Similarly MMK 20:17f).

Not surprisingly, Nāgārjuna's understanding of the Buddhist teaching has often been compared to Ludwig Wittgenstein's analogy of the ladder: His own philosophy, says Wittgenstein, is like a ladder; once climbed up, it is no longer needed (*Tractatus Logico-Philosophicus* 6:54). In Nāgārjuna's case, the model was surely the Buddha's own comparison of his teaching with a raft that is only needed to cross over to the other shore, and should not be clung to thereafter (see above p. 40; in MMK 24:11 Nāgārjuna indirectly refers to the sūtra containing this parable). He summarises his understanding of Buddha's teaching in his famous theory of the 'two truths':

> The teaching of the *Dharma* by the various *Buddhas* is based on the two truths; namely, the relative (worldly) truth and the absolute (supreme) truth.
>
> Those who do not know the distinction between the two truths cannot understand the profound nature of the Buddha's teaching.
>
> Without relying on everyday common practices (i.e., relative truths), the absolute truth cannot be expressed. Without approaching the absolute truth, *nirvāṇa* cannot be attained.
>
> (MMK 24:9f; Inada, 1970, p. 146)

Buddha's teaching, insofar as it appears to give an accurate description of reality, should be understood as a relative or 'worldly ensconced' truth. It is not literally true, not true in the absolute or 'supreme' sense. The supreme or ultimate truth is unconceivable and ineffable, but without understanding the ultimate truth, *nirvāṇa* is not attained. The insight into the transconceptual, ineffable nature of ultimate truth is brought about through the relative truth of the Buddha's teaching with its inherent propensity for overcoming all views including itself. This is the reason why the Buddha's teaching is a 'relative' or 'ensconced' truth: its truth lies in its instrumental function to overcome the delusion that any of our views would adequately represent ultimate reality. In later Mahāyāna Buddhism the theory of the 'two truths' has often been merged or identified with the idea of the 'skilful means' used by a Bodhisattva to gradually guide deluded beings to the highest insight: the insight into the ultimate, ineffable nature of reality.

For Nāgārjuna the attainment of *nirvāṇa* presupposes the understanding of ultimate truth and thus the liberation from the delusion of confusing our customary conceptual representations of reality with its true nature. He designates this liberation as 'the blissful appeasement of conceptual representation (*prapañca*)' (MMK 25:24; see also MMK 18:4f; 18:9; 22:15 and MMK dedicatory verses). The use of this formula provides us with an illuminating clue to the background of Nāgārjuna's hermeneutics. For on the one hand, this terminology ('blissful appeasement of the *prapañca*') is linked to those Buddhist texts which deal with 'formless' meditation as the way to experience Nirvāṇa (e.g. AN 4:174 and 6:14) and on the other hand, to the very similar tradition of contemplative practice and mystical experience as it is testified to in Māṇḍūkya-Upaniṣad (cf. above p. 58f). Nāgārjuna seems to put his radical logical criticism of all views, including Buddhist views, at the service of a similarly radical transconceptual mystical practice and experience.

If the Buddhist teachings are not absolutely but only relatively true, does this then mean that all the Māhāyana teachings about Bodhisattvas, transcendent Buddhas and Buddha Lands are unreal? Now if one were to take these teachings as literally accurate descriptions of reality, they are certainly not absolutely true. But this is also the case with ordinary ideas as that there are 'really' trees or mountains or houses or 'selves'. Not a single statement about reality can count as *absolutely* true because they are all, without exception, constructed of deceiving concepts. This, however, does not entail, conversely, that all statements are relatively true. Some are simply and totally false, devoid of any capacity whatsoever to guide beings to the insight into ultimate truth – and in that sense all these Mahāyāna doctrines are certainly more true (on the level of relative truth!) than any other rival teachings or doctrines or everyday assumptions. It is virtually axiomatic in Mahāyāna Buddhism that the adequate linguistic response in the face of ultimate truth is silence (see for example Vn 9). But among the last and highest things we can say before we must pass over to silence is that reality, in its true nature, is Bodhisattva-like, is a pure Buddha Land, or indeed, *is* Buddha.

Yogācāra Idealism?

Within the Madhyamaka School the philosophical debates after Nāgārjuna centred to a large extent on issues concerning 'relative truth'. Is its function best fulfilled through a deliberate deconstruction of all views, along with its self-annulment? Or is it permissible to engage in some sort of positive and constructive reasoning as well (as long as it is not forgotten or denied that ultimately truth cannot be expressed)? While the Madhyamaka School was split over this question, the second major school of Mahāyāna philosophy, the Yogācāra or Vijñānavāda School, focussed on the epistemological issues resulting from the teaching of universal emptiness: Which are the mental mechanisms producing our habitual, illusory perception of the world, and how can these be overcome so that true insight might be attained or experienced? To exemplify some of their ideas, I will turn briefly to Vasubandhu, one of their major early representatives.

Like many Yogācāra thinkers and Yogācāra scriptures, Vasubandhu distinguishes 'three' aspects or 'natures' (*trisvabhāva*) of all beings and uses this as a starting point. For him (as already in the *Saṃdinirmocana Sūtra*, see Powers, 1995, pp. 95–127) the three natures of all beings are simply three different ways of designating their emptiness or 'naturelessness'. First, everything has an 'imagined nature' (*parikalpita-svabhāva*), in other words, what the thing appears to be in our conventional, deluded perception. The 'imagined nature' is an indication of emptiness inasmuch as that which we imagine the thing to be is not real. Second, everything has an 'other-dependent nature' (*paratantra-svabhāva*), in that everything depends on something else for its being (as explained in the Buddhist teaching of Dependent Origination). The 'other-dependent nature' is an indication of emptiness inasmuch as a thing's dependence on something else proves that it does not exist by itself and thus lacks 'own-being'. Third, everything has an 'absolutely accomplished nature' (*pariniṣpanna-svabhāva*), which is its ultimate, ineffable nature. This too is an indication of universal emptiness inasmuch as it directs us beyond the imagined, unreal 'self-natures' imposed by the deluded mind.

For Vasubandhu the great value of this distinction of three natures, or better: three ways of signifying 'naturelessness', lies in its suggestion of a strategy for overcoming illusion. Here the point of departure is the second, the 'other-dependent nature': By realising the complete (inter-) dependency of everything one will understand the unreal, illusory nature of our ordinary conceptual distinctions. The conceptual representation of reality has always a 'dualistic' character, in so far as every concept is constructed via its distinction from another concept. The understanding of the complete inter-dependency of 'everything' (or of all concepts) therefore reveals the unreality of all duality, and through understanding the artificial, unreal character of duality one understands the 'imagined nature' of everything. From here one can proceed to the true, the 'absolutely accomplished nature', for this is then understood as the utter absence of duality (see *Trisvabhāva-Nirdeśa* 24f; Kochumuttom, 1989, pp. 107–111). Everything perceived and thought of within a dualistic framework, that is through conceptual distinctions, is of an 'imagined nature'. In this light everything is 'mind only' or 'mere mental representation of consciousness' (*Viṃśatikā* 1; Kochumuttom, 1989, p. 166). Such statements have led many interpreters to the view that Yogācāra is a form of metaphysical idealism or idealistic monism. But for Vasubandhu, the insight that everything – insofar as it is dualistically conceived – is merely 'mind' or 'thought' would apply as well to that quasi-idealistic conception – and thus it would be equally erroneous:

> Through the perception that there is only thought,
> There arises the non-perception of knowable things;
> Through the non-perception of knowable things,
> There arises the non-perception of thought, too.
> (*Trisvabhāva-Nirdeśa* 37; Kochumuttom, 1989, p. 124)

Mind, too, whether one's own mind or other minds, must not be understood within the conceptual scheme of subject-object duality (see also *Viṃśatikā* 21). As long as one postulates mind as the sole reality one is still treating it as a 'graspable' object (*Triṃśatikā* 27f). In order to 'see' true reality, all duality needs to be abandoned – including idealistic or monistic conceptions (for these would still be 'dualistic'). Only then can a non-dualistic, a non-conceptual, form of insight be realised:

> That indeed is the supramundane knowledge
> When one has no mind that knows,
> And no object for its support; …
>
> That itself is the pure source-reality,
> Incomprehensible, auspicious and unchangeable;
> Being delightful, it is the emancipated body,
> Which is also the truth(-body) (*dharmakāya*) of the great sage.
> (*Triṃśatikā* 29f; after Kochumutton, 1989, p. 160)

Yogācārins have called this enlightened realization the 'transmutation' or 'revolution of the basis' (*āśraya-parāvṛtti*). Now, the interpretation of this 'transmutation' varies. At times it is merely understood as the complete and lasting cessation of those forces in consciousness which produce karmic tendencies and defilements and are responsible for the construction of illusion. But the 'transmutation of the basis' can also be presented as a kind of purification, as in the above verses, so that in enlightenment the original purity of mind – which is not different from the original purity or luminosity of everything – is restored by being freed from the defilements which have covered it. Then the 'pure source-reality' of everything shines forth. In any event it is assumed that such a state can be achieved only through meditative practice, as the Saṃdinirmocana Sūtra tersely states:

> … minds that do not meditate cannot know reality just as it is, whereas those that have meditated can do so.
> (Powers, 1995, p. 187)

For further reading: Cabezón (1994), King (1999), Kochumuttom (1989), Nagao (1991), Pye (1978), Sprung (1973), Streng (1967).

13

Tantric Buddhism

The illusory character of all conceptual distinctions (including that between Saṃsāra and Nirvāṇa); or the inconceivable but nevertheless auspicious and luminous character of true reality; or the Buddha-Nature not only of sentient beings but of all beings – such Mahāyāna Buddhist ideas had far-reaching implications for a new understanding and re-formation of Buddhist practice within the general framework of the Mahāyānic Bodhisattva ideal. A particularly salient example of this is the rise of Tantric Buddhism.

What is Tantrism?

The term 'Tantrism' refers to a specific religious movement and set of practices which achieved prominence in Hinduism and Buddhism during the second half of the first millennium CE. Some of the oldest Tantric scriptures, however, were presumably already composed between the third and fifth century CE, and several Tantric ideas and motifs have their roots in ancient Vedic traditions (particularly from the Atharvaveda) and perhaps even in pre-Vedic fertility cults.

'Tantra' literally means 'loom' or 'warp' but has also acquired the metaphorical meaning of the 'underlying principle' or the 'main point' of a set of teachings or a system of religious practice. According to its own self-understanding, Tantrism reveals the deepest – and hidden – meaning of the Dharma. Its ideas and practices are documented in a large group of scriptures called '*tantras*'. Though the Hindu tantras and the Buddhist tantras are clearly distinct texts, and though (as far as we know) neither of the two traditions made use of the tantras of the other, they nevertheless display many features in common. Both employ erotic imagery, for example, and both think in terms of a female-male polarity. Moreover we find striking similarities in their ritual practices (*sādhana*). The latter include the use of geometrical structures (*yantras* and *maṇḍalas*) to delineate real or imagined sacred spaces, the use of sacred formulas or syllables (*dhāraṇīs* and *mantras*) and special gestures (*mudrās*), the visualization of a chosen deity and the critical significance of an initiation by a Tantric master (*gūru*). The latter, along with the claim of presenting the hidden and deepest sense of the teaching (often expressed in ambiguous or encoded symbolic language), gives Tantrism its esoteric character. A further common feature is that both Hindu and Buddhist tantras aim at the acquisition of magical/supernatural powers (including forms of sorcery and alchemy) – at least as an intermediary spiritual goal. Moreover, Tantric spiritual practice testifies to the conviction that what are usually considered as unwholesome factors, such as aggression or desire, can be put to use within Tantric spiritual training and thereby transformed into wholesome energies. In conjunction with this conviction we find in both Hindu and Buddhist Tantrism certain antinomian tendencies expressed not only in unconventional lifestyles but also in ritual practices which can involve, for example, the consummation of forbidden and impure substances, like alcohol, meat or excrement, and the performance of sexual acts.

Particularly this antinomian trend – whether manifested merely symbolically or imaginatively, or lived-out in concrete practice – has often made Hindu and Buddhist Tantrism the target of severe criticism or outright rejection from the more conservative or mainline strands within both traditions. Nevertheless at some periods and in certain regions Tantrism became quite strong – or even the dominant form of Hinduism and Buddhism. Centring our discussion now on Buddhism, we find traces of Tantrism (mostly dating from the late first millennium and early second millennium) throughout the Buddhist world, whether in Indonesia, Sri Lanka, China or Korea. But it was in Bihar and Bengal in North India where Tantric Buddhism first flourished. Here the Pāla Dynasty (760–1142 CE) vigorously supported Tantrism, and the monastic universities of Vikramaśīla and Odantapurī became its vibrant centres. From here Tantric Buddhism was exported to Tibet where it was carefully preserved, highly venerated, practiced and further developed up to the present day. From Tibet it reached Mongolia which likewise became a stronghold of Tantric Buddhism (of the Tibetan type) and it even survived suppression by the communist regime in the second half of the 20th century. In a more moderate form, Tantric Buddhism also made its way to China and its neighbouring countries, though within the areas of Chinese cultural influence it persisted only in Japan, in the form of the old and once powerfully important school of Shingon-Buddhism.

Tantric Buddhism

A large number of Buddhist tantras have been preserved, either in their original language or in Tibetan, Mongolian and Chinese translations. The Tibetan canon contains about 500 tantras classified into four different groups: (1) *Kriyā Tantras* (tantras of 'action'), (2) *Caryā Tantras* (tantras of 'observance'), (3) *Yoga Tantras* (tantras of 'union') and (4) *Anuttarayoga Tantras* (tantras of 'ultimate union'); the latter is further divided into so-called 'Father Tantras' (*Yogottara Tantras* = 'higher yoga tantras') and 'Mother Tantras' (*Yoganiruttara Tantras* = 'highest yoga tantras') (see Williams with Tribe, 2000, pp. 202–17; Skilton, 1997, pp. 140–2).

Though this classification roughly reflects the chronological order in which the texts first emerged, its primary significance lies in its differentiation of the content of the texts. Kriyā Tantras, by far the largest group, deal primarily with ritual-magical ways of attaining a variety of worldly benefits or averting worldly mischief. In this sense the Tantric master thereby satisfies one of the classical Vedic goals: the pursuit of material well-being and power (*artha*). The very small group of Caryā Tantras focuses on the cult of Vairocana Buddha, who is presented as the central and principal figure within a schema of five supranatural Buddhas (see below). Yet here too, the aspiration to acquire supernatural powers for mundane purposes is quite pronounced. The Yoga Tantras likewise focus on Vairocana and on such related Bodhisattvas as Mañjuśrī, the famous and popular Bodhisattva of wisdom. However, in this group of texts we can see an obvious and remarkable shift in the goal of Tantric practice. The acquisition of supernatural powers is now subordinate to and in the service of the attainment of Buddhahood. These two tantra-groups, the Caryā and the Yoga, became the central texts of Shingon, the Japanese school of Tantric Buddhism. In the fourth class of tantras, the Anuttarayoga Tantras, it is no longer Vairocana but Buddha Akṣobhya who occupies the centre of attention (though in the Mother Tantra subdivision he is accompanied and sometimes replaced by various other divine figures). Here the goal is unquestionably the swift attainment of Buddhahood – or better: the swift realization that one *is* Buddha. Yet the means towards this end are fairly unusual, for it is in the two subdivisions of the Anuttarayoga Tantras that the antinomian tendencies and the widespread use of erotic imagery come to the fore. Famous and influential texts like the *Guhyasamāja Tantra*, the *Hevajra Tantra* or the *Caṇḍamahāroṣaṇa Tantra* belong to this class. Within the Tantric tradition these shifts of emphasis among the four classes of Buddhist tantras have often been seen as reflecting a spiritual progression wherein the practitioner gradually advances from the exclusively exterior aims of the Kriyā Tantras to the ultimate and highest aim of interior realization of the Anuttarayoga Tantras. The inner dynamism of this ascent is nicely expressed in traditional imagery: In the Kriyā Tantras the deities are laughing; in the Caryā Tantras the deities are gazing at each other; those of the Yoga Tantras are holding hands, and in the Anuttarayoga Tantras they are finally united in sexual union (see Wayman, 1997, p. 221f).

It is in the Anuttarayoga Tantras that the symbol of the '*vajra*', meaning 'diamond' or 'thunderbolt', comes into frequent use. The *vajra* is a multi-layered symbol which can indicate power ('thunderbolt'), the indestructibility of enlightenment and adamantine luminosity of ultimate reality ('diamond') and also universal emptiness (since the instrument serving as the *vajra* in Tantric ritual is shaped like two hollow bulbs which are connected). Within the context of erotic symbolism the *vajra* represents the male genital, while the *lotus* correspondingly symbolizes the vulva. The prominence of the *vajra*-symbol within some tantras has led at times to the identification of all Tantric

Buddhism as '*vajrayāna*' (the 'Diamond Vehicle'). Yet this can be misleading if one ignores the fact that the content of the Anuttarayoga Tantras is in some respects quite different from other Tantric texts.

The doctrinal framework of the Buddhist tantras is generally Mahāyānic. The Tantric practitioner, *yogin* (male) or *yoginī* (female), is usually understood as someone following the Bodhisattva-ideal, striving to combine the perfection of wisdom (*prajñā*: the insight into universal emptiness) with skill-in-means (*upāya:* the knowledge of how to realise and efficaciously exercise compassion, *karuṇā*). In the Anuttarayoga Tantras and related writings the inner complementarity and unity of these two major Bodhisattva virtues is symbolically expressed as the sexual union of a Buddha, who represents *skill in means/compassion*, with a female consort representing the *perfection of wisdom* (see Figure 7). Every Buddhist Sūtra usually opens with a description of the location and occasion for the Buddha's communication of the particular text. In the Anuttarayoga Tantras this setting is the sexual union of Buddha with his consort – who is highest wisdom: 'Thus have I heard: at one time the Lord reposed in the vagina of the Lady of the Vajra-sphere – the heart of the Body, Speech and Mind of all Buddhas' (see Snellgrove, 2002, p. 152).

The classification of highest wisdom as female is accompanied by an extraordinary praise of women in general – something which is otherwise virtually unheard-of in a Buddhist context. The Caṇḍamahāroṣaṇa Tantra (8:35ff), for example, can say:

> Women are heaven; women are Dharma;
> and women are the highest penance.
> Women are Buddha; women are the Saṅgha;
> and women are the Perfection of Wisdom.
>
> (George, 1974, p. 82)

Inasmuch as Mahāyāna Buddhism in general sees the perfection of wisdom as the source of all Buddhas – for this 'perfection' is enlightenment and makes a Buddha a Buddha – Tantric texts can identify the highest wisdom as the *mother* of all Buddhas, so that the aspect of female fertility is vitally present in the metaphor. The vulva becomes the *mahāmudrā*, the 'great symbol' referring to absolute reality itself. Not only the Buddhas but all reality (because in the end all reality *is* Buddha) shares the one ultimate Buddha-Nature and has therefore a single creative source (see HT 1:8:39–41). Several Tibetan texts can thus characterize the ultimate reality not only as 'sovereign' and 'all-creating' but also as a motherly reality (see Neumaier-Dargyay, 1992, pp. 28ff). 'Prajñā is called the Mother, because she gives birth to the world', says the Hevajra Tantra (1:5:16; Snellgrove, 1971, p. 62).

In response to the question of how 'loving-kindness' or 'benevolence' (*maitrī*), the first of the four divine mental states (see above p. 54), is initially brought about, the eminent Tibetan Tantric master Gampopa (1079–1153)

10. The union of wisdom and compassion.

explains that it results from 'the memory of benefits received'. The one being from whom each of us received the first and most fundamental benefits is our mother: She gave us life, raised us, taught us about the world and suffered for us. The love for her can be extended to all beings if we remind ourselves that during the long course of *saṃsāra* all have once been our mother (see Guenther, 1970, pp. 92–4). Ultimately all beings are permeated by the universal Buddha-Nature and it is the all-encompassing activity of the Buddha-Nature that they reflect (ibid. pp. 2f, 273f)

The Mahāyānic teaching of the universal Buddha-Nature (see above pp. 110ff) is of particular importance for Tantric spiritual practice, for it was this idea that provided the basis for a divergent approach to the 'defilements', the roots of spiritual and moral evil: If everything shares the Buddha-Nature this will hold for the defilements themselves. Therefore the spiritual task consists not in the eradication of the defilements but in the discovery of their specific share in the universal Buddha – so that they may be transformed into their own true luminous nature. In this light 'greed' can be seen as having at its root the longing for ultimate bliss and satisfaction; sexual 'lust' as originating in the powerful desire to overcome duality; 'hatred' as a projection of what ultimately is revulsion towards one's own deluded state, etc.

The schema of the Five Buddhas (*pañcatathāgatas*) and the way they are arranged within specific maṇḍalas provides the fundamental symbolic key not only to the integration of macrocosmic and microcosmic aspects of the universal Buddha-Nature, but also to an understanding of the spiritual evils as part and parcel of the powerful and wholesome creative energies of the universal Buddha. Within the structure of the maṇḍala, each of the first four Buddhas is assigned to one of the major directions while the fifth (usually Vairocana or Akṣobhya) occupies the centre. This signifies the immanence and all-pervasiveness of the Buddha-Nature, while the transcendent aspect of the Buddha-Nature is sometimes expressed by introducing a sixth Buddha who, as the 'primordial Buddha' (*ādibuddha*), transcends and encompasses all others.

Since the macrocosmic reality is mirrored in each of its microcosmic substructures, the Five Buddhas not only represent the universal Buddha-Nature but equally so the Buddha-Nature of each individual. Thus each one of the Five Buddhas is associated with one of the five *skandhas*, i.e. the five constituents of the human individual (see above pp. 36): Vairocana with consciousness, Akṣobhya with material form, Ratnasambhava with feeling, Amitābha with perception and Amoghasiddhi with constructing forces/volition. Further, the Five Buddhas correlate with five specific defilements and the corresponding forms of wisdom which inhere in each defilement and into which the defilement shall be transformed – that its true Buddha-Nature may shine forth: 'Anger is transformed into mirrorlike wisdom, arrogance becomes the wisdom of equality, desire becomes discriminating awareness, jealousy turns into all-accomplishing wisdom, and ignorance becomes the panoramic wisdom of all-encompassing space' (Shaw, 1995, p. 26f). These correspondences vary within the different tantras and their respective traditions, and they become greatly amplified and elaborated upon through the introduction of still further correlative groups of 'five': five colours, five identifying emblems, five gestures, five syllables, five consorts, five Bodhisattvas, five elements, five bodily centres of energy (*cakras*), etc. (see

Williams with Tribe, 2003, pp. 209–29; Snellgrove, 2002, pp. 189–213). These schemata are meant to aid the practitioner in understanding the interdependence of all things and discovering their Buddha-Nature. Within the Tantric ritual these correlations and connections are dramatically enacted, liturgically performed and reproduced – and thereby realised.

The sacred space of a specific maṇḍala is either physically created or mentally visualized. Through the utterance of a particular syllable or mantra the respective Buddha or a related deity is called forth and the practitioner identifies him- or herself with the 'chosen deity' (*iṣṭadeva* or *yidam*) – 'chosen' either with the help of a master or through oracle-like practices (e.g., throwing a flower onto a maṇḍala and seeing in which deity's field it lands). This identification is understood as the unfolding of the corresponding aspect of reality within oneself. Through a range of visualization tasks, and supported by diverse sets of ritual gestures, recitations and offerings together with various yogic practices, particular processes of spiritual transformation are made graphic, acted out and thereby triggered or reinforced. During Tantric practice, meditative visualization may undergo a transformation into supraconscious states resembling the traditional contemplative states of formless meditation (see above p. 58f), from which the practitioner re-emerges as someone in whom the specific deity – i.e. a particular aspect of the universal Buddha-Nature – assumes form, in order that compassionate work for the liberation of all beings may be carried out most powerfully.

Antinomian Tendencies

Traditionally Tantric ritual is not an open, public practice, but confined to a narrow circle of specially selected adepts who need to be empowered and initiated into their practice by a Tantric master. The ritual practices of the Anuttarayoga Tantras require initiations designated as particularly secret. These rituals and their initiation ceremonies involve the performance of sexual acts, the consumption of impure substances – alcohol, meat (even human flesh), urine, faeces, semen, vaginal fluids, etc. – and the corresponding texts contain exhortations which seem to encourage the violation of fundamental rules of Buddhist morality. The Guhyasamāja Tantra (5:5:4f) offers an example:

> ... those who take life, who take pleasure in lying, who always covet the wealth of others, who enjoy making love, who purposely consume faeces and urine, these are worthy ones for the practice.
>
> (Snellgrove, 2002, p. 170f)

Similar statements are found in a number of Anuttarayoga Tantras. The texts demonstrate a full awareness of the shocking nature of such statements. The Guhyasamāja Tantra, for instance, describes how the Bodhisattvas, upon hearing the just-quoted pronouncement, were puzzled and frightened, and even swooned. The provocation is intentional. It is crucial to understand that such Tantric texts are not denying the morally false and spiritually dangerous character of transgressive acts. They do however insist that within the context of Tantric practice, and given a correspondingly correct understanding, such acts are spiritually efficacious and beneficial: 'The same terrible action which leads people to hell, undoubtedly leads them to Release if it is done together with Method' (CT 7:24; George, 1974, p. 79). What does that mean?

One influential line of interpretation holds that such shocking statements are to be read entirely as extreme forms of figurative language. 'Killing living beings', for example, refers to overcoming saṃsāric existence; 'lying' means speaking relative truth; 'stealing', the development of the Bodhisattva-mind; 'the 'women' to which one shall resort are nothing but the four divine states (loving-kindness, compassion, sympathy and equanimity); and 'drinking alcohol' means to experience highest bliss. (For a classical example of this view see the position of the 'Bri-gung-pa-School in Sobisch, 2002, p. 375–9.) Sometimes the tantras themselves support this kind of interpretation, as when the Hevajra Tantra (2:3:30) explains that 'taking life' refers to the stopping of conceptual thinking in meditation, 'for the thought is the life'; or that 'lying' refers to the Bodhisattva's vow to save all beings, for there are in truth neither any beings to be saved nor any being to save them (as already declared in the Prajñāpāramitā Sūtras – see above p. 118).

Yet a purely metaphorical interpretation is problematic, in that it does not really explain the necessity of using such provocative images for otherwise entirely acceptable points. Nor can it explain the graphic and detailed instructions for the ritual performance of transgressive acts in a number of tantras. These instructions, it is sometimes said, should be understood as referring only to the practice of visualisation: Under certain conditions and within a supervised meditational framework, the practitioner should imagine the transgressive acts as a means of becoming aware of the corresponding 'likes and dislikes' within his or her own mind, that these tendencies may be transformed into wholesome spiritual energies. This way of understanding the transgressive acts is frequently found in monastic settings where the monks or nuns, bound by the monastic rule, did not feel entitled to actually perform such acts.

Another line of interpretation however does not hesitate to understand the transgressive acts as something that is indeed to be carried out, given the right method or circumstances. One argument declares that transgressive acts are justified and even required when motivated by compassion and performed as 'skilful means' by a Buddha or Bodhisattva (examples from Tantric texts may be found in Snellgrove, 2002, p. 175f). This idea is firmly rooted in the Mahāyānic Bodhisattva-ideal (see above p. 100) and is well-documented in texts far older than the Anuttarayoga Tantras, such as the *Upāyakauśalya Sūtra* (see Tatz, 1994). To be sure, there are situations in which people, out of compassion, find acts like lying, stealing or even killing unavoidable and morally justified. Some classical Mahāyāna scriptures extend this reasoning to sexual acts, as when a Bodhisattva consents to marriage so as to prevent the suicide of a lovesick girl (see Tatz, 1994, p. 34f); and the *Vimalakīrtinirdeśa* and the *Gaṇḍavyūha Sūtra* tell of Bodhisattvas who become courtesans 'in order to win men over … with the hook of desire' (Thurman, 1976, p. 71). Even in these relatively simple examples the justifying logic behind them is quite strained; in the far more complex Tantric examples involving sexual acts and the consumption of forbidden or impure substances, etc., the logic would be strained to the breaking point. The justification cannot refer directly to the realization of compassion but only indirectly: To the extent that these methods contribute to the practitioner's own spiritual development on the path to Bodhisattva perfection, they are indirectly beneficial to other sentient beings as well. But how and why can they fulfil this function?

Here the tantras make use of the homeopathic principle of curing like with like: 'Just as water that has entered the ear may be removed by water and just as a thorn may be removed by a thorn, so those who know how, remove passion by means of passion itself. (…) so the wise man renders himself free of impurity by means of impurity itself' (*Cittaviśuddhiprakaraṇa*, see Conze, 2000, p. 221; see also HT 2:2:46–51). The idea here is that within the framework of Tantric ritual and meditative practice under the supervision of a knowledgeable master, a limited and controlled use of transgressive acts can be permitted so as to lay bare the roots of one's defilements and transform them into corresponding aspects of the Buddha-Nature, of which they are but perverted manifestations. Thus a second principle, underlying the first, is that ultimately there are no impurities. Everyone and everything is Buddha, everything is pure in a sense which goes beyond the conventional distinctions between pure and impure, good and bad, etc. (see Saraha, Dohākośa 106; Conze, 2000, p. 238). When, for instance, the practitioner consumes forbidden and impure substances he or she should abandon all thoughts of 'edible' or 'inedible', of 'to be done' or 'not to be done' (CT 7:18; HT 1:7:24). What takes place then is a symbolic but nevertheless real act of going beyond duality, of liberating oneself from any attachment to conventional distinctions.

The motif of transcending duality also underlies the ritual performance of sexual union. Tantric texts praise orgasm not simply as a moment of 'blissful delight' but also as an experience which is 'profound' and 'vast' inasmuch as 'it is neither self nor other' (Saraha, *Dohākośa* 96; Conze, 2000, p. 237). Or as the female Tantric master Sahajayoginīcintā writes:

> In stages, because of the taste of desire,
> One ceases to know who is the other and
> What has happened to oneself.
> The lovers experience an inexpressible bliss
> They never experienced before.
>
> (Shaw, 1995, p. 186f)

Overcoming the barriers between self and other, thereby detaching oneself from dualistic, conceptual thinking, is understood as the realization of the most basic attributes of wisdom and compassion. If sexual union is achieved in this spirit the Tantric texts do not hesitate to equate it with enlightenment (e.g. CT 8:50): Freeing oneself from dualistic thinking is liberation from Saṃsāra, the compassionate identification of oneself with all others is not clinging to Nirvāṇa. Hence Tantric texts view their practice as fully in accord with the Bodhisattva ideal of remaining neither in Saṃsāra nor in Nirvāṇa (see above p. 99).

The Siddha

Broadly speaking, the ideal pursued by Tantric Buddhists is still the Bodhisattva ideal – and yet when a being actually manifests the Tantric ideal, it reveals a dimension and quality of its own in the person of the Siddha, the 'perfected' or 'accomplished' one, who has acquired higher supernatural capabilities and knows how to use them on the Tantric path. The unconventional lifestyle of Tantric Siddhas demonstrates their freedom from Saṃsāra as well as from Nirvāṇa; their mastery of supernatural powers is a sign of their unobstructed unity with the ultimate reality of everything. 'Free from learning and ceremony and any cause of shame, the yogin wanders, filled with great compassion in his possession of a nature that is common to all beings', says the Hevajra Tantra (1:6:23; Snellgrove, 1971, p. 65).

In traditional Tantric records (see, for example, Dowman, 1985) the Siddhas are often presented as Buddhist lay-people, both male and female, from all layers of society. They usually live with a partner of the other sex, though hermits (at least for some period of their lives) can also be found among them. Despite an individualist lifestyle they maintain close contact with either their guru or their own disciples. They hold more or less regular communal gatherings, often at cremation grounds, where they assemble to celebrate Tantric feasts. Some of the great Siddhas are presented as former monks who have abandoned their monastic life for spiritual reasons – Nāropa (11th cent.) is a famous example. Tradition claims that he was a highly learned monk and for some time even the abbot of the monastic university of Nālandā – a post which he quit so as to become a true practitioner instead of a scholar. He 'gave up all his belongings and books' and became the disciple of the Tantric guru Tilopa, and after many years of training he became able to act 'like a small child, playing, laughing, and weeping with the children' (Guenther, 1963, pp. 27, 89). Another famous Tantric, Padmasambhava (8th–9th cent.), is said to have successfully exercised his extraordinary supernatural powers to achieve the conversion of the Tibetan people (for a translation of his legendary biography see Evanz-Wentz, 1975). He too is closely associated with Nālandā, and likewise presented as a monk who abandoned celibate life. Nevertheless, Tantric Siddhas do not call the institution of monastic life into question. Padmasambhava, for instance, despite his own renouncement of celibacy, participated in the founding of a Buddhist monastery in Tibet. The Siddhas are often portrayed in such a way as to appear neither as proper monastics nor as ordinary laypeople. Like bees – to use a favourite Tantric image – they taste and enjoy the nectar of sensual pleasures without becoming attached to it. As Saraha, another of the great 8th-century Tantrics, puts it: 'Do not sit at home, do not go to the forest, but recognize mind wherever you are' (Conze, 2000, p. 238). Obviously the Tantric ideal of going beyond all dualities considerably relativized the traditional Buddhist distinction between monastics and laypeople without, however, doing away with it.

Frequently Tantric Siddhas exhibit a sovereign neglect of social conventions and – this time in line with traditional Buddhism – reject the barriers of the caste system. In this regard it is indeed illuminating to find the Hevajra Tantra relating the ritual consumption of forbidden and impure substances to the Tantric practitioner's attitude towards the members of the different castes. In the same way as the yogin should not avoid any impure food, he should converse with 'men of all castes' – 'for his mind conceives no distinctions' (HT 2:3:45ff; Snellgrove, 1971, p. 98). Somewhat controversial among contemporary historians of religion is the question as to whether the Tantric praise of women corresponds to a more egalitarian approach than is found in non-Tantric Buddhism. Whereas the majority of Western scholars tends to deny this, even holding that women were generally exploited and instrumentalised by male practitioners for ritual purposes, Miranda Shaw has presented considerable counter-evidence, arguing that 'the radical intent of Tantra's religious vision … is that *women and men can attain liberation together*' (Shaw, 1994, p. 204; for a more sceptical view see Young, 2004).

Tantric Buddhism will presumably remain a controversial phenomenon (which is partly in line with its own intentions). Without a doubt it has demonstrated a startling facility for integrating seemingly disparate and incongruous elements. Its spiritual practices and aims include the principal values of the Vedic tradition *(dharma*, *artha* and *kāma)* as well as the śramaṇic goal of *mokṣa* (salvation/liberation: see pp. 13, 16). It combines ancient fertility-cult motifs with sophisticated yogic meditation techniques and highly philosophical speculations with anti-intellectual and blatantly corporeal practices. Yet while this integrative capacity is seen by some as its extraordinary strength, making Tantrism in their eyes the consummation of Indian religious and cultural life, it is assessed by others as a sign of extraordinary weakness, as the last symptom of Buddhist decadence in India which finally led to its ruin.

Similarly controversial, Tantra's unconventional and antinomian tendencies can be viewed (not without reason) as the wellspring of 'spontaneity and new vitality' (Dowman, 1985, p. 2) and as the therapeutic attempt 'to master desires by immersion in them rather than flight from them' (Shaw, 1994, p. 21). On the other hand, it is difficult to deny that these very same tendencies harbour serious dangers, insofar as they may lend themselves to the legitimation of practices which are hardly experienced as expressions of 'great compassion' by those who become their victims. It is certainly alarming when the Caṇḍamahāroṣaṇa Tantra declares that the Tantric practitioner 'although he may kill a hundred Brāmans, ... will not be stained by sin' (CT 7:24; George, 1974, p. 79), or when some Tantric scholastics argue that killing other beings cannot constitute a moral transgression, for under the aspect of universal emptiness neither the killer nor the victim are ultimately real (see Sobisch, 2002, p. 435ff). The history of Tibet records several, sometimes lengthy periods of violent struggle between different orders and monasteries, and in the process of converting Mongolia Tantric Buddhists justified the use of violence against non-Buddhist shamanic circles (see Kollmar-Paulenz, 2003). On the whole, however, the religious history of Tibet has been comparatively peaceful, and by and large Tantric Buddhism fostered a mentality which sees violence as an evil to be avoided as far as possible. Probably the best illustration of this has been the unambiguously non-violent stance of the 14th Dalai Lama in the face of the violent suppression suffered by the Tibetan people during the 20th century.

For further reading: Bharati (1993); Dowman (1985); Shaw (1995); Singh (2004); Snellgrove (2002); White (2000); Williams with Tribe (2000, pp. 192–244); Young (2004).

14

Buddhism in China and Japan

Buddhism and the Chinese Civilisation

In India Buddhism arose as part of the Śramaṇa movement and reflected its longing for final liberation from the potentially endless series of rebirths and redeaths. In China however there was no belief in reincarnation nor anything akin to it. To make their message intelligible Buddhists had to adapt it to the Chinese cultural context. If the Dharma was not to remain an exotic alien element, it would have to be related to and expressed with indigenous ideas. Transplanting Buddhism onto Chinese soil thus involved the hermeneutic challenge of reformulating it against the background of China's vigorous and highly developed cultural-religious traditions: Confucianism and Taoism.

In the first place, there was the tremendous task of translating Buddhist scriptures into Chinese – more precisely, of finding or creating a suitable terminology that could render the highly specific doctrinal and philosophical concepts of Indian Buddhism into Chinese without losing too much of their original meaning and religious flavour. The early translators employed Taoist terminology rather excessively and indiscriminately; only gradually were ways found to give the Buddhist concepts a more distinctive profile. Yet that too entailed the rethinking and reformulation of Buddhist ideas vis-à-vis Taoism. Non-Mahāyānic forms of Buddhism proved less adaptable and thus, despite their missionary efforts, did not manage to establish themselves lastingly or to gain any significant influence in China. In contrast, Mahāyāna Buddhism regarded some of its own teachings as basically consistent with Taoist philosophy and thus was better equipped to expound the Dharma in Taoist terms. Yet by emphasising those aspects of Buddhism which displayed the strongest affinity with Taoism, Buddhism did indeed lay itself open to considerable Taoist influence.

Buddhist ideas of universal 'emptiness' (*śūnyatā*) and 'suchness' (*tathatā* – as the true, ultimate nature of everything), together with the identification of 'suchness' with Buddha-Nature (either as the Dharma-body [*dharmakāya*] or as the Buddha-germ [*tathāgatagarbha*]) were particularly accentuated so as to conform to the Taoist belief in the one ineffable *Tao* as the 'mother of the ten thousand things' (*Tao Te King* 1). The Taoist experience of intimate unity with nature was held to be comparable to Buddhist enlightenment; indeed, it virtually amounted to the discovery that one's true, supra-individual self is actually the universal Buddha-Nature, the true source and essence of everything, present in everything – 'analogous to the salt in water', as the famous Zen text of the *Ten Ox-herding Pictures* says (Kapleau, 1980, p. 316). Under Taoist influence, Buddhism now articulated its understanding of enlightenment in a way startlingly reminiscent of the classical upaniṣadic teaching of the oneness of *ātman* and *brahman* (see the famous metaphor of salt dissolved in water in *Chāndogya Upaniṣad* 6:13) – a teaching which Indian Buddhism had once so vehemently rejected.

Awakening to one's true nature as non-different from everything else's true nature was increasingly interpreted along the lines of the Taoist concepts of 'non action' (*wu-wei*) and 'spontaneity' (*tzu-jan*): The awakening could not be brought about through intentional effort of the individual self but had to happen *'of itself'*, as a spontaneous, natural break forth of true reality itself. Buddhists had rejected the upaniṣadic Brahman-Ātman teaching as (supposedly) inconsistent with their own teaching of 'not-self' (*anātman*). But they were open to the corresponding Taoist ideas because the Taoist understanding of naturalness and spontaneity opposed calculated action on the part of the individual self in favour of the 'original self' – and for Mahāyāna Buddhists this 'original self' was nothing else but the Buddha-Nature.

By and large the resulting symbiosis of Mahāyāna Buddhism and Taoism proved extremely fruitful from the spiritual point of view, and triggered a number of creative developments in Buddhism both within China itself and in the larger context of Chinese cultural influence: Korea, Vietnam and, in particular, Japan. Yet this was not achieved without 'blood, sweat and tears'. Initially, the closeness of the two traditions manifested itself in competing superiority claims, creating a strained situation of dangerous rivalry. From the second century CE onwards, Taoists promulgated a legend according to which the Buddha had been no one else than Lao-tzu, the semi-mythological founder of Taoism. After his disappearance from China, so the legend, Lao-tzu went to India where, as the Buddha, he disseminated his teachings and converted the 'barbarians'. Hence it is nothing but Lao-tzu's wisdom which they now bring back to China as the Buddha's Dharma. Apparently, the Buddhists did not at first protest against such an appropriation, though from the fourth century onwards, once Buddhism had become widespread and gained considerable strength, they attacked the legend as a vicious and deliberate Taoist fabrication for which those who had invented it were to suffer in the Buddhist hells. In turn, Buddhists now presented Lao-tzu as a 'disciple of the Buddha'.

The tensions did not remain at the level of reciprocal polemics. In the sixth century, under the rule of the Liang dynasty in South China, when Buddhism enjoyed the full support of the court, all Taoist temples were closed and ordained Taoist monks were forced back into lay-status in the name of Buddhist superiority. For their part, Taoists instigated several local persecutions of Buddhists during the fifth and sixth century. The seventh and eighth centuries witnessed numerous official moves to reassert the primacy of Buddhism, though in 844–5 Buddhism was subjected to severe persecution, aiming not at the total annihilation of Buddhism but at seriously reducing its enormous economical power. More than 4500 monasteries were closed and about 250,000 monks and nuns disrobed. Buddhism survived, though it never regained its former strength (see Eichhorn, 1973).

The great persecution was largely inspired by Confucian circles which had long suspected Buddhism of violating the key Confucian virtues of filial piety and loyalty to the sovereign. Did not the powerful Saṅgha show a tendency to develop into a state within the state? And were not Buddhist monastic ideals in conflict with family values? Monastic celibacy in particular clashed with the moral obligation of providing one's ancestors with descendants. On the other hand, the Buddhist virtue of compassion resonated well with the Confucian ideal of humanity or benevolence (*jen*), and Confucians acknowledged the various charitable activities of the Buddhist monasteries such as hospitals or almshouses for the poor. In contrast to Confucianism however Buddhism saw compassion not merely as a moral virtue. Its place was firmly grounded in the larger soteriological context of the Bodhisattva ideal. And this Buddhist insistence on deliverance or liberation met again with suspicion among Confucians, whose primary concern lay with the things of this world.

A major Buddhist contribution to the religious life of China was the veneration of Buddhas and Bodhisattvas, among whom the most popular were Buddha Amitābha and his associate Bodhisattva Avalokiteśvara, often venerated in female form as Kuan-yin (see Palmer and Ramsay, 1995). While Avalokiteśvara was called upon as a divine helper in every worldly need, and Kuan-yin in particular as the 'giver of children', Amitābha became increasingly a cosmic saviour figure. Both figures represent compassion: Avalokiteśvara/Kuan-yin the divine compassion for people in worldly need and sorrow, and Amitābha the divine compassion as saving grace. Neither Confucianism nor Taoism had ever given ultimate reality such a decidedly personal expression as Buddhism did. Contrary to the widespread Western cliché according to which Buddhism is exclusively associated with impersonal or non-personal concepts of transcendence, Buddhism in fact introduced a powerful personal element into the religious life of China.

T'ien-t'ai, Hua-yen and Nichiren

Initially, almost all philosophical schools of Indian Buddhism had their counterparts in China. The first schools to show a more distinct Chinese character (though a clear dependence on Indian traditions persisted) are the two sister-systems of T'ien-t'ai and Hua-yen. Both had to deal with the same two vital issues: Since the Buddhist Sūtras had been brought to China without any systematic order, and since the Chinese knew very little of their Indian background and historical genesis, the first major question was how to harmonise the often very different or even contradictory teachings of the numerous Sūtras; the second was how to understand the meaning of the central Mahāyānic idea of 'emptiness' given the divergent interpretations offered by the different Indian philosophical schools. Underlying both questions was a call for systematization, and this is what the two schools of T'ien-t'ai and Hua-yen provided.

In their interpretation of 'emptiness' both schools emphasised the 'suchness' (*tathatā*) of things – not however as the ineffable true nature of their reality as distinct from their phenomenal appearance, but as their true nature *in conjunction with* their appearance. According to Chih-i (538–97), the founder of the T'ien-t'ai school, 'suchness' is understood in three steps: At first one recognizes the provisional nature of ordinary appearance (form) and thereby understands emptiness. In the next step one sees that emptiness too is empty, i.e. it does not indicate some other substantial reality next to or behind the ordinary world. This leads to the third insight, formulated in the Heart Sūtra: Emptiness is not different from form and form not different from emptiness. Both, emptiness *and* form, in non-discriminating unity, constitute the true suchness of things. Chih-i calls this third step the understanding of the 'middle'. This 'middle' can unite the manifoldness of forms with their oneness in emptiness; it is 'the principle of one-is-all and all-is-one' – and that, in essence, is what Buddha-Nature means: Everything, not only sentient beings, shares the Buddha-Nature. Its full realization constitutes enlightenment which Chih-i expressed as 'the three thousand worlds in one thought-instant' (see Unno, 1997, p. 350).

Building upon a similar view the Hua-yen school arrived at the interpenetration and reciprocal inclusion of everything in everything. Every form is what it is only in relation to other forms. The father is a father only in relation to the son, and the son is a son only in relation to the father, etc. This classical position of the Madhyamaka school (see above p. 119) is understood by the Hua-yen school as implying that, ultimately, everything exists only in complete dependence upon and interconnectedness with everything else – and in that sense 'one is all'. At the same time, everything is empty of any own being – and in that sense 'all is one'. Oneness is real only in this *total interpenetration* in which every single particle of the universe mirrors the totality of the universe, for its being is nothing but the reflection of the whole in each single point. The truth of the 'all is one' lies in the 'one is all'. Oneness as thoroughgoing interconnectedness, without remainder, is the universal Buddha-Nature.

A major representative of this school, Fa-tsang (643–712), illustrated this fundamental thought with his famous 'mirror hall'. He constructed a room made up of ten huge mirrors, covering each of the four walls, the four corners plus the floor and ceiling – all the mirrors facing each other. He then put a Buddha statue and a light in the centre. The reflections of all the mirrors are found in each one of them – a complete mutual interpenetration manifesting the one Buddha-Nature in a virtual infinity of figures, each empty of own-being while at the same time entailing the whole (see Chang, 1972, p. 22–4). Fa-tsang's 'mirror hall' had been built after the classical model of 'Indra's Net', related in the Indian Avataṃsaka Sūtra: An infinite net hangs in the heavenly abode of god Indra. In each 'eye' of the net is a glittering jewel whose surface mirrors the infinity of all other jewels together with the infinite reflections of the whole in each one of them (see Cook, 1991, p. 2).

Chih-i believed that Buddha, after his enlightenment, had initially given his insight expression in the Avataṃsaka Sūtra, a huge collection of various Mahāyāna texts. However, since few were able to understand this Sūtra, the Buddha – according to Chih-i – adapted his teachings to the capacity of his listeners: he began with the non-Mahāyāna Sūtras, followed by the Mahāyāna teachings on the Bodhisattva ideal, then by the Perfection of Wisdom Sūtras. Finally, as the climax of his doctrine, the Buddha proclaimed the Lotus Sūtra in conjunction with the Mahāyāna Mahāparinirvāṇa Sūtra. Accordingly the Lotus Sūtra was venerated by the T'ien-t'ai school as the superior revelation providing the scheme for the integration of all the other Buddhist doctrines into the 'one vehicle' of universal Buddhahood. The Hua-yen school, however, insisted on the primacy of the Avataṃsaka Sūtra as most clearly expressing the doctrine of total interpenetration. Each of the two schools regarded all other Buddhist scriptures as 'skilful means', whose merely provisional value consisted in preparing the way for the exalted insights of its own key text.

T'ien-t'ai and Hua-yen exerted considerable influence on the further development of Chinese Buddhism. But whereas in China they gradually disintegrated in the aftermath of the great persecution of the ninth century, in Japan they lived on as distinct schools: T'ien t'ai as the *Tendai* and Hua-yen as the *Kegon* school. Tendai became the root of one of the most robust strands of Japanese Buddhism even today – i.e. the whole cluster of schools relying on the Lotus Sūtra and tracing their teachings back to Nichiren Shōnin (1222–82).

Nichiren, originally a monk of the powerful Tendai monastery on Mount Hiei near Kyoto, defended the supremacy of the Lotus Sūtra with a fervency hitherto unknown. Having also studied the teachings of Kegon (Hua-yen) and Shingon (the Japanese form of Tantric Buddhism), he acknowledged the closeness of both schools to the highest truth but blamed them for not recognizing that their own insights find their ultimate and exclusive foundation only in the Lotus Sūtra.

Nichiren's argument takes off from the enormous diversity of the Buddhist Sūtras: Since their teachings are often incompatible they cannot all be equally true. For Nichiren the essential truth, the 'bone and marrow' of all Buddhism, consists in just two doctrines: the beginninglessness or eternity of Buddhahood, and the idea of 'the three thousand worlds in one thought-instant' (see Nichiren, 2003, pp. 235, 251). Both doctrines culminate in the non-difference of *saṃsāra* and *nirvāṇa*, or as Nichiren puts it (in Hua-yen manner), in 'the mutual possession of the ten worlds': The first nine worlds are the six forms of *saṃsāric existence* (denizens of hells, demons, animals, humans, titans, gods) plus the three courses of Buddhist practice as 'hearers', 'pratyekabuddhas' and 'Bodhisattvas'. The tenth 'world' is *nirvāṇic existence*, the Buddha. According to Nichiren, the Lotus Sūtra is the only one that fully and unambiguously 'reveals that the nine worlds are all present in beginningless Buddhahood and that Buddhahood is inherent in the beginningless nine worlds' (Nichiren, 2003, p. 235).

If other schools like Kegon and Shingon claim the same doctrines they are in fact close to the truth but unable to justify it, for they cannot properly ground these doctrines in their own key scriptures – either because their scriptures exclude the so-called *icchantikas* (see above, p. 43) and thus fail to acknowledge the Buddhahood of *all* beings; or deny the beginninglessness of Buddhahood in disregarding the teaching of the Lotus Sūtra that Śākyamuni (Siddhārtha Gautama) attained enlightenment before all times; or divert attention to other Buddhas like Amida, Vairocana, etc.. For Nichiren all Buddhist scriptures are but dim reflections of the one truth revealed in the Lotus Sūtra (see Nichiren, 2003, p. 235), and all other Buddhas are but emanations of the one true Buddha, Śākyamuni (ibid. p. 256). The true mirror of the cosmos is its true revelation in the Lotus Sūtra, and just as the one true Buddha is present in everything, so he *is* each of the 69,384 characters of this text. The one and only Buddha is therefore truly venerated through this scripture. In consequence, Nichiren established the veneration of the title of the Lotus Sūtra as the highest form of practice. As the supreme *mantra* the syllables of the title ('*myōhō-renge-kyō*') constitute the most concentrated condensation and 'materialisation' of the Buddhist truth. The practice of chanting it is the realization of our true nature in unity with all nature:

> The function of fire is to burn and give light. The function of water is to wash away filth. The winds blow away dust and breathe life into plants, animals, and human beings. The earth produces the grasses and trees, and heaven provides nourishing moisture. The five characters of Myoho-renge-kyo are also like that. They are the cluster of blessings brought by the Bodhisattvas of the Earth, disciples of the Buddha in his true identity.
>
> (Nichiren, 2003, p. 218)

The unmistakable spirit of Taoist 'naturalness' and 'spontaneity' shines through this understanding of Buddhist practice as joined with Nichiren's interpretation of the Bodhisattva ideal.

With respect to the latter, Nichiren was radical. He was convinced that the welfare of the nation depends on the establishment and protection of the highest truth. The slightest divergence from true revelation will ultimately end with its being completely abandoned (see Nichiren, 2003, p. 239) and the inevitable consequence will be chaos and immense suffering. Out of compassion for the country Nichiren thus saw it as his duty – a tremendously burdensome duty – to attack all other schools of Buddhism because of their failure to recognize the Lotus Sūtra as the only true basis of revelation. Even the use of violence could be justified for the protection of the true Dharma, and he seriously called for the political authorities to desist from supporting the other schools or even to ban them, and to promote exclusively the Lotus Sūtra. The result, however, was that Nichiren himself was exiled, barely escaping execution, and had to spend several years in dire circumstances. This however did not weaken his firm resolve to be 'the pillar of Japan, … the eyes of Japan, … the great ship of Japan', 'father and mother to all the people' (Nichiren, 2003, pp. 276f, 287). It is not surprising that the political dimension of religious persuasion has always been particularly strong in the Lotus schools which followed in Nichiren's footsteps.

Zen Buddhism

Nichiren criticised Zen Buddhism for its alleged neglect of all scriptures (see Nichiren, 2003, p. 258). On meditation alone – so Nichiren's key objection – no decisive doctrinal conclusions can be established (see Nichiren, 2003, p. 276). Indeed, Bodhidharma, who according to the Zen Buddhist tradition brought the true spirit of Buddhism from India to China in the 6th century, is credited with the following verse:

> A special transmission outside the scriptures;
> Not founded on words and letters;
> By pointing directly to [one's] mind
> It lets one see into [one's own true] nature and [thus] attain Buddhahood.
>
> (Dumoulin, 1988, p. 85)

This is, and has always been understood as, Zen in a nutshell: Not doctrinal erudition is the goal, not learnedness in the scriptures, but the direct experience of one's true nature as Buddha-Nature. 'Mind is Buddha' or 'this very mind is Buddha' has become a frequent maxim of Zen Buddhism. Scriptures are like the 'finger pointing to the moon', as a famous Zen-metaphor has it. Scriptures speak of the wisdom from which they emerge. Having found this wisdom within oneself one no longer depends on the written word (see Yampolsky, 1967, p. 149). Through meditation one gains direct access to one's Buddha mind, the source of all scriptures. This conviction is reflected in the name of the school: *Zen* is the Japanese term for the Chinese word *ch'an* which is the short form of the Chinese pronunciation of the Sanskrit term *dhyāna*, i.e. 'meditation'.

A major theme of Zen Buddhism is how to understand meditational practice in relation to Buddha-Nature. If Buddhahood is our true nature – 'this very mind' – then why is there any need to strive for Buddhahood at all? What is the point of Buddhist practice? The most obvious answer seems to be the one suggested by the classical Yogācāra image wherein the defilements must be cleared away so that the originally pure mind can shine forth, and this idea did indeed prevail in early Zen (Ch'an) Buddhism in China. Increasingly, however, this 'answer' itself became a principal target of Zen's own criticism, as expressed in a famous story about Hui-neng, the Sixth Patriarch of Chinese Ch'an. Shen-hsiu, Hui-neng's learned rival in the succession to the Fifth Patriarch, had demonstrated the degree of his wisdom with a poem:

> The body is the Bodhi tree,
> The mind is like a clear mirror.
> At all times we must strive to polish it,
> And we must not let the dust collect.
> (Yampolsky, 1967, p. 130)

Hui-neng, himself an illiterate assistant in the monastery's kitchen, replied to this with a counter-poem of which three different versions are transmitted (see Yampolsky, 1967, p. 132):

> The mind is the Bodhi tree,
> The body is the mirror stand.
> The mirror is originally clean and pure;
> Where can it be stained by dust?

Another version reads:

> Bodhi originally has no tree,
> The mirror also has no stand.
> Buddha-Nature is always clean and pure;
> Where is there room for dust?

The final version (which became the most popular one) is the same as the second version – except for the changes in the third line (see Yampolsky, 1967, p. 94, fn. 14):

> Bodhi originally has no tree,
> The mirror also has no stand.
> From the first not a thing is.
> Where is there room for dust?

The three versions of Hui-neng's poem present an ever sharper and more comprehensive critique of the traditional idea that practice is an act of constant purification – whereas if the mind is the Buddha-Nature, and as such 'always clean and pure', how could it be stained by any dust? What defilements would any practice have to remove? The second version denies that enlightenment (*bodhi*) and mind have any substantial support; they are grounded in emptiness – as the third version explicitly concludes: 'From the first not a thing is ...'. If everything is Buddha-Nature because everything is empty, how can there be any distinction between mirror and dust at all? In emptiness there is no difference between Buddha-Nature and defilements. 'Good friends, the very passions are themselves enlightenment', teaches Hui-neng, and: 'When all things are illumined by wisdom and there is neither grasping nor throwing away, then you can see into your own nature and gain the Buddha Way' (Yampolsky, 1967, pp. 148f).

This attitude of neither attachment nor detachment – expressing the Bodhisattva ideal of being attached neither to Saṃsāra nor to Nirvāṇa – can be realised only by abandoning the traditional conception of practicing *for the sake of a* particular goal. The realization must happen spontaneously or instantaneously – as in the Taoist approach. It is this conviction which underlies the long dispute in early Ch'an Buddhism as to the so-called 'sudden' or 'gradual enlightenment'. The traditional idea of a gradual progress towards the goal of enlightenment through constant practice is rejected as an expression of exactly that kind of dualistic thinking from which one is liberated in enlightenment. True enlightenment is only attained in the abandonment of such ideas. As one of the more systematic Zen treatises says:

> Q: What method must we practise in order to attain deliverance?
> A: It can be attained only through a sudden Illumination.
> Q: What is a sudden Illumination?
> A: Sudden means ridding yourselves of deluded thoughts instantaneously. Illumination means the realization that Illumination is not something to be attained.
>
> (Blofeld, 1973, p. 43)

The 'deluded thoughts' stand for any form of dualistic, discriminative thinking. Enlightenment, the liberation from 'deluded thought', thus presupposes the relinquishment of any idea that enlightenment is 'something to be attained', something from which we are presently separated. 'The Ox has never really gone astray, so why search for it?' says the text of the Ox-herding pictures (Kapleau, 1980, p. 314).

This view triggered a new understanding of Buddhist practice. The most profane and ordinary acts could become authentic practice if 'seen as a primordial manifestation of Buddha-Nature' (Wright, 1999, p. 36). Formal meditation still had its place, but it was now understood as an exercise in relinquishing any kind of dualistic thinking – either by 'just sitting' and nothing else, or by meditating upon a *koan*, i.e. a riddle, paradoxical question or puzzling story demanding a spontaneous reaction which would show that the practitioner had left discriminative thought behind – as for example: 'Without words or without silence transgressing, how can one be unmistakably one with the universe?' (Mumonkan 24).

Under Taoist influence various arts also came to be regarded as genuine practice in which one's Buddha-Nature can manifest – painting, for example, or calligraphy, ikebana, pottery, martial arts and the famous practice of the tea ceremony. The principle is always the same: training in one of these arts shall lead the practitioner to a state of mind which enables him or her to bring about a natural, spontaneous, completely un-*art*ificial performance of the particular act.

Despite all these innovations, Zen did not lose its connection with the traditional forms of Buddhist practice, as can be seen in the Japanese Zen-master Dōgen (1200–53). The key motif of his own spiritual search is also the central theme of Zen: If all beings possess Buddha-Nature, then why did all the Buddhas and Bodhisattvas *practise* in their search for enlightenment (see Dumoulin, 1990, p. 52)? Like Nichiren, Dōgen began his religious career as a monk of the Tendai monastery on Mt. Hiei. He later joined the Zen movement and travelled to China to deepen his practice. After a sort of enlightenment experience he returned to Japan and became the founder of the Sōtō line of Zen Buddhism. His quest came to completion with his insight into the non-difference of practice and enlightenment: He discovered that the true manifestation of original enlightenment *is* the traditional striving for it; 'one's initial negotiation of the Way in itself is the whole of original realization' (Dumoulin, 1990, p. 79). Thus Dōgen could instruct his followers in quite traditional terms:

> Now, since you have left home and joined the family of the Buddha and become monks, you should learn the practice of the Buddha. To learn the practice and maintain the way is to abandon ego-attachment and to follow the instructions of the teacher. The essence of this is being free from greed. To put an end to greed, first of all, you have to depart from egocentric-self. In order to depart from egocentric-self, seeing impermanence is the primary necessity.
>
> (Shōbōgenzō-zuimonki 1:4; Okumura, 1987, p. 26)

'Seeing impermanence' is for Dōgen to be fully aware of each moment's brevity as the brevity of our own being: 'Remember that you are alive only today in this moment' (Shōbōgenzō-zuimonki 2:14; Okumura, 1987, p. 94). Time is being, and for Dōgen, the former Tendai monk, each moment in all its brevity nevertheless contains the totality of being and time (see Shōbōgenzō 20: Uji; see Tanahashi, 2000, pp. 69–76). For this reason, enlightenment is already and truly manifested in a practice which is persistently striving for it as something yet to come. The flying bird is one with the sky and the fish is one with the water, yet no matter how far they fly or swim they never reach an ‘end’. And so for us: We can always make progress in our practice, which *is* enlightenment, towards some infinitely greater end. It is true that wind reaches everywhere, but this, explains Dōgen, is no reason not to use a fan. On the contrary, fanning is precisely the experience of the wind reaching everywhere (see Shōbōgenzō 1: Genjō Kōan; see Tanahashi, 2000, pp. 35–9).

Pure Land Buddhism

The third major strand of Chinese and Japanese Buddhism, after the Lotus schools and Zen, is the Pure Land tradition. According to general Mahāyāna belief, a Bodhisattva, having attained Buddhahood, will manifest his own pure Buddha-land over which he presides and in which he creates optimal conditions for the beings’ progress to enlightenment (see above pp. 112ff). In the Indian Sukhāvatīvyūha Sūtra Buddha Śākyamuni tells the story of Buddha Amitābha (‘Amida’ in Japanese) who, while he was still the Bodhisattva Dharmākara, had vowed to create a pure land where all beings would easily and quickly attain enlightenment and into which they can be reborn if they sincerely aspire to be born there, entrust themselves to his vow and call his name.

In China the veneration of Amida Buddha developed into a flourishing and popular feature of Buddhist practice. Simple and ordinary people who felt unable to pursue a monastic career called upon Amida’s name, confident that he would guide them from their deathbed to rebirth in his marvellous land. But within monastic circles too the veneration of Amida, the meditation on him and the visualisation of his Pure Land became popular practices. Chih-i, the founder of T’ien-t’ai, taught the meditation on Amida as one of the approved practices, and masters like Tao-ch’o (562–645) and Shan-tao (613–681) expounded the theory and practice of recitation and meditation in the Pure Land tradition. T’an-luan (467–542), who had been trained in the Chinese branch of the Madhyamaka school and was also experienced in Taoist practices, contributed significantly to the tradition’s philosophical and doctrinal development. He interpreted Amida Buddha and his Pure Land as a manifestation and revelation of ultimate ineffable reality. As T’an-luan understands the narrative of Amida, it is not that the human being strives for the ultimate, but that the ultimate reaches out to the human being. T’an-luan’s writings became a decisive source of inspiration for Shinran (1173–1262), who developed the deepest and most radical understanding of this thought.

Shinran was a contemporary of Nichiren and Dōgen, and like these a former Tendai monk from Mt. Hiei. Dissatisfied over his lack of spiritual progress, he left the Tendai order and became a disciple of Hōnen (1133–1212), who taught Pure Land Buddhism in Kyōto. In 1207 Hōnen’s community was abolished, the master and his disciples were separated and exiled. During his exile Shinran married Eshin-ni and founded a family. From his point of view this was not a return to lay-status but an act of deliberately transcending the distinction between monastics and laity as something that had become irrelevant in face of Amida's all-encompassing compassion.

If, as Buddhism always taught, self-centredness is at the root of all our problems, then we cannot save ourselves through our own effort, through our 'self-power' (*jiriki*), argues Shinran. Any attempt to do so must necessarily fail. To increase one's religious efforts will only mean to increase self-centredness. The greatest piety is often only concealing tremendous arrogance and vanity:

> … those who wish to be born into the Pure Land have only thoughts of deceiving and flattering. Even those who renounce this world have nothing but thoughts of fame and profit. Hence, know that we are not good persons, nor persons of wisdom; that … within, the heart is ever empty, deceptive, vainglorious, and flattering. We do not have a heart that is true and real
>
> (Shinran, 1997a, p. 466)

Our only hope, then, is not to rely on 'self-power' but on 'other-power' (*tariki*), i.e. on Amida's vow, although in truth we are incapable of fulfilling even the three conditions attached to the vow: We lack *sincerity*, *trust* and genuine *aspiration* for the Pure Land. The virtue of Amida, on the other hand, manifests the perfection of sincerity; he trusted in reaching his goal when he made his vow, and aspired for the Pure Land that he wanted to create out of his boundless compassion. Thus it is Amida himself who has the triple mind that we need to fulfil the condition for rebirth in his Pure Land. So even our faith (*shinjin*) in Amida's vow must and does come from Amida. Out of compassion he directs his mind to us that we might share his mind. This can happen when we realise in despair our total inability to produce any good, hear the liberating message of Amida's boundless compassion, and then spontaneously gain faith. This faith *is* the manifestation of Amida's heart in us. Calling Amida's name (the practice called *nembutsu*) is not one more condition that we would have to fulfil; it is rather the natural sign of gratefully receiving faith.

Shinran's understanding of faith as sharing in Amida's mind implies that rebirth into the Pure Land and the attainment of enlightenment has, in a sense, already taken place in the one instant in which true faith arises. In this regard, Shinran sees the Pure Land tradition in line with the Zen notion of 'sudden enlightenment' (see Shinran, 1997, p. 534). At the same time, this faith is confidently expecting birth into the Pure Land as a future event. The structural similarity to Dōgen's claim that enlightenment is already present precisely in the process of being seriously sought, is evident.

Yet Shinran goes still further. In the Pure Land tradition there was the expectation that after achieving enlightenment in the Pure Land, the Bodhisattvas would return to the ordinary saṃsāric world and work for the liberation of all others. If genuine faith means receiving Amida's mind and manifesting it in the saying of his name, then the person of faith becomes a visible sign of Amida's saving presence. In pointing others to the only source of our salvation the true believer is a vehicle of Amida's presence in this world and thereby participates in Amida's compassionate Bodhisattva activity. For what greater service could be rendered to other beings than to point them towards Amida? In that sense, the arising of faith means not only an instantaneous rebirth into the Pure Land, but equally so the return to this world as a Bodhisattva. And once again, all this occurs only inasmuch as we faithfully expect it in the future – as Amida's gift. Only in pointing completely away from us towards Amida is his Bodhisattva work manifesting in and through us. For Shinran, the non-difference of Nirvāṇa and Saṃsāra is real and realised in this paradoxical structure of faith.

Participating through faith in Amida's mind does not mean that the defilements disappear; rather, their function is completely transformed. They now serve as constant reminders of our utter dependence on Amida, thereby deepening our faith. In that sense Shinran can say that if even the good people are saved, how much more so the evil ones – for the 'good' 'fail to entrust themselves wholeheartedly to Other Power' (Shinran, 1997, p. 663). And thus, insofar as our defilements drive us to wholehearted trust in Other Power they make no small contribution to the manifestation of Amida in our hearts and thereby make us participate in his Bodhisattva activity. While the idea of any spiritual achievements of one's own will only boost the ego, the realization of one's utter depravity forces one to turn to Amida as the sole hope. 'I ... am sinking in an immense ocean of desires and attachments and lost in vast mountains of fame and advantage' confesses Shinran (Shinran, 1997, p. 125). Even if his reliance on Amida should prove groundless and lead him to hell, says Shinran, he would have no regrets. For 'I am incapable of any other practice, so hell is decidedly my abode whatever I do.' He has no other choice than 'simply accept and entrust myself' (Shinran, 1997, p. 662).

But who or what is Amida? Following T'an-luan, Shinran understands Amida as the supreme manifestation of ultimate reality. T'an-luan distinguishes between the *dharmakāya* in its ineffable suchness and the *dharmakāya* as skilful means which are made manifest in the two form-bodies of the *saṃbhogakāya* and *nirmāṇakāya*. (On the three Buddha-bodies see above pp. 108ff.) Hence, the *dharmakāya* is not different from the two form-bodies; these are rather the sacramental means through which the ultimate becomes present. What in itself is inexpressible makes itself accessible to us in expressing itself in the form of Amida and of Amida's manifestation in Śākyamuni Buddha. Amida – or better: the boundless compassion which he represents – is thus the highest possible expression of what is ultimately inexpressible. It is the one Buddha-Nature that 'fills the hearts and minds of the ocean of all beings', including 'plants, trees, and land' (Shinran, 1997, p. 461). This universal Buddha-Nature is realised spontaneously (*jinen*), of

15

Buddhism and Modernity

The Challenge of Modernity

The global civilisation prevailing in our world today displays quite distinctive features which did not exist when the major strains of Buddhism (or of any other world religion) took shape. Buddhism, like all the others, faces the challenge of responding to this new situation in constructive, creative, critical and self-critical ways.

On the one side – and it could be called the practical side – contemporary life is marked by the tremendous technological advances of the last 200 years, advances which have brought countless advantages in such fields as medicine, food technology, education, information, traffic, etc. Unfortunately many of the positive results have had negative 'side-effects', creating new problems and/or expanding old problems to a new and previously unknown magnitude. Progress in medicine and food technology has led to an explosion of the global population which, if it continues at its present rate – or even accelerates – constitutes a major threat to all life on this planet. Technological progress brought an overwhelming improvement in the life standard of so many human beings, an unparalleled expansion of knowledge, a hitherto unknown array of communications and mobility options, but at the same time, coupled with the population boom, it caused the global ecological crises, which, if nothing is undertaken to effectively counter it, will clearly develop into a global tragedy. To be sure, technological advances have provided humanity with exciting new possibilities, but some of these entail horrific new threats as well, such as the threat of global extinction through modern weapons. Others throw up completely new ethical questions, as for example the moral issues resulting from genetic engineering. What is more, technological advances have made us aware of the bitter fact that not all parts of the world are equally enabled to enjoy technology's benefits, and of the scandalous fact that the poverty of the one group contributes to the wealth of the other group.

On the other side – the cognitive side – our global situation is marked by a particular approach to human knowledge most clearly expressed in the European Enlightenment: the spirit of critical and unrestricted rational enquiry. It is this spirit that made possible the extraordinary success of science which is behind the startling technological progress. This same spirit set in motion a ruthless questioning, criticising, reassessment and reconstruction in key areas of human culture and tradition – in the way we understand history, law, politics, social behaviour and religion. At least in some parts of the world enlightened criticism and restructuring have led to forms of legal protection, political co-determination and individual autonomy of which former generations had hardly dared to dream. And this spirit has certainly engendered a global increase of a moral sensibility which fosters human rights and gender equality, and rejects racial, sexual and religious discrimination. Yet the spirit of ruthless criticism is also accompanied by a potential for relativising, undermining or even sacrificing those utterly fundamental values which had hitherto served as the very foundation of human societies: belief in the good, the true and the holy. In this context our heightened global awareness of religious diversity becomes extremely important: Will the perception of that diversity corroborate the relativist claim that none of the religions is ultimately trustworthy, that they are just cultural relicts, remnants of bygone days, not jewels of wisdom but colourful and often bizarre trinkets? Or will it demonstrate the wealth and variety of ways in which humans could and still can, with rational justification, ground their lives in a reality deeper than that which appears on the surface?

In dealing with the ambivalence of the modern world, religious reactions have run at times to two extremes: total rejection and opposition, or total surrender and adaptation. For the most part, however, the religions have struggled to find balanced and nuanced responses, displaying the courage not only to criticise aspects of modernity but to be self-critical as well – self-critical precisely in the light of modernity's insights and achievements. In any event it would seem that the religions can evade a differentiated struggle with modernity only at the price of their own irrelevance and decline.

Buddhists of all schools have taken up this challenge, working towards a 'critical reflection upon Buddhist experience in the light of contemporary understanding and critical reflection upon contemporary understanding in the light of Buddhist experience' (Jackson and Makransky, 2000, p. 19). For the remainder of this chapter, I can only indicate, somewhat roughly and summarily, a few examples of where and how contemporary Buddhists have taken up the challenge of modernity. Since the important areas of politics and human rights were already addressed in Chapter 9, I will focus here on the challenges presented by feminism, ecology, scientific materialism and religious diversity.

The Challenge of Feminism

The role of 'Women in Buddhism' was carefully investigated in Diana Paul's groundbreaking and foundational book of the same name (1985; 1st ed.

1979), and further studies of the subject followed. Most influential has been Rita Gross's pioneering formulation of the principles of Buddhist feminism on the basis of historical research: 'Buddhism after Patriarchy' (Gross, 1993). Whereas Paul had cogently described the inconsistency between the basic Buddhist principle of non-attachment to all forms, on the one hand, and Buddhism's male bias in doctrine, practice and history, on the other, Gross treats this normatively – from a Buddhist perspective – not merely as an inconsistency but as a 'massive intolerable contradiction' (Gross, 1993, p. 215) which needs to be amended.

Ambivalent positions regarding the status of women are indeed all too obvious. While Buddhism stresses the basic equality of all humans and denounces contrary tendencies in Brahmanism, Buddhist texts at times disparage rebirth as a woman: For one thing, rebirth as a woman usually entails more suffering (which to some extent of course is simply a reflection of women's subordinate social position; see SN 37:3). For another, women are seen as more prone to the defilements than are men (e.g. AN 4:80; for a list of examples from Mahāyāna texts see Dayal, 1932, p. 223f). Although early Buddhism (and perhaps the Buddha himself) set up the female order, thus permitting women to embark on a religious career, the fact remains that the nuns are subordinate to the monks in almost every regard, and the establishment of the female order is even charged with having accelerated the decline of the Dharma (see above pp. 75f). Though Buddhism acknowledges that women *as women* can attain enlightenment and become *arhats,* the Buddhist tradition (with virtually no exceptions) nevertheless affirms that a Buddha has to be male and that a woman can become a Buddha only after a male rebirth. Accordingly, there are, for instance, no women in Amida's Pure Land (see Gōmez, 2002, pp. 74, 170).

This restriction of Buddhahood to men is particularly unfortunate in Mahāyāna Buddhism where, other than in Theravāda, the universal goal is to be a Bodhisattva, i.e. to become a Buddha. By implication then the supreme religious aim, Buddhahood, involves the overcoming of female existence. The conviction that a Buddha must be male is anchored in a mythological framework which confines all outstanding 'roles' – whether good or evil – to males. It is impossible that a woman can be a Buddha, a universal ruler (*cakravartin*), god Indra, god Brahmā, or Māra, the tempter and a Buddha's chief antagonist (see MN 115:15; Ñāṇamoli and Bodhi, 2001, p. 929). Of the thirty-two extraordinary bodily marks unique to a Buddha and a *cakravartin,* the tenth requires that his 'male organs are enclosed in a sheath' (DN 30:1:2; Walshe, 1995, p. 441). This obviously implies that the Buddha has to have male genitals (even if in an unusual manner). On the basis of these traditional premises the necessary maleness of a Buddha has been reasserted frequently throughout Buddhist history, though there are cases where this restriction is relativised, undermined or even out-and-out rejected. In the Saṃyutta Nikāya (5:2) paying attention to sexual identity is criticised in the name of the Not-Self teaching. In Mahāyāna Buddhism, the influential Vimalakīrtinirdeśa Sūtra tells of a goddess (Vn 7) who exchanges roles with her male dialogue partner, Śāriputra (one of the Buddha's chief disciples): She magically transforms herself into him, and him into herself, thus demonstrating to him that in the light of universal emptiness 'in all things, there is neither male nor female' (Thurman, 1976, p. 62). In the 'Sūtra of Sāgara, the Nāga King' the view that Buddhahood cannot be attained in a female body is explicitly rejected with the argument that highest enlightenment and the true Dharma are 'neither male nor female' (see Paul, 1985, p. 235f). These insights notwithstanding, cases where women are unambiguously designated as Buddhas, are extremely rare. Most can be found in Tantric Buddhism (see Shaw, 1994, pp. 27f, 105), where in one instance a woman is even praised as manifesting the thirty-two marks while yet being a 'beautiful woman' (see ibid. p. 119).

How should we interpret the blatant discrepancy between central Buddhist insights on the one side and the traditional restriction of Buddhahood to the male gender (together with all the other forms of gender-inequality) on the other? It is temptingly easy to ascribe all this solely to the patriarchal cultural settings in which Buddhism developed – too easy, for Buddhism has demonstrated its ability to resist other features of its cultural context, as for example the caste system (even if not always with thoroughgoing consistency). So what within Buddhism itself made an accommodation to prevailing sexist norms acceptable, despite its own better insights?

A frequently discussed explanation finds that ascetic practice is linked to a misogynist mentality. Indeed, there is ample scriptural, let alone psychological, evidence that women were seen as a threat for Buddhist monks, either because they might lure them back into lay status, or seduce the monks into violating their celibacy. Sometimes, as for example in the Ugraparipṛcchā, even Buddhist laymen are advised to regard their own wife as 'impure, … stinking, … disagreeable, … an enemy, … an executioner, … an ogre, … a demon, … a hag'. For wives, says this text, are 'an occasion for the construction of lustful thoughts, … of malicious thoughts, … an obstacle to insight' (see Nattier, 2003, pp. 248ff). Misogynist tendencies are obviously indicative of the problems *male* Buddhists have with their sexuality, which might also explain why in Buddhist Tantrism, with its integration of sexuality into spiritual practice, the pendulum could swing to the opposite pole by declaring women collectively as 'heaven' and 'highest wisdom', as 'Buddha, Dharma and Saṇgha' (see above p. 130).

There are texts which exhibit a more balanced view, at least insofar as they offer a reciprocal perspective. Aṅguttara Nikāya 1:1, for instance, declares that no sight is so able to obsess the mind of a man as the sight of a woman, and no sight so able to obsess the mind of a woman as the sight of a man (see Nyanaponika and Bodhi, 1999, p. 33). Yet if there was indeed such a clear and balanced acknowledgement of the spiritual challenge caused by the attractiveness of the other sex on *both* sides, then why do we find so many misogynist and so few misandrist texts? The most likely answer: The male perspective is dominant because men dominated the institutional structures of Buddhism. Buddhist feminists, like their counterparts in other religious traditions, are therefore not only working towards an equal access of women to a game in which men set the rules, but towards a change of the rules themselves (see Gross, 1993, 225f). This involves a number of practical issues. From this perspective, the restitution of the nuns' order in Theravāda Buddhism, for example, can be only a very preliminary goal, and will even prove counterproductive if the supremacy of the monks is not abolished at the same time. (For a range of innovative activities of women in Buddhism see Tsomo, 2000).

But how strong is the Buddhist interest in demanding, and even actively struggling for, radical reforms within its own institutions and within society? According to Rita Gross, Buddhism lacks the impetus of a 'prophetic voice' exercising powerful social criticism in the name of justice and righteousness, and has therefore been too lax with regard to social circumstances that contradict its own insights and ideals (see Gross, 1979, p. 134f). In this regard, Buddhism could learn from the Abrahamic religions. On the other hand, Buddhism has also something to teach. It holds the important message for feminists 'that basic human sufferings and existential anxieties are not patriarchy's fault and will not be eliminated in post-patriarchal social conditions' (ibid., p. 133).

The Challenge of Ecology

In their anti-Western and, more specifically, anti-Christian polemics some Buddhists have claimed that the biblical idea of subjugating nature (see Genesis 1:28) and the (supposedly) consequent Western project of conquering nature, are not only alien but 'abhorrent' to the nature-friendly attitude of Buddhism (e.g. D.T. Suzuki, quoted in Harris, 2000, p. 130). The so-called 'Eco-Buddhist' conviction that a solution to our ecological crises must involve the replacement of the Judaeo-Christian worldview with a Buddhist one has met with much approval among environmentalists. However, there is ample evidence that the Buddhist tradition, for the most part, favoured a pro-civilisation attitude not very different from what we find in Western traditions (see Harris, 2000). It is also important to realise that most contemporary environmental problems have been unintentional side-effects of rather beneficial developments and not maliciously intented. But today we can no longer be innocently naive. We are now fully aware of the ecological implications of our 'civilising' activities and need to review them in that light. Given the relative newness of the ecological crisis, Mary Evelyn Tucker, an ecologist with long experience, has aptly described the current situation as a challenge to *all* religions, a challenge calling upon them to enter their 'ecological phase' with a self-critical enquiry into what in their respective traditions might be conducive and what obstructive to a global, multidisciplinary effort to arrive at effective ecological solutions (see Tucker, 2003; Tucker and Grim, 2001).

In the attempt to ground an ethic of ecological concern in Buddhist teachings and tradition, two lines of exploration have been brought forward. The first is linked to the general protection of nature implicit in the first *śīla,* which is the precept not to harm or kill sentient beings (see above pp. 64ff); the second line of exploration relates to the doctrine of universal interdependence, understood as a most powerful spur to wholistic thinking.

Now, the first precept has always included animals, and in the spirit of Buddhist compassion and loving-kindness, the ideal here is not only not to harm animals but also actively to protect them and do them good. Indeed their protection is explicitly listed among the principle duties of the ideal Buddhist ruler, as we have seen, (see above pp. 85f). Benevolence towards animals is rooted in a feeling of deepest solidarity with them as fellow saṃsāric beings – and in fact as one's own kin, for in the immeasurably long course of the saṃsāric past each being has at some point has been related to all others (see above p. 68). Although plants and material objects are not seen as possible forms of reincarnation and hence not considered sentient beings as such, they too must be protected for they provide the basis and *lebensraum* of animals and humans (and other sentient beings such as ghosts, who were assumed to inhabit trees).

But does the restoration of an eco-system, the preservation of an endangered species or the re-cultivation and re-creation of extinct ones, even make sense from a Buddhist perspective? After all, existence as an animal is not seen as a desirable form of rebirth, and in the Pure Land, as a sort of Buddhist ideal world, there are not only no women but also no 'real' animals (see above, p. 113; on this whole paragraph see Schmithausen, 1991 and 1997). Yet in Thailand Buddhist monks have been actively involved in the restoration of eco-systems – in reforestation projects, for example. Some monks even symbolically 'ordained' trees in order to protect them and protest against deforestation. While clothing trees in monastic robes certainly exceeds what is acceptable according to strict monastic rule, it is nevertheless a spectacular way of expressing the dignity and importance of nature (see Harris, 2000, p. 118; Harvey, 2000, pp. 177–185).

The complexity of ecological systems and the interconnectedness of all their components is something that any serious ecological ethics has to take into account. In her classical study, 'Mutual Causality in Buddhism and General Systems Theory' (Macy, 1991), Joanna Macy argued that Buddhism is particularly amenable to the development of a comprehensive ecological worldview ('deep ecology'). For, according to Macy, it stresses not only causality and dependence but *reciprocal* causality and *inter*-dependence. However, Macy's attempt to demonstrate this for the early Buddhist understanding of the principle of dependent origination (see above pp. 46ff) has been convincingly refuted as untenable (see Schmithausen, 1997, pp. 56ff). The idea of reciprocal, interdependent causality emerged only with the Madhyamaka argument of logical, conceptual interdependence (the cause is a cause only in relation to the effect and conversely, etc.; see above pp. 122f), and only thereafter it did become critically important in some Mahāyāna branches, particularly in its Chinese forms such as Hua-yen. Moreover, the ecological usefulness of this philosophical idea is moot. While there are serious concerns that the idea of *total* interpenetration might even be counterproductive since it seems to negate any substantial distinction between ecologically harmful and beneficial factors (see Harris, 2000, p. 125) and may not have clear practical implications (see Schmithausen, 2000, pp. 62–70), there are also those who appreciate its positioning of the human being within the overall scheme – not as opposed to nature but as part of nature – and its implicit emphasis of human co-responsibility within an overarching non-anthropocentric perspective (see the contributions of Odin and Barnhill to Tucker and Williams, 1997, and the discussion in James, 2004, pp. 58–105).

The Challenge of Scientific Materialism

In a thoughtful essay the Tibetan Buddhist scholar Thupten Jinpa (Jinpa, 2003, pp. 79ff) distinguishes three different Buddhist attitudes to Western science: Buddhism and science are seen either as *rivals*, or as *allies*, or as *partners*. To some extent, at least, this reflects the actual historical sequence: In the first encounter with Western scientific findings Buddhists often reacted adversely, largely because these were used by Christian missionaries as polemical weapons to argue that Buddhism rests on an obsolete worldview (for some samples see Cabezón, 2003, pp. 41ff; Thelle, 1987, pp. 32f). It was not long however before Buddhism's apologists turned the tables, arguing that Buddhism, and not Christianity, is compatible with the findings of science and, even more importantly, with its spirit of experience-based free enquiry. A particularly prominent and influential representative of this rather typical modernist view was the Sri Lankan scholar K.N. Jayatilleke (1920–1970). Yet the conviction that Buddhism and science are antagonistic has not entirely disappeared, and those who still hold it do so because they identify modern science with a materialistic worldview and refute it with the traditional Buddhist arguments against the classical materialism of the Cārvākas (see Jinpa, 2003, p. 79f; see also above pp. 17, 28).

The understanding of Buddhism and science as partners is to some extent the result of a more differentiated view in which Buddhists have learned to distinguish between the scientific method as a formidable means of increasing our knowledge and understanding of the world on the one hand, and scientific materialism's ideological claim to be the only possible worldview consistent with modern science on the other. But clarifying just what the ideological implications and limitations of scientific findings really are, and exploring the extent to which scientific research might itself receive valuable impulses from traditional religious ideas, could well set the stage for a fruitful dialogue between Buddhism and science as partners. In this context, the relationship between traditional Buddhist ontology (analysis of 'being') and modern molecular physics, as well as that between Buddhist epistemology (analysis of knowledge) and modern cognitive sciences are of particular interest (see the contributions to Wallace, 2003).

Meanwhile, the dispute over scientific materialism is increasingly becoming an ideological debate within Buddhism itself. Many Buddhists, especially (though by no means exclusively) those with a Western background, have themselves assumed a reductionist worldview and now reinterpret Buddhism along these lines. This is particularly evident with regard to the possibility of an afterlife and the related question of the nature of mind (see Wallace, 2003, pp. 10–27; Siderits, 2001).

A number of Buddhists today have publicly claimed that rebirth (or any other form of afterlife) is no longer credible. Keiji Nishitani, a prominent representative of the Kyoto School (a contemporary Japanese branch of Buddhist philosophy) has called reincarnation a 'myth' and a 'pre-scientific illusion' which is now best understood as a radical way of expressing the essential impermanence of all life (see Nishitani, 1982, 173ff). Similar views have been taken by Francis Cook (see Cook, 1989), Whalen Lai (Lai, 2001), Roger Jackson (Jackson, 2000) and others. Likewise, several twentieth-century Pure Land Buddhists, like Naotaro Nonomura or Daiei Kaneko, propose an interpretation of the Pure Land as entirely a symbol of *this-worldly* human realization (see Kigoshi, 2004). Against this, other Buddhists, like K.N. Jayatilleke (1969) or Gunapala Dharmasiri (1988, p. 179f.), have expressed their confidence in the literal truth of reincarnation – not necessarily in the full-blown variant with all its hells and heavens, but as a factual assumption about the continuance of human striving beyond death until the final goal of Nirvāṇa is reached. Like Francis Story (1975), they find this belief corroborated by parapsychological research into apparent recollections of previous lives (see Stevenson, 1966). Still others attempt a sort of middle position, demanding at least a partial 'demythologisation' of traditional Buddhist concepts of afterlife while leaving the question as to whether there might be some form of afterlife deliberately open (see Buddhadāsa, 1989, pp. 132–5), or speculating about new ways of conceiving of 'afterlife', e.g. in terms of process philosophy (see Yokota, 2000).

What happens to Buddhism if it is understood along the lines of 'scientific materialism'? It turns from an impressive religion into an impressive psychology, from metaphysical faith into aesthetic poetry (see the 'confession' of Roger Jackson in Jackson, 2000, pp. 220, 240f). Would this imply any loss? The philosopher of religion John Hick has pointed out that such a reductionist view of Buddhism would transform 'the Buddha's teaching from good to bad news', for there would no longer be any hope for the vast numbers of people who failed to attain Nirvāṇa in this life (see Hick, 1989). Yet there is more: Nirvāṇa itself would no longer be the unconditioned deathless reality but simply a name for some sort of very conditioned and fragile psychological state. The non-difference between Nirvāṇa and Saṃsāra would no longer mean, as it did for Nāgārjuna, that Sāṃsāra is elevated to the level of Nirvāṇa as equally mysterious, but that Nirvāṇa is reduced to a sort of Saṃsāra no longer understood as a 'cycle of rebirth', and no longer emanating any mystery whatsoever.

David Loy, speaking for Buddhists who have lost their 'belief in a transcendent dimension', suggests that the accompanying existential 'lack' might be mended by 'a *this-worldly* transcendence of self' – which means abandoning all futile attempts to 'ground myself' by realising that 'I have always been fully grounded in so far as I am nondual with the world' (Loy, 2002, p. 213f). Loy claims that his suggestion is in line with the tradition of universal emptiness, and particularly its understanding in Hua-yen. Yet his proposal is not without its problems: Traditionally the realization of one's non-duality with 'the world' was part and parcel of the realization that 'the world' itself is non-dual – that is, the world itself is not other than unconditioned *transcendent reality*. If this latter dimension is negated and the world reduced to its phenomenal appearance, the 'realization of nonduality' will merely function as one more surrogate, and hardly be able to fill the existential 'lack' which Loy has so aptly described.

The Challenge of Religious Diversity

In current discussions of religious diversity the most frequently told story is probably the old narrative of the blind-born men, each of whom grabs hold of an elephant at a different part of its body. An elephant is like a post, says the one who touches the leg. No, it's like a storeroom, replies he who touches the belly. A third, touching the end of the tail, holds that it is like a broom – and so on. Hotly denying each other's claims, they finally end up fighting 'with their fists'. Today this story is usually offered as a religious response to the non-religious challenge forcefully advanced by David Hume and other critics of religion: Since all religions equally deny each other's claims, none of them is trustworthy, let alone credible. Our story responds to this challenge with the idea that religious claims are incompatible only if the limited perception expressed in each one of them is mistaken for the whole truth. Religions should refrain therefore from any attempt to absolutise their own teachings – such is the moral of the story *as it is told today*. But hardly anyone is aware that this story, in all its numerous versions, goes back to the Buddhist Pāli Canon where it appears with quite a different moral. In addition to the blind men, we find here a king with healthy eyes who clearly sees what the elephant is truly like, and is thus amused at the spectacle of the others' fighting. Now, the text makes it fairly clear who the king with healthy eyes is, for it is given to the Buddha to comment that the various religious teachers of the time are like 'people who see only one side of things' and thus 'engage in quarrels and disputes' (Ud 6:4; Ireland, 1997, p. 89). Far from illustrating any kind of religious equality, then, the point is that the other teachers, but not the Buddha, are attached to their partial views, do not know what the true Dharma is like and are unable to cross the stream of Saṃsāra (see Ud 6:5). In its original version the story thus exemplifies exactly the kind of attitude to religious diversity against which its contemporary versions are usually directed.

Traditionally the Buddhist attitude towards other religions has been either *exclusivist*, denying them any insight that would enable salvation or liberation, or *inclusivist*, granting them liberating insight of an inferior degree. While the latter view has only rarely been applied to non-Buddhist religions, it was typical of the approach taken to other schools or branches of Buddhism. Mahāyāna asserted its superiority over non-Mahāyāna schools (pejoratively designated as 'Hīnayāna' = 'inferior vehicle'); Theravāda asserted its superiority over Mahāyāna (where too much Hindu influence had supposedly rendered it heretical); and each Mahāyāna school asserted its own superiority over all others, ranking them hierarchically according to their respective levels of realization (all of which were lower than its own). Though a growing number of contemporary Buddhists are now willing to extend an inclusivist position to non-Buddhist religions as well (see Kiblinger, 2005), there are also several Buddhists (see Buddhadāsa, 1967, pp. 12ff; Abe, 1985; Takeda, 2004; Tanaka, 2005) who tend towards a *pluralist* acceptance of at least some other religions as equal, acknowledging that they incorporate different but equally liberating forms of insight and ways of practice (for an elucidation of exclusivist, inclusivist and pluralist approaches see Schmidt-Leukel, 2005a).

This pluralistic development results from a growing involvement of Buddhism in inter-faith dialogue. To some extent *ecumenical* dialogue among different branches of Buddhism has been furthered through the establishment of the World Fellowship of Buddhists (WFB) in 1950. However, it is worth noting that these exchanges apparently proceed more effectively not within or between the traditionally Buddhist countries but rather among the various Buddhist communities living as minorities in the West – i.e. living in a situation where Buddhist minorities simply cannot afford the luxury of mutual rivalry, and where the atmosphere in the society-at-large fosters real opportunities for improving mutual knowledge and understanding.

The greatest progress has been made in the dialogue between Buddhism and *Christianity* (for a broad and detailed overview, see Brück and Lai, 2001; for a brief summary, see Schmidt-Leukel, 2005b, pp. 1–26). Several study centres in Asia, for instance, the Nanzan Institute for Religion and Culture in Nagoya, Japan, or the Ecumenical Institute for Study and

Dialogue in Colombo, Sri Lanka, and flourishing academic associations in the West, such as the American Society for Buddhist-Christian Studies or the European Network of Buddhist-Christian Studies, have helped this dialogue to develop and deepen on all levels. Christians have benefited from Buddhist meditation practice as well as from the spiritual wisdom of Buddhist teachings, and in its encounter with Buddhism Christianity has rediscovered its own mystical heritage. Buddhists have received important impulses from Christian social involvement as well as from Christian intellectual/theological approaches to the various challenges of modernity. One highly significant form of exchange is the inter-monastic dialogue (see www.dimmid.org), dedicating to promoting a mutually fruitful and enriching sharing of monastic experience in both religions.

Yet Buddhist-Christian relations are still weighed down by the burden of the past as Christians, with the support of the colonial powers, attempted so often to triumph over Buddhism, at times even by violent means; and Buddhists, in reaction, also resorted to occasional violence, as was massively the case in Japan and to a lesser extent in China. Today, the aggressive missionising practices of evangelical Christians in the name of their exclusivist claims evoke painful memories and poison the atmosphere between Buddhists and Christians in a number of Asian countries, particularly in Korea and Sri Lanka, thereby undermining the progress of dialogue.

Most recently the importance of Buddhist-*Jewish* dialogue has considerably increased in light of the fact that there is a surprisingly high number of Jews among Western converts to Buddhism (see Linzer, 1996; Kasimow *et. al.*, 2003). Like Christians, Jews too find themselves rediscovering their own mystical tradition through their encounter with Buddhism, and are deeply enriched through meditative practices as exercises in 'slowing down' – reminiscent of the idea of 'Sabbath' (see Green, 2003). It is too early to speculate about the nature of the inspiration which Buddhists may draw from their encounter with Judaism, yet two issues might be worth mentioning: Tibetans in exile have developed an interest in how Jews managed to keep their tradition alive despite being separated from their land for so long. And Norman Fisher, a Zen teacher of Jewish background, has recently made the startling admission: 'If Buddhism is strong on liberation and self-realization, it is weak on relationship' (Fischer, 2003, p. 259). No doubt that this is an area where Judaism has much to teach.

Buddhism's relationship with *Islam* has been more or less strained ever since the Muslim invasions of India and the destruction of major Buddhist centres by Muslim troops. The Kālacakratantra, a late Indian Tantric scripture, gives an indication of the sentiments and mood of many Buddhists at that time when it promises them a final military victory over the Muslim forces and the destruction of their 'barbarian religion' (see Newman, 1995, p. 288). On the Muslim side, Buddhists were perceived either as polytheists or as atheists, with the result that their religion could hardly be accepted as a genuine manifestation of divine revelation. There were, though, exceptions to this, and we even find attempts to identify the Buddha with the prophet *Dhu'l-kifl* mentioned in the Qur'an (21:85f; 38:48). The Islamic mystics in India, the Sufis, have often shown a real interest in the meditative practices of Buddhists, though there are almost no signs of any serious Buddhist-Muslim dialogue. This might be about to change, however. In the wake of the Taliban's demolition of the Buddha images of Bamiyan a continuing series of Buddhist-Muslim dialogues has been set in motion (see Yi and Habito, 2005). Additionally, Daisaku Ikeda, spiritual mentor of the Nichiren-Buddhist Soka Gakkai, and Majid Tehranian, a Muslim and Professor of International Communication at the University of Hawaii, have published a Buddhist-Islamic dialogue on 'Global Civilization' (see Ikeda and Tehranian, 2003), in which the primary focus falls on an exploration of shared beliefs and goals in questions of ethics and fundamental human values.

Most problematic is perhaps the relationship between Buddhism and *Hinduism*, and part of the problem is that both sides tend to deny the existence of the problem. The history of Buddhist-Hindu relations is not only replete with mutual accusations (starting with the frequent polemical snipes at Brahmanism in the Pāli-Canon and the subsequent denunciation of the Buddha as a heretic in Hindu texts) but also with records of violent clashes. Following a war against the Hindu Tamils in Sri Lanka, King Duṭṭhagāmaṇī (2nd cent. CE) was comforted by Buddhist monks with the words that the thousands of Hindus who had been killed were 'not more to be esteemed than beasts' (Mhv 25:110; see Geiger, 1912, p. 178); and Hindu records relate that Sudhanvan (8th cent. CE), a king in Central India, was encouraged by the great Hindu philosopher Kumārila to exterminate all Buddhists in his realm (see Hazra, 1995, p. 387). The conflict between Buddhist Sinhalese and Hindu Tamils in Sri Lanka today is not only an ethnic conflict; there is also a religious component grounded in mutual fears, stemming from the conflicts of the past, and enflamed by the supposed need to defend one's own religion against that of the other (for the Buddhist perspective see Bartholomeusz, 2002).

Notwithstanding the long record of mutual polemic and hostilities, it cannot be denied that Buddhism and Hinduism have drawn much inspiration from one another throughout their histories, and one finds developments in both traditions which would have been unthinkable without the impulse coming from the other side. Still, the seeming impassibility of the traditional barriers, together with the mutual unwillingness to admit that there is a problem at all, have had the net effect of blocking any sincere and open-minded dialogue. Once again, it was Daisaku Ikeda who together with Karan Singh published a pioneering venture into such a dialogue (see Singh and Ikeda, 1988), though so far this initiative has not had any successors.

One, and perhaps *the*, crucial topic of the Buddhist dialogues with Judaism, Christianity, Islam and theistic Hinduism concerns the understanding of ultimate reality. Are Buddhist views of the Ultimate compatible with those of theistic religions which understand the Ultimate as a personal God? They might be seen as compatible if, on the one hand, it is not forgotten that Nirvāṇa refers not merely to an unconditioned state but to an unconditioned reality; and if, on the other hand, the personal features of God are relativised by the time-honoured proviso that God, strictly speaking, is inconceivable and ineffable, and that personalist God-talk is therefore expressive of a specific form of God-experience rather than expressive of God's nature in itself. Through its own ways of experiencing the Ultimate and letting the human life be transformed by it, Buddhism has much to offer and share with other religions. In the long run, however it remains to be seen whether Buddhism will continue to identify itself with the sighted king helping to liberate the blind from their partial insights by teaching them the superior truth about the elephant (or teaching them the modern variant thereof: that in reality there is no elephant); or whether it will come to understand itself as one way among other ways – each of which might collectively deepen and broaden its own mode of understanding by listening to and sharing what all of the others have learned through their own partial experiences.

If Buddhism's encounter with Modernity makes one thing unmistakably clear it is that 'Understanding Buddhism' is not only a task for non-Buddhists but very much so for Buddhists themselves.

For further reading: Gross (1993); Harvey (2000); Jackson, Makransky (2000); Keown (2000); Kiblinger (2005); Tucker, Williams (1998); Wallace (2003).

Bibliography

Abe, M. (1985) 'A Dynamic Unity in Religious Pluralism: A Proposal from the Buddhist Point of View', in Hick, J. and Askari H. (eds) *The Experience of Religious Diversity*, Aldershot: Gower Publishing, pp. 163–90

Anesaki, M. (1916) *Nichiren, the Buddhist Prophet*, Cambridge: Harvard University Press

Aronson, H.B. (1980) *Love and Sympathy in Theravāda Buddhism*, Delhi: Motilal Banarsidass

Aung, S.Z. and Rhys Davids, C.R.F. (1969) *Points of Controversy or Subjects of Discourse being a Translation of the Kathā-Vatthu from the Abhidhamma-Piṭaka*, London: Pāli Text Society

Bartholomeusz, T. (2002) *In Defense of Dharma: Just-War Ideology in Buddhist Sri Lanka*, Richmond: Curzon

Bechert, H. (1966, 1967, 1973) *Buddhismus, Staat und Gesellschaft in den Ländern des Theravāda Buddhismus* (Schriften des Instituts für Asienkunde in Hamburg, vols XVII/1, XVII/2, XVII/3), Frankfurt am Main/Berlin: Otto Harrassowitz

Bechert, H. and Gombrich, R. (eds) (1984) *The World of Buddhism*, London: Thames and Hudson

Bendall, C. and Rouse, W.H.D. (transl.) (1971) *Śikshā-Samuccaya: A Compendium of Buddhist Doctrine Compiled by Śāntideva*, Delhi: Motilal Banarsidass (repr.)

Benz, E. (1966) *Buddhism or Communism: Which Holds the Future of Asia?* London: George Allen and Unwin

Bharati, A. (1993) *Tantric Traditions*. Revised and enlarged edition of *The Tantric Tradition*, Delhi: Hindustan Publishing Corporation

Blofeld, J. (transl.) (1973) *The Zen Teaching of Hui Hai on Sudden Illumination: A Complete Translation of the Tu Wu Ju Tao Yao Mên Lun and of the previously unpublished Tsung Ching Record,* London: Rider & Company

Bodhi, B. (transl.) (2000) *The Connected Discourses of the Buddha:: A Translation of the Saṃyutta Nikāya*, Boston: Wisdom Publications

Brockington, J.L. (1998) *The Sacred Thread: Hinduism in its Continuity and Diversity*, Edinburgh: Edinburgh University Press

Bronkhorst, J. (1986) *The Two Traditions of Meditation in Ancient India*, Stuttgart: Franz Steiner Verlag

Brück, M. von and Lai, W. (2001) *Christianity and Buddhism: A Multi-Cultural History of Their Dialogue*, Maryknoll: Orbis

Buddhadāsa, B. (1967) *Christianity and Buddhism*, Bangkok: Sinclaire Thompson Memorial Lecture, 5th Series

Buddhadāsa, B. (1989) *Me and Mine: Selected Essays of Bhikkhu Buddhadāsa*, ed. D.K. Swearer, Albany: SUNY

Burton, D. (2004) *Buddhism, Knowledge and Liberation: A Philosophical Study*, Aldershot: Ashgate

Cabezón, J.I. (1994) *Buddhism and Language: A Study of Indo-Tibetan Scholasticism*, Albany: SUNY

Cabezón, J.I .(2003) 'Buddhism and Science: On the Nature of the Dialogue', in Wallace, B.A. (ed.) *Buddhism and Science: Breaking New Ground*, New York: Columbia University Press, pp. 35–68

Cahill, P.J. (1982) *Mended Speech: The Crisis of Religious Studies and Theology*, New York: Crossroad

Carter, R. and Palihawadana, M. (transl.) (1987) *The Dhammapada: A New English Translation with the Pāli Texts and the First English Translation of the Commentary's Explanation of the Verses*, New York and Oxford: Oxford University Press

Carrithers, M. (1983) *The Buddha*, Oxford: Oxford University Press
Ch'en, K. (1972), *Buddhism in China: A Historical Survey*, Princeton: Princeton University Press
Chappell, D. (ed.) (1999) *Buddhist Peacework: Creating Cultures of Peace*, Boston: Wisdom Publications
Chandrkaew, C. (1982) *Nibbāna: The Ultimate Truth of Buddhism*, Bangkok: Mahachula Buddhist University
Chang, G C.C. (1972) *The Buddhist Teaching of Totality: The Philosophy of Hwa Yen Buddhism*, London: Allen and Unwin
Collins, S. (1982) *Selfless Persons: Imagery and Thought in Theravāda Buddhism*, Cambridge: Cambridge University Press
Collins, S. (1998) *Nirvana and Other Buddhist Felicities: Utopias of the Pali imaginaire*, Cambridge: Cambridge University Press
Conze, E. (1959) *Buddhist Scriptures*, London: Penguin Books
Conze, E. (1980) *A Short History of Buddhism*, London: Allen & Unwin
Conze, E. (1995) *The Perfection of Wisdom in Eight Thousand Lines & Its Verse Summary*, San Francisco: Four Seasons Foundation (5th repr.)
Conze, E. (ed.) (2000) *Buddhist Texts Through the Ages*. In collaboration with I.B. Horner, David Snellgrove and Arthur Waley, Oxford: Oneworld (repr.)
Conze, E. (2001) *Buddhism: Its Essence and Development*, Birmingham: Windhorse
Cook, F.H. (1989) 'Memento Mori: The Buddhist Thinks about Death', in Davis, S. (ed.) *Death and Afterlife*, Houndmills: Macmillan, pp. 154–76
Cook, F.H. (1991) *Hua-yen Buddhism: The Jewel Net of Indra*, University Park, PA and London: Pennsylvania State University Press
Crosby, K. and Skilton, A (transl.) (1995) *Śāntideva: The Bodhicaryāvatāra*, Oxford: Oxford University Press
Dayal, H. (1932) *The Bodhisattva Doctrine in Buddhist Sanskrit Literature*, London: Paul Kegan
Dharmasiri, G. (1988) *A Buddhist Critique of the Christian Concept of God*, Antioch: Golden Leaves Publishing
Dharmasiri, G. (1989) *Fundamentals of Buddhist Ethics*, Antioch: Golden Leaves
Dhirasekera, J. (1982) *Buddhist Monastic Discipline: A Study of its Origin and Development in relation to the Sutta and Vinaya Pitakas*, Colombo: Ministry of Higher Education Research Publication Series
Dowman, K. (1985) *Masters of Mahāmudrā: Songs and Histories of the Eighty-Four Buddhist Siddhas*, Albany: SUNY
Dumoulin, H. (1988) *Zen Buddhism: A History: Vol. 1: India and China*, New York–London: Macmillan
Dumoulin, H. (1990) *Zen Buddhism: A History: Vol. 2: Japan*, New York–London: Macmillan
Eckel, M.D. (1997) 'Is There a Buddhist Philosophy of Nature?', in Tucker, M.E. and Williams, D.R. (eds) *Buddhism and Ecology: The Interconnection of Dharma and Deeds*, Cambridge, MA: Harvard University Press, pp 327–49
Eichhorn, W. (1973) *Die Religionen Chinas* (Die Religionen der Menschheit 21), Stuttgart: Kohlhammer
Emmerick, R.E. (transl.) (1970) *The Sūtra of the Golden Light: Being a Translation of the Suvarṇabhāsottamasūtra*, London: Luzac
Evans-Wentz, W.Y. (1975) *The Tibetan Book of the Great Liberation*, Oxford: Oxford University Press (repr.)
Fischer, N. (2003) 'Calling, Being Called', in Kasimow, Keenan and Klepinger Keenan (eds) (2003), pp. 251–60
Flood, G. (2002) *An Introduction to Hinduism*, Cambridge: Cambridge University Press
Foard, J., Solomon, M. and Payne, R. (eds.) (1996) *The Pure Land Tradition: History and Development*, Berkeley: Asian Humanities Press
Fuchs, R. (transl.) (2000) *Buddha Nature: The Mahāyāna Uttaratantra Shastra by Arya Maitreya. With Commentary by Jamgön Kongtrül Lodrö Thayé*, Ithaca, NY: Snow Lion Publications
Gard, R.A. (1961) *Buddhism*, New York: George Braziller

Geiger, W. (transl.) (1912) *The Mahāvaṃsa or The Great Chronicle of Ceylon*, Oxford: Pali Text Society

George, C.S. (1974) *The Caṇḍamahāroṣaṇa Tantra: A Critical Edition and English Translation, Chapters I–VIII*, New Haven: American Oriental Society

Gethin, R. (1998) *The Foundations of Buddhism*, Oxford: Oxford University Press

Gombrich, R. (1988) *Theravāda Buddhism: A Social History from Ancient Benares to Modern Colombo*, London: Routledge & Kegan

Gomez, L.O. (1996) *The Land of Bliss: The Paradise of the Buddha of Measureless Light*, Honolulu: University of Hawaii Press

Gowans, C.W. (2003) *Philosophy of the Buddha*, London–New York: Routledge

Green, A. (2003) 'To Learn and to Teach: Some Thoughts on Jewish-Buddhist Dialogue', in Kasimow, Keenan and Klepinger Keenan (eds) (2003), pp. 231–42

Griffiths, P.J. (1987) *On Being Mindless: Buddhist Meditation and the Mind-Body Problem*, LaSalle: Open Court (repr.)

Griffiths, P.J. (1994) *On Being Buddha: The Classical Doctrine of Buddhahood*, Albany: SUNY

Griffiths, P.J. (1997) 'Indian Buddhist Meditation', in Takeuchi (ed.) (1997), pp. 34–66

Grosnick, W.H. (1995) 'The Tathāgatagarbha Sūtra', in Lopez (ed.) *Buddhism in Practice*, Princeton: Princeton University Press, pp. 92–106

Gross, R. (1993) *Buddhism After Patriarchy: A Feminist History, Analysis and Reconstruction of Buddhism*, Albany: SUNY

Guenther, H. von (transl.) (1963) *The Life and Teaching of Nāropa*, Oxford: Oxford University Press

Guenther, H. von (transl.) (1970) *Jewel Ornament of Liberation*, London: Rider & Co.

Habito, R. (2005) *Experiencing Buddhism: Ways of Wisdom and Compassion*, Maryknoll: Orbis

Halbfass, W. (2000) *Karma und Wiedergeburt im indischen Denken*, München: Diederichs

Harris, E. (1997) *Detachment and Compassion in Early Buddhism* (Bodhi Leaves 141), Kandy: Buddhist Publication Society

Harris, I. (2000) 'Buddhism and Ecology', in Keown, D. (ed.) *Contemporary Buddhist Ethics*, Richmond: Curzon, pp. 113–135

Harrison, P. (1992) 'Is the Dharma-kāya the Real "Phantom Body" of the Buddha?', in *Journal of the International Association of Buddhist Studies* 15, pp. 44–94

Harvey, P. (1998) *An Introduction to Buddhism: Teachings, History and Practices*, Cambridge: Cambridge University Press (repr.)

Harvey, P. (2000) *An Introduction to Buddhist Ethics: Foundations, Values, Issues*, Cambridge: Cambridge University Press

Harvey, P. (2004) *The Selfless Mind: Personality, Consciousness and Nirvāṇa in Early Buddhism*, London–New York: Routledge Curzon (repr.)

Hazra, K.L. (1995) *The Rise and Decline of Buddhism in India*, New Delhi: Munshiram Manoharlal Publishers

Hick, J. (1989) 'Response to Cook', in Davis, S. (ed.) *Death and Afterlife*, Houndmills: Macmillan, pp. 177–9

Hirakawa, A. (1990) *A History of Indian Buddhism: From Śākyamuni to Early Mahāyāna*, Honolulu: University of Hawaii Press

Hoffmann, H. (1961) *The Religions of Tibet*, London: Allen & Unwin

Hookham, S.K. (1991) *The Buddha Within: Tathagatagarbha Doctrine According to the Shentong Interpretation of the Ratnagotravibhaga*, Albany: SUNY

Huong, B.G. (2004) *Bodhisattva and Śūnyata: In the Early and Developed Buddhist Traditions*, Delhi: Eastern Book Linkers

Ikeda, D. and Tehranian, M. (2003) *Global Civilization: A Buddhist-Islamic Dialogue*, London–New York: British Academic Press

Inada, K.K. (1970) *Nāgārjuna: A Translation of his Mūlamadhyamakakārikā with an Introductory Essay*, Tokyo: Hokuseido Press

Ireland, J.D. (transl.) (1997) *The Udāna & The Itivuttaka*, Kandy: Buddhist Publication Society

Jackson, R. (2000) 'In Search of a Postmodern Middle', in Jackson R. and Makransky, J. (eds) *Buddhist Theology: Critical Reflections by Contemporary Buddhist Scholars*, Richmond:

Curzon, pp. 215–46
Jackson, R. and Makransky, J. (eds) (2000) *Buddhist Theology: Critical Reflections by Contemporary Buddhist Scholars*, Richmond: Curzon
James, S.P. (2004) *Zen and Envirolmental Ethics*, Aldershot: Ashgate
Jayatilleke, K.N. (1969) *Survival and Karma in Buddhist Perspective* (The Wheel Publication 141/2/3), Kandy: Buddhist Publication Society
Jinpa, T. (2003) 'Science As an Ally or a Rival Philosophy? Tibetan Buddhist Thinkers' Engagement with Modern Science', in Wallace, B.A. (ed.) *Buddhism and Science: Breaking New Ground*, New York: Columbia University Press, pp. 71–85
Jones, K. (1989) *The Social Face of Buddhism: An Approach to Political and Social Activism*, London: Wisdom Publications
Kapleau, P. (1980) *The Three Pillars of Zen*, London: Rider and Co (rev. and expanded)
Kasimow, H., Keenan, J.P. and Klepinger Keenan, L. (eds) (2003) *Beside Still Waters: Jews, Christians, and the Way of the Buddha*, Boston: Wisdom Publications
Kawamura, L.S. (ed.) (1981) *The Bodhisattva Doctrine in Buddhism*, Waterloo, Ontario: Wilfried Laurier University Press
Keenan, J.P. (transl.) (1992) *The Summary of the Great Vehicle by Bodhisattva Asaṅga* (BDK English Tripitaka 46–III), Berkeley: Numata Center for Buddhist Translation and Research
Keown, D.V., Prebish, C.S. and Husted, W.R. (eds) (1998) *Buddhism and Human Rights*, Richmond: Curzon
Keown, D. (ed.) (2005) *Contemporary Buddhist Ethics*, Richmond: Curzon
Kern, H. (transl.) (1963) *Saddharma-Puṇḍarīka or The Lotus of the True Law* (SBE 21, repr.), New York: Dover Publications
Kiblinger, K.B. (2005) *Buddhist Inclusivism: Attitudes Towards Religious Others*, Aldershot: Ashgate
Kigoshi, Y. (2004) 'Shin Buddhist Doctrinal Studies and Modernization. A Dispute over the Understanding of the Pure Land', in Barth, H.-M. et. al. (eds) *Buddhismus und Christentum vor der Herausforderung der Säkularisierung*, Hamburg: EB-Verlag, pp. 89–101
King, R. (1999) *Indian Philosophy: An Introduction to Hindu and Buddhist Thought*, Edinburgh: Edinburgh University Press
King, S.B. (1991) *Buddha Nature*, Albany: SUNY
Kochumuttom, T.A. (1989) *A Buddhist Doctrine of Experience: A New Translation and Interpretation of the Works of Vasubandhu the Yogācārin*, Delhi: Motilal Banarsidass (repr.)
Kollmar-Paulenz, K. (2003) 'Der Buddhismus als Garant von "Frieden und Ruhe". Zu religiösen Legitimationsstrategien von Gewalt am Beispiel der tibetisch-buddhistischen Missionierung der Mongolei im späten 16. Jahrhundert', in *Zeitschrift für Religionswissenschaft* 11, pp. 185–207
Kornfield, J. (1977) *Living Buddhist Masters*, Santa Cruz: Unity Press
Krishna, D. (1996) *The Problematic and Conceptual Structure of Classical Indian Thought about Man, Society and Polity*, Delhi: Oxford University Press
Küng, H. (ed.) (1996) *Yes to a Global Ethic*, London: SCM
La Vallée Poussin, L. de (1936–7) 'Musīla et Nāradā: le chemin du Nirvāṇa', in *Mélanges chinois et bouddhiques* 5, pp. 189–222
Lai, W. (2001) 'A Renewal of Samsara (Rebirth) – New Heaven, New Earth, and New Hell in Buddhist China', in Schweidler, W. (ed.) *Wiedergeburt und kulturelles Erbe–Reincarnation and Cultural Heritage*, Sankt Augustin: Academia Verlag, pp. 133–54
Lindtner, C. (1982) *Nagarjuniana: Studies in the Writings and Philosophy of Nāgārjuna*, Copenhagen: Akademisk Forlag
Lindtner, C. (1999) 'Madhyamaka Causality', in *Hōrin: Vergleichende Studien zur japanischen Kultur: Comparative Studies in Japanese Culture* 6, pp. 37–77
Linzer, J. (1996) *Torah and Dharma: Jewish Seekers in Eastern Religions*, Northvale: Jason Aronson
Loy, D. R. (2002) *A Buddhist History of the West: Studies in Lack*, Albany: SUNY
Makransky, J.J. (1997) *Buddhahood Embodied: Sources of Controversy in India and Tibet*, Albany: SUNY
Matthews, B. (1994) *Craving and Salvation: A Study in Buddhist Soteriology* (Bibliotheca Indo-Buddhica Series 135, repr.), Delhi: Sri Satguru Publications

Meadows, C. (1986) *Ārya-Śūra's Compendium of the Perfections: Text, Translation and Analysis of the Pāramitāsamāsa*, Bonn: Indica et Tibetica Verlag

Müller, F.M. (transl.) (2000) *Wisdom of the Buddha: The Unabridged Dhammapada*, Mineola, NY: Dover Publications (repr.)

Nagao, G.M. (1991) *Mādhyamika and Yogācāra: A Study of Mahāyāna Philosophies*, Albany: SUNY

Ñāṇamoli, B. (transl.) (1999) *The Path of Purification (Visuddhimagga) by Bhadantācariya Buddhaghosa*, Seattle: BPS Pariyatti Editions

Ñāṇamoli, B. and Bodhi, B. (transl.) (2001) *The Middle Length Discourses of the Buddha: A Translation of the Majjhima Nikāya*. 2nd edn, Boston: Wisdom Publications

Nattier, J. (2003) *A Few Good Men: The Bodhisattva Path according to 'The Inquiry of Ugra' (Ugraparipṛcchā)*, Honolulu: University of Hawaii Press

Neumaier-Dargyay, E.K. (1992) *The Sovereign All-Creating Mind – the Motherly Buddha: A Translation of the Kun byed rgyal po'i mdo*, Albany: SUNY

Newman, J. (1995) 'Eschatology in the Wheel of Time Tantra', in Lopez, D.S. (ed.) (1995) *Buddhism in Practice*, Princeton, NY: Princeton University Press, pp. 284–289

Nichiren (2003) *The Writings of Nichiren Daishonin*, ed. by The Gosho Translation Committee, Tokyo: Soka Gakkai

Nishitani, K. (1982) *Religion and Nothingness*, Berkeley: University of California Press

Nyanaponika, T. (1971) *The Heart of Buddhist Meditation*, New York: Samuel Weiser

Nyanaponika, T. and Bodhi, B. (transl.) (1999) *Numerical Discourses of the Buddha: An Anthology of Suttas from the Aṅguttttara Nikāya*, Walnut Creek: AltaMira Press

O'Flaherty, W.D. (1981) *The Rig Veda: An Anthology*, London: Penguin Books

Okumura, S. (transl.) (1987) *Shōbōgenzō-zuimonki: Sayings of Eihei Dōgen Zenji recorded by Koun Ejo*, Kyōto: Sōtō-Zen Centre

Orzech, C.D. (1998) *Politics and Transcendent Wisdom: The 'Scripture for Humane Kings' in the Creation of Chinese Buddhism*, University Park, PA: Pennsylvania State University Press

Palmer, M. and Ramsay, J. with Kwok, M.-H. (1995) *Kuan Yin: Myths and Revelations of the Chinese Goddess of Compassion*, London: Thorsons

Pande, G.C. (1999) *Studies in the Origins of Buddhism*, Delhi: Motilal Banarsidass

Pandit, M.L. (1993) 'Nirvāṇa as the Unconditioned', in *Being as Becoming: Studies in Early Buddhism*, New Delhi: Intercultural Publications

Panikkar, R. (1978) *The Intrareligious Dialogue*, New York: Paulist Press

Paul, D. (1985) *Women in Buddhism: Images of the Feminine in Mahāyāna Tradition*, 2nd edn, Berkeley: University of California Press

Pérez-Remón, J. (1980) *Self and Non-Self in Early Buddhism*, The Hague: Mouton Publishers

Perera, L.P.N. (1991) *Buddhism and Human Rights: A Buddhist Commentary on the Universal Declaration of Human Rights*, Colombo: Karunaratne & Sons

Powers, J. (transl.) (1995) *Wisdom of Buddha: The Saṁdhinirmocana Sūtra*, Berkeley: Dharma Publishing

Prebish, S. (1996) *Buddhist Monastic Discipline: The Sanskrit Prātimokṣa Sūtras of the Mahāsāṃghikas and Mūlasarvāstivādins*, Delhi: Motilal Banarsidass

Pye, M. (1978) *Skilful Means: A Concept in Mahāyāna Buddhism*, London: Duckworth

Pye, M. (1979) *The Buddha*, London: Duckworth

Radhakrishnan, S. and Moore, C.A. (1989) *A Source Book in Indian Philosophy*, Princeton: Princeton University Press (repr.)

Rhys Davids, C.A.F. (transl.) (1909) *Psalms of the Early Buddhists. Psalms of the Sisters*, London: Pali Text Society

Rhys Davids, T.W. and Oldenberg, H. (transl.) (1881) *Vinaya Texts: Part I*, Sacred Books of the East series, vol. 13, Oxford: Clarendon Press

Ruegg, D.S. (1981) *The Literature of the Madhyamaka School of Philosophy in India*, Wiesbaden: Otto Harrasowitz

Runzo, J. and Martin, N.M. (2001) *Ethics in the World Religions*, Oxford: Oneworld

Saddhatissa, H. (transl.) (1987) *The Sutta-Nipāta*, London: Curzon Press (repr.)

Schlingloff, D. (1987) 'Die Bedeutung der Symbole in der altbuddhistischen Kunst', in Falk, H. (ed.) (1987) *Hinduismus und Buddhismus: Festschrift für Ulrich Schneider*, Freiburg:

Hedwig Falk, pp. 309–328

Schmidt-Leukel, P. (ed.) (2004a) 'War and Peace in Buddhism', in *War and Peace in World Religions: The Gerald Weisfeld Lectures 2003*, London: SCM-Press, pp. 33–56

Schmidt-Leukel, P. (2004b) 'Buddhism and the Idea of Human Rights', *Studies in Interreligious Dialogue* 14, pp. 216–234

Schmidt-Leukel, P. (2005a), 'Exclusivism, Inclusivism, Pluralism: The Tripolar Typology – Clarified and Reaffirmed', in Knitter, P. (ed.) *The Myth of Religious Superiority: Multifaith Explorations of Religious Pluralism,* Maryknoll: Orbis, pp. 13–27

Schmidt-Leukel, P. (ed.) (2005b) *Buddhism and Christianity in Dialogue: The Gerald Weisfeld Lectures 2004*, London: SCM

Schmidt-Leukel, P. (ed.) (2006) *Buddhism, Christianity and the Question of Creation: Karmic or Divine?* Aldershot: Ashgate

Schmithausen, L. (1981) 'On some aspects of descriptions or theories of "Liberating Insight" and "Enlightenment" in early Buddhism', in Bruhn, K. and Wezler, A. (eds) (1981) *Studien zum Jainismus und Buddhismus*, Wiesbaden: Franz Steiner Verlag, pp. 199–250

Schmithausen, L. (1991) *Buddhism and Nature: The Lecture delivered on the Occasion of the EXPO 1990. An Enlarged Version with Notes,* Tokyo: The International Institute for Buddhist Studies

Schmithausen, L. (1997) 'The Early Buddhist Tradition and Ecological Ethics', *Journal of Buddhist Ethics* 4, pp. 1–74

Schmithausen, L. (1999) 'Aspects of the Buddhist Attitude Towards War', in Houben, J.E.M. and Van Kooji, K.R. (eds) *Violence Denied: Violence, Non-Violence and the Rationalization of Violence in South Asian Cultural History*, Leiden: Brill, pp. 45–67

Schmithausen, L. (2000) 'Buddhism and the Ethics of Nature – Some Remarks', *The Eastern Buddhist: New Series* 32, no. 2, pp. 26–78

Schumacher, E.F. (1993) *Small is Beautiful: A Study of Economics as if People Mattered*, London: Vinage

Schweitzer, A. (1936) *Indian Thought and Its Development*, London: Hodder & Stoughton

Seth, V. (1992) *Study of Biographies of the Buddha: Based on Pāli and Sanskrit sources*, New Delhi: Parimal Publications

Shaw, M. (1995) *Passionate Enlightenment: Women in Tantric Buddhism*, Princeton: Princeton University Press (4th repr.)

Shinran (1997a) *The Collected Works of Shinran: Vol. I: The Writings*, Kyoto: Jōdo Shinshū Hongwanji-ha

Shinran (1997b) *The Collected Works of Shinran: Vol. II: Introduction, Glossaries and Reading Aids*, Kyoto: Jōdo Shinshū Hongwanji-ha

Siderits, M. (2001) 'Buddhism and Techno-Physicalism: Is the Eightfold Path a Program?', *Philosophy East & West* 51, pp. 307–14

Singh, N.K. (2004) *Buddhist Tāntricism*, Delhi: Global Vision Publishing House

Singh, K. and Ikeda, D. (1988) *Humanity at the Crossroads: An Inter-cultural Dialogue*, Delhi: Oxford University Press

Skilton, A. (1997) *A Concise History of Buddhism*, Birmingham: Windhorse Publications

Smith, W.C. (1978) *The Meaning and End of Religion*, San Francisco: Harper & Row

Smith, W.C. (1979) *Faith and Belief*, Princeton: Princeton University Press

Smith, W.C. (1981) *Towards a World Theology: Faith and the Comparative History of Religion*, Maryknoll: Orbis

Smith, W.C. (1997), *Modern Culture from a Comparative Perspective*, ed. by J.W. Burbidge, Albany: SUNY

Snellgrove, D. (1971) *The Hevajra Tantra: A Critical Study: Part I: Introduction and Translation*, London: Oxford University Press (repr.)

Snellgrove, D. (2002) *Indo-Tibetan Buddhism: Indian Buddhists and their Tibetan Successors*, Boston: Shambala (repr.)

Sobisch, J.-U. (2002) *Three-Vow Theories in Tibetan Buddhism: A Comprehensive Study of Major Traditions from the Twelfth through Nineteenth Centuries*, Wiesbaden: Dr. Ludwig Reichert Verlag

Sprung, M. (ed.) (1973) *The Problem of Two Truths in Buddhism and Vedānta*, Dordrecht–Boston: D. Reidel Publishing

Stcherbatsky, T. (1988) *The Central Conception of Buddhism and the Meaning of the World "Dharma"*, repr. of the 1st edn (1922), Delhi: Motilal Banarsidass

Stury, F. (1975) *Rebirth as Doctrine and Experience: Essays and Case Studies*, Kandy: Buddhist Publication Society

Streng, F. (1967), *Emptiness: A Study in Religious Meaning*, Nashville–New York: Abingdon Press

Streng, F. (1985), *Understanding Religious Life*, 3rd edn, Belmont: Wadsworth Publishing

Stevenson, I. (1966) *Twenty Cases Suggestive of Reincarnation*, New York: American Society for Psychical Research

Studholme, A. (2002) *The Origins of Oṃ Maṇipadme Hūṃ: A Study of the Kāraṇḍavyūha Sūtra*, Albany: SUNY

Swanson, P. (1989) *Foundations of T'ien-t'ai Philosophy: The Flowering of the Two Truths Theory in Chinese Buddhism*, Berkeley: Asian Humanities Press

Swearer, D. (ed.) (1989) *Me and Mine: Selected Essays of Bhikkhu Buddhadāsa*, Albany: SUNY

Takeda, R. (2004) 'Mutual Transformation of Pure Land Buddhism and Christianity', in Bloom, A. (ed.) *Living in Amida's Universal Vow: Essays in Shin Buddhism*, Bloomington: World Wisdom, pp. 255–87

Takeuchi, Y. (1983) *The Heart of Buddhism: In Search of the Timeless Spirit of Primitive Buddhism*, New York: Crossroad

Takeuchi, Y. (1997) *Buddhist Spirituality I: Indian, Southeast Asian, Tibetan, and Early Chinese*, New York: Crossroad

Takeuchi, Y. (1999) *Buddhist Spirituality II: Later China, Korea, Japan, and the Modern World*, New York: Herder & Herder.

Tambiah, S. (1976) *World Conqueror and World Renouncer: A Study of Buddhism and Polity in Thailand Against a Historical Background*, Cambridge: Cambridge University Press

Tanahashi, K. (ed.) (2000) *Enlightenment Unfolds: The Essential Teachings of Zen Master Dōgen*, Boston: Shambala

Tanaka, K. (2005) 'Acceptance of the Other as a similarly valid path and awareness of one's self-culpability: a deepening realization of my religious identity through dialogue', *Buddhist-Christian Studies* 25, pp. 41–6

Tatz, M. (1994) *The Skill in Means (Upāyakauśalya) Sūtra*, Delhi: Motilal Banarsidass

Thelle, N.R. (1987) *Buddhism and Christianity in Japan: From Conflict to Dialogue, 1854–1899*, Honolulu: University of Hawaii Press

Thomas, E.J. (1952) *The Perfection of Wisdom: The Career of the Predestined Buddhas*, London: John Murray

Thomas, E.J. (1992) *The Life of Buddha as Legend and History* (repr. of the 3rd edn, London, 1949), New Delhi: Munshiram Manoharlal Publishers

Thurman, R. (transl.) (1976) *The Holy Teaching of Vimalakīrti: A Mahāyāna Scripture*, University Park, PA: Pennsylvania State University Press

Tsomo, K.L. (ed.) (2000) *Innovative Buddhist Women: Swimming Against the Stream*, Richmond: Curzon

Tucker, M.E. and Williams, D. (eds) (1997) *Buddhism and Ecology: The Interconnection of Dharma and Deeds*, Cambridge, MA: Harvard University Press

Tucker, M.E. and Grim, J.A. (2001) *Religion and Ecology: Can the Climate Change?* Issued as *Daedalus*. Journal of the American Academy of Arts and Sciences Vol. 130, No. 4.

Tucker, M.E. (2003) *Worldly Wonder: Religions Enter Their Ecological Phase*, Chicago and La Salle: Open Court

Unno, T. (1997) 'San-lun, T'ien-t'ai, and Hua-yen', in Takeuchi (ed.) (1997) pp. 343–65

Vetter, T. (1988) *The Ideas and Meditative Practices of Early Buddhism*, Leiden: Brill

Victoria, B. (1997) *Zen at War*, New York: Weatherhill

Wallace, B.A. (ed.) (2003) *Buddhism and Science: Breaking New Ground*, New York: Columbia University Press

Walshe, M. (transl.) (1995) *The Long Discourses of the Buddha: A Translation of the Dīgha Nikāya*, Boston: Wisdom Publications

Watts, J., Senauke, A. and Santikaro, B. (eds) (1998) *Entering the Realm of Reality: Towards Dhammic Societies*, Bangkok: International Network of Engaged Buddhists

Wayman, A. (1997) 'The Diamond Vehicle', in Takeuchi (ed.) (1997) pp. 219–41

vakayāna – the 'vehicle of the hearers'; pejorative term used by →Mahāyāna Buddhists for the pre- and non-Mahāyāna schools
aviravāda – forerunner of the Theravāda school
pa – symbolic tomb containing relics; places for ritual veneration of the →Buddha
khāvatī – 'Land of Happiness', the name of the Pure Land created by →amida Buddha
yatā – 'emptiness'; central religious / philosophical term in →Mahāyāna Buddhism: all beings/entities are empty of 'own nature' (substance, essence)
tra – (Sutta) a Buddhist text, usually claimed to render the Buddha's teachings
ntra – literally: 'loom' or 'warp', also 'underlying principle' or 'main point'; a class of Buddhist scriptures belonging to Buddhist →Tantrism
ntrism – religious movement and set of doctrines/practices which achieved prominence in Hinduism and Buddhism during the second half of the first millennium CE
thāgata – the 'Thus-Gone'; alternative title for the →Buddha
hāgatagharba – 'germ', or 'embryo', or 'womb' of the Tathāgata; the Buddha-Nature in every (sentient) being
hatā – 'suchness', true or ultimate reality as it is beyond conceptual representation
eravāda – the 'Way of the Elders', major form of Buddhism in South-East Asia of ancient, pre-Mahāyāna descent
ien-t'ai – influential Chinese and Japanese (Tendai) school of Buddhism focussed on the Lotus-Sūtra
kāya – the 'Three Bodies' of a →Buddha; one of the principal doctrines in later →Mahāyāna about the different levels of reality/existence of Buddha
svabhāva – 'three' aspects or 'natures'; central concept in the →Yogācāra school of philosophy concerning the nature of reality and its mental representation
ṇā – (Pāli: taṇhā) 'thirst'; the wrong, unsatisfied existential orientation; together with →avidyā the root of the human predicament
aniṣads – group of Hindu texts (composed between c. 600 and 300 BCE), influenced by ideas from the →Śrāmaṇas and incorporated into the →Vedas as their concluding sections
āsaka – Buddhist layman
āsikā – Buddhist laywoman
āya – (skilful) 'means'; a Buddha's or Bodhisattva's compassionate use of intellectual and practical means for the sake of unenlightened beings
irocana Buddha – principal supranatural →Buddha in some classes of →Tantras
jra – 'diamond' or 'thunderbolt'; multilayered symbol and ritual instrument in Buddhist →Tantrism
ajrayāna – 'Diamond Vehicle'; teachings of a specific class of Buddhist →Tantras; also used as designation for Tantric Buddhism in general
edas – collection of sacred texts composed between c. 1,200 and 300 BCE; in Hinduism seen as containing divine revelation
ijñānavāda – 'Consciousness-School'; philosophical school of →Mahāyāna Buddhism (also called →Yogācāra)
naya – the 'rule' or 'discipline' of Buddhist monks and nuns
isuddhimagga – major work of →Theravāda orthodoxy, composed by Buddhaghosa (5th cent. CE)
ama – in Buddhist mythology a deity closely associated with death
antra – geometrical representation of cosmological ideas, used for meditative and ritual practice in Hinduism and Tantric Buddhism
ogācāra – 'Yoga-Practice' school; philosophical school of Mahāyāna Buddhism (also called →Vijñānavāda)
ogin – male Tantric practitioner
oginī – female Tantric practitioner
azen – in →Zen Buddhism the practice of just 'sitting in meditation', without using an object (e.g. a →koan)
en – Japanese form of the Chinese →Ch'an school

Weber, M. (1958) *The Religion of India: The Sociology of Hinduism and Buddhism*, Glencoe, Ill.: Free Press

White, D.G. (ed.) (2000) *Tantra in Practice*, Princeton, Oxford: Princeton University Press

Wijayaratna, M .(1990) *Buddhist Monastic Life According to the Texts of the Theravāda Tradition*, Cambridge: Cambridge University Press

Williams, P. (1989) *Mahāyāna Buddhism: The Doctrinal Foundations*, London and New York: Routledge

Williams, P. with Tribe, A. (2000) *Buddhist Thought: A Complete Introduction to the Indian Tradition*, London: Routledge

Wright, D.S. (1999) 'Four Ch'an Masters', in Takeuchi (ed.) (1999) pp. 33–43

Yampolsky, P.B. (transl.) (1967) *The Platform Sutra of the Sixth Patriarch: The Text of the Tun-Huan Manuscript with Translation, Introduction, and Notes*, New York: Columbia University Press

Yi, L. and Habito, M.R. (eds.) (2005) *Listening. Buddhist-Muslim Dialogues 2002–2004*, Taipei: Museum of World Religions Development Foundation

Yokota, J.S. (2000) 'Understanding Amida Buddha and the Pure Land. A Process Approach', in Hirata D. (ed.) *Toward a Contemporary Understanding of Pure Land Buddhism: Creating a Shin Buddhist Theology in a Religiously Plural World*, Albany: SUNY pp. 73–100

Young, S. (2004) *Courtesans and Tantric Consorts: Sexualities in Buddhist Narrative, Iconigraphy, and Ritual*, New York–London: Routledge

Zimmermann, M. (2000) 'A Mahāyānist Criticism of Arthaśāstra: The Chapter on Royal Ethics in the *Bodhisattva-gocaropāya-viṣaya-vikurvaṇa-nirdeśa-sūtra*', in *Annual Report of The International Research Institute for Advanced Buddhology at Soka University for the Academic Year 1999* (ARIAB 3), Tokyo: Soka University, pp. 179–211

Glossary

abhijñā – higher or supernatural powers
ādibuddha – primordial Buddha; designation for ultimate reality in later Mahāyāna and Tantric Buddhism
Akṣobhya – one of the →pañcatathāgata, the 'Five Buddhas' of the Tantric →maṇḍala
Amida – Japanese name for Buddha Amitābha (→pañcatathāgata); principal Buddha in →Pure Land Buddhism
amṛta – (Pāli: amata) the 'deathless'; synonym for →nirvāṇa
anātman – (Pāli: anattā) 'not-self' or 'not the →ātman'
arhat – (Pāli: arahat) one who reached enlightenment; highest religious goal in →Theravāda Buddhism
artha – 'wealth' or 'power'; one of the traditional Vedic (→Vedas) goals in life
āśraya-parāvṛtti – 'transmutation' or 'revolution of the basis'; designation for enlightenment in the →Yogācāra school
ātman – 'self'; in the →Upaniṣads the designation for the presence of the ultimate (→brahman) within each individual
Avalokiteśvara – 'Kuan-yin' in China, 'Kwannon' or 'Kannon' in Japan; literally 'who hears the cries of the world': one of the most venerated →Bodhisattvas in →Mahāyāna Buddhism
Avataṁsaka-Sūtra – Indian →Mahāyāna text; basic scripture of the →Hua-yen school
avidyā – (Pāli: avijjā) ignorance, delusion; together with →tṛṣṇā the root of the human predicament
bhavacakra – the 'Wheel of Becoming'; traditional Buddhist depiction of the →saṃsāra
bhikṣu – (Pāli: bhikkhu) Buddhist monk
bhikṣunī – (Pāli: bhikkhuṇī) Buddhist nun
bhūmi – stage of level of the spiritual development of a →Bodhisattva
bodhi – awakening, enlightenment

bodhicitta – the 'enlightenment mind'; the initial awakening of a →Bodhisattva's altruistic mind
Bodhisattva – 'enlightenment being'; a Buddha-to-be; the principal religious ideal in →Mahāyāna Buddhism
Bodhisattvayāna – the 'Bodhisattva Vehicle'; different term for →Mahāyāna
Brahmā – one of the chief Indian deities (→deva)
brahman – in the →Upaniṣads term for ultimate divine reality
Brāhmaṇa – Brahmin, member of the priest-caste
Buddha – the 'Awakened One' or 'Enlightened One'
cakravartin – a world emperor according to Buddhist mythology
Cārvākas – early Indian school of materialists
Ch'an – 'meditation' school; important Chinese →Mahāyāna school, in Japan known as →Zen
Dalai Lama – 'Ocean (of wisdom) Teacher'; title of the head of the →Geluk order
dāna – 'giving' or 'generosity'; the first and foundational virtue (→pāramitā) of a →Bodhisattva
deva – Indian 'god' or 'deity'; according to Buddhism a possible form of reincarnation
dhāraṇīs – magical formula used in →Mahāyāna and →Tantrism
dharma – (Pāli: dhamma) (1) cosmic 'law', but also an individual's duty; studying the dharma is one of the traditional Vedic (→Veda) goals in life; (2) the Buddha's teaching; (3) an entity or one of its constituents
dharmakāya – 'Dharma-body', the most profound of the 'Three Buddha Bodies' (→trikāya); in later →Mahāyāna term for ultimate reality
Dharmaguptaka – one of the early pre-Mahāyāna schools
dhyāna – meditative absorption, divided in form-based absorption (rūpya dhyāna) and 'formless absorption' (ārūpya dhyāna).
duḥkha – (Pāli: dukkha) 'suffering'; technical Buddhist term for the human predicament
Geluk – school of Tibetan Buddhism
gūru – 'teacher', spiritual master
Hīnayāna – 'Small' or 'Inferior Vehicle'; pejorative term used by →Mahāyāna Buddhists for the pre- and non-Mahāyāna schools
Hua-yen – Chinese school of Mahāyāna (in Japan: Kegon), based on the teaching of the →Avataṁsaka-Sūtra
icchantika – a being lacking any potential for enlightenment; the existence of icchantikas was a disputed question in →Mahāyāna
Indra – one of the chief Indian deities (→deva)
Jains, Jainism – ancient Indian religion originating in the →Śrāmaṇa movement.
Jātakas – literary genre; stories about the Buddha's previous lives
Kagyü – school of Tibetan Buddhism
kāma – sensual, particularly erotic pleasure; one of the traditional Vedic (→Vedas) goals in life
karma – 'deed'; originally the efficacious performance of ritual sacrifice; in Buddhism the spiritual effects (upon the mind and upon the form of rebirth) of our behaviour in thoughts, words, and deeds.
karuṇā – compassion (mahākaruṇā = 'great compassion); key attitude of a →Bodhisattva
kōan – (Chin.: kung-an) a puzzling or paradoxical statement, question, story, etc. Used as object of some forms of →Zen meditation
Kṣatriya – a member of the 'warrior' caste
Lotus-Sūtra – →Saddharmapuṇḍarīka-Sūtra
Madhyamaka – 'Middle Way' school; Mahāyāna Buddhist philosophical school based on the teachings of Nāgārjuna (2nd/3rd cent. CE)
mahāmudrā – the 'great symbol'; set of specific Tantric teachings and practices in Tibetan Buddhism focussed on the realization of ultimate reality
Mahāsaṅghika – a cluster of early pre-Mahāyāna schools which anticipated some →Mahāyāna teachings
Mahāyāna – 'Great Vehicle' or 'Eminent Vehicle'; major branch of Buddhism first appearing between 100 BCE – 100 CE.

maṇḍala – geometrical configuration, often a particular arrangement of the Five Bu (→pañcatathāgatas)
mantra – sacred syllable or set of syllables used in →Mahāyāna and Tantric practic
Māra – in Buddhist mythology an evil deity; the tempter, associated with the bonds pleasures and death
maitri – (Pāli: metta) love, loving kindness
Maitreya – in Buddhist mythology the future Buddha following →Siddhārtha Gaut
Milindapañha – influential pre-Mahāyāna philosophical /doctrinal treatise
mokṣa – salvation, liberation
mudrā – gesture, usually of the hand(s), with symbolic and ritual meaning
nirmāṇakāya – 'transformation body', the human manifestation of the →Buddha, three Buddha-Bodies (→trikāya)
nembutsu – Japanese short form for 'Namu Amida Butsu', the formula for the inv Amida Buddha
nirvāṇa – (Pāli: nibbāna); 'extinction'; technical Buddhist term for unconditioned reality in and through which existence in →saṃsāra is terminated
Nyingma – school of Tibetan Buddhism
Pāli Canon – canonical collection of the Theravāda school
pañca śīla – the 'five precepts': abstention form killing, stealing, sexual miscondu intoxicants
pañcatathāgata – the 'Five Buddhas': Vairocana, Akṣobhya, Ratnasambhava, Am Amoghasiddhi, a micro-macrocosmic symbol, particularly in Buddhist →Tantris
pāramitā – 'perfection' or 'virtue', to be accomplished by a →Bodhisattva
prajñā – (Pāli: paññā) wisdom
Prajñāpāramitā Sūtras – 'Perfection of Wisdom-Sūtras'; group of early Mahāyā
praṇidhāna – the formal vow(s) of a →Bodhisattva to work for the liberation of a
prapañca – plurality, proliferation; philosophically: the conceptual, diversified re of reality
prātimokṣa – recitation formula containing the monastic rules
pratītyasamutpāda – (Pāli: paṭiccasamuppāda) the Buddhist teaching of 'Depend tion'
Pratyekabuddha – 'Solitary Buddha'; someone who finds enlightenment for him not establish a →saṅgha
Pure Land Buddhism – major form of East Asian Buddhism focussed on →Amid and Amida's Pure Land →Sukhāvatī
puruṣa – primordial 'man'; in Hinduism a designation of ultimate reality
puruṣa-myth – mythological narrative related in Ṛg-Veda 10:90 about the creatio world out of the sacrifice of the →puruṣa
Saddharmapuṇḍarīka-Sūtra – 'Sūtra of the Lotus of the True Law' = 'Lotus- Sū influential early Mahāyāna text
sādhana – ritual / spiritual practice in →Tantrism
Sakya – school of Tibetan Buddhism
Śākyamuni – 'the wise from the Śākyas'; alternative name for →Siddhārtha Gaut
samādhi – concentration, meditation
saṃbhogakāya – 'enjoyment body' or 'body of communal enjoyment'; the Budd supranatural being, one of the three Buddha-Bodies (→trikāya)
saṃsāra – the cycle of rebirth and redeath (reincarnation)
saṅgha – the Buddhist community; in a narrow sense: Buddhist monks and nuns
Shingon – Japanese school of Buddhist →Tantrism
siddha – 'perfected' or 'accomplished' one; term for the religious ideal of Buddhi →Tantrism
Siddhārtha Gautama – Pāli: 'Siddhattha Gotama' (roughly 560–480 or 450–370 'Buddha'; founding figure of Buddhism
śīla – (Pāli: sīla) morality, ethic
Sōtō – a Japanese →Zen school
Śrāmaṇas – (Pāli: samaṇas = 'strivers') early Indian movement of ascetics and wo renouncers

Index